Pediatric Forensic Evidence

David L. Robinson

Pediatric Forensic Evidence

A Guide for Doctors, Lawyers and Other Professionals

 Springer

David L. Robinson
Department of Paediatrics
Queen's University Hospital
Romford, Essex
United Kingdom

ISBN 978-3-319-45335-4   ISBN 978-3-319-45337-8   (eBook)
DOI 10.1007/978-3-319-45337-8

Library of Congress Control Number: 2017958970

Printed on acid-free paper

This Springer imprint is published by Springer Nature
The registered company is Springer International Publishing AG
The registered company address is: Gewerbestrasse 11, 6330 Cham, Switzerland

Foreword

Doctors, lawyers, and others concerned with child protection ask similar questions and seek similar answers: what is the nature of harm done, if physical abuse, the force required for a given injury and the reaction of the child in the aftermath? Does the account provided fit with the injuries observed and the developmental stage of the child? Is the cause on balance likely to arise from accident, intention, or an underlying medical condition?

Cross-examination in Court is a robust form of clinical governance where the clinicians' evidence is tested with time to reconsider crucial opinions on which may rest the residence of a child, or custodial sentence for an alleged perpetrator. The highest standards of analysis are required based on medical experience, evidence-based medicine and a comprehensive analysis of the international literature.

Medical assessments should reflect those high standards so that an abused child is not returned home, carers of a child with an accidental injury are not falsely accused or that a child with a condition increasing susceptibility to bruising or fractures is not left undiagnosed.

The vast majority of carers, from whatever walk of life, love, nurture and protect their children. A very few, in a momentary loss of control, in an otherwise caring parent cause much-regretted injury. An even smaller number repeatedly hurt their children in what becomes a pattern of abuse.

This book seeks to guide professionals working with children who present with injuries, neglect and other forms of child abuse. The analysis of clinical findings, current literature, and clinical experience are drawn together to assist professionals in diagnosing the cause of injury and other presentations. I hope it will assist doctors, lawyers, the Courts, social workers, health visitors, teachers, the police, nurses and others involved in child protection.

Pediatric Forensic Evidence is the result of many years' experience working with children and families in an East London hospital receiving over 1,000 children a week through the emergency department (ED) covering a population of 750,000 as well as the analysis of over 400 cases for the Courts.

It is said that a good doctor (and perhaps lawyer) learns from his or her mistakes – a bad one makes the same mistakes with increasing confidence. Our task is to learn, acknowledge our errors and do better on behalf of the children and families under our joint care.

My immense thanks to colleagues both junior and senior who have advised, corrected and contributed material. Also to some exceptional experts, advocates and judges who have added to my knowledge and allowed me time to reflect and reconsider. Finally to the children who have come under my care and to their devoted families with few exceptions.

Romford, UK   David L. Robinson
September 2017

Preface

His Honour Judge Dowse
(Designated Family Judge for Humberside 2007–2016)
Every Child Matters – Every Day Matters

The protection and safety of children is now a large industry. Gone are the days when children were known to be mistreated with impunity. In terms of history, it is not long since children as young as 5 or 6 were sent up chimneys to free them of soot, and worked in mines crawling through tunnels. At the Battle of Trafalgar, some midshipmen were aged 13. These tasks were not 'abuse' in the way we see it now. They were simply a part of life. They would certainly be regarded as abuse to-day.

Animals appear to have been conferred greater protection from abuse than children. The RSPCA was formed in 1824, but the NSPCC was not formed until 1884 (then known as the London Society for the Prevention of Cruelty to Children) being granted a Royal Charter in 1895. In fact, London took its lead from the Liverpool SPCC which was formed the year before. The first known criminal case of child abuse was brought by the RSPCA and, by stretching the bounds of ingenuity, involved a charge which referred to the mistreatment of 'a little animal'. A concerned neighbour could no longer bear the screams of the child during its daily beating.

From the middle of the nineteenth century the vulnerability of children was increasingly recognised and statutes were introduced which recognised the importance of their protection and welfare. Legal reference books on infants were rare. *Simpson on Infants* was revised in 1908 and had its last edition in 1926. The 1908 edition reflected considerable change in attitudes towards children. The Prevention of Cruelty to Children Act 1889 and the Children Act 1908 conferred responsibilities concerning children on local authorities and the 1908 Act dealt with many aspects of child care and protection, including, as an example, suffocation by overlaying in the parents' beds. If the parent was drunk, then the parent would be regarded as having neglected the child.

As time has moved on, the increasing recognition for Child Protection has meant the need for a greater understanding by professionals as to how neglect has occurred or injury has been caused. At the front line of this need lies the medical profession which is tasked to assess harm to the child and whether that harm has been caused accidentally, deliberately or by neglect. Social Services, the Police and the Courts all rely on the expertise and experience of the medical profession in seeking to reach conclusions. Explanations from carers for injury may be regarded with suspicion but may be supported by medical diagnosis of disease. Brittle bone cases are an example. Some explanations can often be excluded because the medical practitioner is able to rest on a wealth of experience in practice, and on modern literature made more widely available by computer, to demonstrate that the offered explanation is implausible. The violent parent who claims that his child's head injury was caused by falling off the sofa onto the carpeted floor is generally unaware that there are hundreds if not thousands of such falls logged each year and caused accidentally without the alleged resultant injury. The experienced Paediatrician is able to identify what is a likely cause of injury and what is not.

Those of us who have been involved in Child Protection work also develop with experience an understanding of how children have been harmed. Those of us who are not within the medical profession often have our lay preliminary opinions dislodged by those within it. The greater the understanding we develop of how injury has, or may have been, caused the greater the path to justice. Children are the nation's future. A wrong conclusion reached by any of us in Child Protection work can have lifelong adverse consequences for the child, its parents and siblings and the extended family.

Oh how I wish Dr. Robinson's book had been available for me to read before embarking on Child Protection work. It is a remarkable work in which he brings together a mass of learning providing examples of what should be looked for, and what can be discounted, in determining the cause of injury or harm. It informs the budding Paediatrician (and perhaps a wider medical circle such as GPs) of how to approach an examination of the child and the procedures to be adopted. It reminds us of the importance of taking and recording careful histories and signing, timing and dating them. I recognise when discussing 'injury' that a better description of what is being considered is 'harm'. Injury is not always inflicted physical injury; it may be psychological or it may arise from neglect (malnutrition is an example).

It is difficult to imagine a medical student, a GP or other doctors or specialist nurses, a line managing social worker, a policeman, a barrister, a solicitor, a legal adviser or a judge, involved in Child Protection work, not having access to a copy of *Pediatric Forensic Evidence*. This book appears to have been lovingly and painstakingly prepared. For those involved in this area of work, it is 'a good read'. I was fortunate enough to have the draft as a holiday book. It is packed with outcomes of research and includes anecdotes that should remind us all that pre-conceived conclusions are dangerous and that today's medical science may be tomorrow's history.

I have been privileged to have been asked by Dr. Robinson to prepare the preface to this remarkable work. I commend this book in the expectation that it will become an invaluable instrument in the Child Protection Toolbox.

His Honour Judge Dowse
October 30, 2016

Acknowledgements

My thanks to the following medical experts for their critical review of the text:

Dr. Amaka C Offiah	Reader in Paediatric Musculoskeletal Imaging
	Honorary Consultant Paediatric Radiologist
	Sheffield, UK
Mr. Peter Richards	Consultant Paediatric Neurosurgeon
	Oxford University Hospitals, UK
Dr. Martin Samuels	Consultant Paediatrician
	University Hospital of North Midlands, Stoke-on-Trent, Staffs
	Respiratory Unit, Great Ormond Street Hospital, London, UK
Dr. Andrew Will	Consultant Paediatric Haematologist
	Royal Manchester Children's Hospital, UK

And to the following colleagues at Queens University Hospital (BHRUT), UK:

Dr. Kausik Banerjee	Consultant Paediatrician, (Endocrinology)
Dr. Ambalika Das	Consultant Neonatologist
Dr. Ravikiran Kotian	Consultant Paediatrician
Dr. Khalid Saja	Consultant Haematologist
Dr. Junaid Solebo	Consultant Paediatrician, (Safeguarding)
Ms Kimberley-Swann	Medical Photography
Nigel Collister	Medical Photography
Judy Wang	Medical Librarian

My special thanks to Amaka Offiah, Paediatric Radiologist, who, at short notice reviewed, corrected and contributed to Chapter 3 (Fractures), His Honour Judge John Dowse for expert legal guidance and for writing the Preface, Ambalika Das my close colleague who meticulously read and corrected the text and to Paul Robinson (Consultant Psychiatrist, St. Ann's Hospital, London) who mentored me throughout this project. Thank you to Adam Feinstein (autism researcher, author and academic) for proof-reading and copywriting the final draft.

Thanks also to the following trainees who reviewed and contributed to chapters:

Dr. Dan Crane	Dr. Johanna Gaiottino
Dr. Sahiti Koneru	Dr. Abirami Nimasavayab
Dr. Bushra Rafiq	Dr. Amaki Sogbodjor
Dr. Rupa Vora	

Abbreviations

ADHD	Attention deficit hyperactivity disorder
AHT	Abusive head trauma
ALT	Alanine aminotransferase
ALTE	Apparent life-threatening event
ASD	Autism spectrum disorder
AST	Aspartate aminotransferase
ATNR	Asymmetrical tonic neck reflex
BESS	Benign enlargement of the subarachnoid space
BMI	Body mass index
BPABG	British Paediatric and Adolescent Bone Group
CAMHS	Child and adolescent mental health services
CML	Classic metaphyseal lesion (metaphyseal corner fracture)
CPP	Child protection plan
CPR	Cardiopulmonary resuscitation
CRP	C-reactive protein
CSA	Child sexual abuse
CSF	Cerebrospinal fluid
CT	Computerised tomography
CVS	Covert video surveillance
DAI	Diffuse axonal injury
DEXA	Dual-energy X-ray absorptiometry
DIC	Disseminated intravascular coagulation
DLA	Disability Living Allowance
DNA	Deoxyribonucleic acid
EB	Epidermolysis bullosa
ED	Emergency department
EDH	Extradural haemorrhage (haematoma)
EDS	Ehlers-Danlos syndrome
EPO	Emergency protection order
FASD	Foetal alcohol spectrum disorder
FFLM	Faculty of Forensic and Legal Medicine
FII	Fabricated or induced illness by carers
FTT	Failure to thrive

GORD	Gastro-oesophageal reflux
GP	General Practitioner
HIE	Hypoxic ischaemic encephalopathy
HV	Health Visitor
ICH	Intracerebral haemorrhage (haematoma)
IUGR	Intra-uterine growth retardation
IVH	Intraventricular haemorrhage
LSA	Lichen sclerosus et atrophicus
LSCB	Local Safeguarding Children Board
MLB	Micro-laryngobronchoscopy
MRI	Magnetic resonance imaging
NSAID	Non-steroidal anti-inflammatory drug
OI	Osteogenesis imperfecta
ONH	Oro-nasal haemorrhage
PA	Physical abuse
RAD	Reflex anal dilatation
RCPCH	Royal College of Paediatrics and Child Health
RCR	Royal College of Radiologists
RH	Retinal haemorrhage
RTA	Road traffic accident
SAH	Subarachnoid haemorrhage
SCIWORA	Spinal cord injury without radiological abnormality
SCR	Serious case review
SDH	Subdural haemorrhage (haematoma)
SGH	Subgaleal haemorrhage (haematoma)
SIDS	Sudden infant death syndrome
SPNBF	Subperiosteal new bone formation
SUDC	Sudden unexpected death in childhood
SUDI	Sudden unexpected death in infancy

Contents

General Aspects of Child Protection

Abstract

The needs of the child are paramount. The clinician's first task is to diagnose the cause of symptoms and signs whether accidental, inflicted or the result of an underlying medical condition. Where abuse is diagnosed the task is to safeguard the child and treat the physical and psychological effects of maltreatment.

A child is one who has not yet reached his or her 18th birthday. Child abuse is any action by another person that causes significant harm to a child or fails to meet a basic need. It involves acts of both commission and omission with effects on the child's physical, developmental, and psychosocial well-being.

The vast majority of carers from whatever walk of life, love, nurture and protect their children. A very few, in a momentary loss of control in an otherwise caring parent, cause much regretted injury. An even smaller number repeatedly maltreat their children in what becomes a pattern of abuse. One parent may harm, the other may fail to protect by omitting to seek help. Child abuse whether physical or psychological is unlawful.

Prevalence

There are 11 million children under 18 in England and over 69,000 in care [1]. In 2014–2015 more than 49,000 were identified as needing protection from abuse [2]. The NSPCC estimates that over half a million children are abused in the UK each year.

'Child abuse, sometimes referred to as child abuse and neglect, includes all forms of physical and emotional ill-treatment, sexual abuse, neglect, and exploitation that results in actual or potential harm to the child's health, development or dignity. Within this broad definition, five subtypes can be distinguished – physical abuse; sexual abuse; neglect and negligent treatment; emotional abuse; and exploitation' World Health Organisation, 2016.

© Springer International Publishing Switzerland 2017
D.L. Robinson, *Pediatric Forensic Evidence*, DOI 10.1007/978-3-319-45337-8_1

Many episodes of abuse are not disclosed or recorded. Most bruises disappear within a few days. Fractures are most painful for the first 72 hours. Psychological maltreatment is hard to document and diagnose. However there has been an increase in reporting over recent years probably as a result of improved surveillance rather than an increase in abuse.

Neglect is the commonest reason for a child to be subject to a child protection plan with emotional abuse the second most prevalent. Fewer children are categorised under physical and sexual abuse [3].

Research indicates that child abuse remains both under-recognised and under-recorded. May-Chahal et al. 2005 reported that 90% of young adults interviewed said they came from a warm loving background. Nevertheless abuse was diagnosed in 16% including physical, emotional, absence of carer and contact sexual abuse [4].

Types of Abuse

Physical Abuse

Physical abuse includes injury to the skin, eyes, ears, internal organs, ligaments and bones. It includes hitting, burning, throwing, shaking, poisoning, drowning or suffocating. There may a momentary loss of control or a pattern of repeated abuse. Either way the child suffers due to the actions of the carer. Illness induction is a form of physical abuse where the carer induces symptoms in the child.

Neglect

Neglect is failure to provide food and nutrition, health needs, education, emotional support, safe shelter and living conditions within resources available to a carer. It may be physical (failure to meet basic physical needs), emotional (withholding emotional nurturance), medical (failure to present a child for required medical care), supervisional (failure to protect a child from harm by supervision) or educational (failure to secure a child's education).

Child Sexual Abuse

A child is sexually abused when he or she is forced or persuaded to observe or take part in sexual acts to include on-line activities. The Sexual Offences Act makes it an offence, where a child is under the age of 13 years, for a person to rape (penetration by the penis of a child's vagina, anus or mouth), sexually assault by penetration (penetrating sexually the vagina or anus of a child with a part of the body or object), sexually assault by touch or cause or incite a child to engage in sexual activity [5].

Emotional Abuse

In emotional abuse (psychological maltreatment) the carer fails to provide a nurturing environment for the child's psychological and emotional well-being. The child is affected with risks for developmental/educational delay, anxiety, agitation, depression and social withdrawal.

Fabricated and Induced Illness by Carers (FII)

Fabricated or induced illness is when a carer either seeks out inappropriate medical care when not required or induces symptoms.

Injury Types

The clinician must accurately diagnose the injury, whether a bruise, burn, bite mark, or other trauma. An underlying medical diagnosis must be excluded. Without this, social care, the police and Courts will have inadequate information on which to base their decisions. Table 1.1 lists the categories of injury to be considered. Accurate documentation and a clear diagnosis are the starting points for forensic analysis.

Table 1.1 Injury types

Bleeding from blood vessels:	
Bruise	Escape of blood from damaged blood vessels
Contusion	Alternative description for a bruise
Haematoma	Localised collection of blood outside blood vessels
Petechiae	Small pinpoint bruises on the skin and mucosal surfaces <3mm
Purpura	Red/purple spots that do not blanch on pressure, 3–10mm
Ecchymosis	Purpura larger than 10mm. May be indistinguishable from a bruise
Skin and organ injury:	
Abrasion	Superficial injury of the outer layers of the skin
Scratch	Linear abrasion
Graze	A brush abrasion where the epidermis is scraped off
Incision	A cut from a sharp-edged object
Excoriation	Injury to the skin from scratching, a sharp object or burn
Laceration	Irregular wound caused by blunt trauma
Scar	Fibrous tissue replacing normal tissue after wound healing
Other injury types:	
Avulsion	A structure forcibly detached from its point of insertion
Burn	Injury caused by heat, electricity, chemicals, friction or radiation
Crush	Injury caused by compression
Frostbite	Localised damage to skin and other tissues due to freezing
Penetration	An object pierces the skin creating an open wound
Puncture	A sharp object piercing the skin
Traumatic alopecia	Hair loss caused by an injury to the scalp

Medical Assessment

A comprehensive assessment to include a medical history, examination, careful notes including line drawings, photo-documentation and investigations where indicated (page 7) are essential. Treatment or specialist referrals may be required with follow-up appointments.

The paediatrician will assess the child's physical and psychological needs, make clear diagnoses, provide an opinion regarding the likelihood of abuse and work collaboratively with social care, the police and other agencies.

Assessments should be carried out by a paediatrician with adequate training or trainees closely supervised by the consultant for both the assessment and report [6]. Acute sexual assault requires an urgent assessment. Physical injury should be assessed promptly (within 24 hours), as should any child where the police or social care consider safeguarding to be urgent. Past sexual abuse, neglect or emotional abuse should be assessed within 1–2 days.

Informed consent should be obtained from the child who should be allowed to express his or her wishes. Children and young people may give consent if they are deemed to be Gillick competent (understanding the nature, purpose, benefits, risks and consequences of not proceeding, being able to retain information discussed, able to use this information and communicate their decisions) [7].

The assessment should take place within an age-appropriate environment. Chaperones should be present and language or communication difficulties provided for. A safeguarding pro-forma should always be used. Hospital admission is needed if a child requires treatment, investigation or emergency safeguarding.

All notes must be signed and date stamped. The author may be called to give evidence which may affect the long-term future of a child and its parents.

Medical History

Where injury has occurred a history will be sought from carers to include a timescale of events, circumstances leading up to as well as the mechanism of any injury. If age-appropriate the child should be encouraged to provide an account (Table 1.2).

For physical abuse the medical history depending on the age of the infant or child should include whether Vitamin K was given at birth, conditions associated with easy bruising or fractures in child or family, any history of unusual bleeding or bruising following circumcision or dental extractions and other relevant matters to include drugs administered to the child or family members. (e.g: aspirin or anticoagulants).

Examination

The parent–child interaction, behaviour of the child and any signs of neglect should be recorded. Systems examination should be followed by a careful search for any skin marks or other injuries. Ears and mouth should be carefully inspected. The

Table 1.2 Medical history and account of any injury depending on age

Initial enquiries
Pre-natal, birth, developmental and immunisation history
General health and systems enquiry
Past medical history including medication and allergies
Previous injuries and hospitalisations
School attendance, behaviour and achievement, special educational needs
Family and Social history
Family history of bleeding, bone or other disorders
Family composition and health of family members
Domestic abuse, drug or alcohol problems
Parental mental health, learning difficulties, employment
Previous involvement with children's social care
For older children and young adults
Menstrual and sexual history
Smoking, drug and alcohol use, self-harm, psychiatric issues
Where there is bruising or bleeding
Documentation of Vitamin K administration
Prolonged bleeding at birth from the umbilical stump, Guthrie heel prick, circumcision
Nose bleeds, gum bleeding or menorrhagia
Joint pain, swelling or reluctance to move a limb suggestive of haemarthroses
Where there is a history of reported trauma
If witnessed, date, time, location of where the injury occurred
What were the events leading up to the injury
If bruising, when first seen and by whom
What was the child's reaction to the injury and carers response
The child's account
Where there is no history of trauma
When did the child last appear perfectly well
Date and time of any change in behaviour
How did any illness progress, did symptoms worsen
Who was caring for the child when he or she first developed symptoms
Who were the carers in the hours and days before the child became ill
Was any treatment sought
Reasons for any delay in presentation

Table 1.3 Medical examination

General	Parent-child interaction, affect of the child
Growth	Plot measurements on standard growth charts
Examination	
Skin	Size, location, colour, tenderness, swelling and pattern of any injuries
Scalp	Swellings, cephalhaematomas
	Evidence for skull fracture
	Avulsed hair, bruises or other injuries
	Fontanelles, size and character
Ears	Look for injury over both the front and back of both ears
	Auroscope for injury, foreign bodies, CSF leakage
Eyes	Scleral colour
	Fundoscopic examination for retinal haemorrhages
	Swelling, sub-conjunctival haemorrhage or bruising
Nose	Swelling, bleeding, septal deviation, foreign bodies, CSF leakage
Mouth	Torn frenulum, lacerations or other intra-oral injuries
	Examine teeth for trauma and dental caries
Chest/ Cardiovascular	Signs of deformity, bruising, tenderness
	Pulses, murmurs, chest signs
Abdomen	Tenderness, guarding, bowel sounds, abdominal distention
	Bruises or other skin marks
Back	Bruises
	Midline masses which may represent vertebral injuries
Extremities	Bruises, soft tissue swellings, joint tenderness, deformity and function
Neurology	Assess for cerebral or spinal injury
Genitalia	(if consent is obtained and a forensic examination is not required)
	Document injuries, anal tone or signs of infection
	Tanner stage of sexual development
Development	Brief developmental assessment
Neglect	Document any evidence of emotional abuse and neglect
Body maps	Documentation of skin marks with a diagnosis for each where possible
	Describe the location in relation to anatomic landmarks
	Shape, colour, tenderness or swelling
	Size in millimeters of each mark
	The explanation provided for each mark
Images	Photo-documentation with a standard ruler
	(Hospital Medical or Police photographs)

scalp must be examined as bruises and haematomas under the hair may be missed. Brief visual inspection of external genitalia and anus noting the stage of sexual development is appropriate if consent has been obtained and a specialist CSA examination not required (Table 1.3).

Table 1.4 Investigations and assessments depending on the clinical presentation

Blood	Full blood count
	Coagulation studies
	Liver function tests, amylase, bone biochemistry
	Vitamin D, Parathyroid hormone (PTH) levels
	Toxicology (urine and blood)
Imaging	For children under 2 years of age or older where there is clinical indication: Skeletal survey with follow-up radiographs 10–14 days later
	Neuro-imaging for infants under 12 months or where there is clinical indication
Opinions	Ophthalmology examination for infants under 12 months
	Specialist opinions as necessary
Other	Forensic samples and investigations in collaboration with the Police

A developmental assessment should be conducted including comments as to whether the infant is pre-mobile, beginning to mobilise or ambulant. Weight, height (and head circumference where appropriate) should be plotted on standard growth charts [8].

Opinion and Follow-Up

The individual mark, whether bruise, scar, birth mark or medical condition, must be diagnosed wherever possible and documented in both the medical notes and on body diagrams. Each mark should then be considered individually and an opinion reached as to whether it is accidental, inflicted or whether investigations for a medical diagnosis are required. It is equally important to take an overview of all injuries as well as evidence for neglect and emotional abuse.

Opinions both in the clinical notes and medical reports should also include a differential diagnosis and care plan including follow-up (to reassess growth, signs or on-going health and mental health needs) or specialist referral. Documents should identify the author who should sign/stamp them and include a date and time (24-hour clock).

Named professionals provide advice and ensure that safeguarding training is in place. They work in collaboration with the designated professionals and the Local Safeguarding Board. Designated professionals take the lead on all aspects of safeguarding children across the area. Both should be available to assist paediatricians with assessments and report writing.

Factors that Raise Concerns for Abuse (Table 1.5)

Clinical Examination
The clinician must assess whether the explanation provided matches clinical findings.

Table 1.5 Factors that raise concerns for abuse

Clinical Examination does not match the account of injury
No credible history of a memorable event and its aftermath
Discrepancies in the histories provided
History does not fit with the child's developmental abilities
Delay in presentation
Carer blames a sibling
Family known to children's social care
Repeated attendances for injuries or neglect
Child discloses abuse

No credible history of a memorable event and its aftermath

The absence of a credible explanation raises concerns for inflicted injury. Babies scratch themselves over the face, forehead, arms, sometimes chest and abdomen. They may hit themselves with rattles or other toys and cause a small bruise. A reliable history from the carer is usual. For older children minor injuries may have no explanation and carers may not have been present when they were sustained.

When an inflicted injury has occurred the perpetrator and observer will be aware that excessive force had been applied. A non-observer may see a crying infant but not know why. Infants with metaphyseal bone fractures may scream out in pain at the time of injury but then settle. A history of a change in behaviour may help to date an injury.

Discrepant or vague accounts

A mother reported that her 3-year-old ran across the playground after which she heard a scream. She saw him on the ground, distressed and crying with further pain on attempts to weight bear. In this case a credible history of a memorable event and its aftermath is provided for the subsequently diagnosed tibial toddler fracture.

Accounts given to paramedics, social workers, police and health professionals will be compared and assessed for credibility and consistency. Vague accounts, inconsistencies, or changing stories that differ between carers raise suspicions for abuse.

When an injured child is admitted to hospital, carers will feel distressed, sometimes confused. A mother may not be aware that the father had injured the child 'wracking her brains' for any possible explanation. More detailed histories may emerge later during admission and should not always be interpreted as a changing history. An account of accidental injury should never be rejected in advance of police and social care enquiries (Fig. 1.1).

Fig. 1.1 A 4-year-old child was brought to ED with multiple facial bruises. Carers stated that she had fallen from a table in the pub garden (pictured) injuring her face. She was immediately presented for medical care. Paediatricians did not accept the explanation and child protection proceedings were commenced. On the final day of the Court hearing parents obtained a video-recording from the pub landlord showing the child falling and severely injuring herself. A carer's explanation should never be rejected prior to comprehensive analysis and investigations by police and social care

Delays in presentation

Most children with significant accidental injuries are presented promptly for care. When a child has been abused, carers may delay presentation in the hope that symptoms will resolve. Some children are brought by an adult not present at the time of injury, whilst others are never presented for care.

A carer may try to treat a burn at home, presenting the child only when it fails to heal or becomes infected. Whilst this may be interpreted as medical neglect, learning or emotional difficulties in the carer or lack of transport may induce them to wait, watch and treat at home.

> A 3-year-old girl with special needs was found to have a high fever and be reluctant to drink. Her mother comforted her at 8am but could not recall reviewing the child until 5pm, at which time she found her not breathing. A postmortem confirmed streptococcal septicaemia. Medical neglect in this case led to the death of a child with a treatable illness.

Developmental stage of the child

When the history provided does not fit with the child's developmental abilities concerns for abuse are raised. Infants beginning to mobilise start exploring their environment with an increased risk of accidental injury.

Carer blames a sibling

Children may be coerced into blaming a sibling for an injury. Reports that an injury occurred during play-fighting or that a sibling fell on an infant should be carefully assessed. Children can, and do, injure each other during rough play. A bite mark reported to have been caused by a child may be distinguished from that of an adult by a forensic odontologist.

Rosenthal and Doherty (1984) reviewed 10 pre-school children who either seriously injured siblings or attempted to do so. Skull and leg fractures, extensive bruising, lacerations, and stab wounds were recorded [9].

> A 6-month-old was brought to the emergency department (ED) with significant facial bruising. The mother reported that she went into the garden to hang up the washing seeing her 3-year-old close and lock the garden door from the kitchen. When she attempted to open the door from the garden side she saw him throwing toys and other items at the infants face. Paediatricians considered the account was implausible and child protection investigations were commenced. Police visiting the home observed the 3-year-old locking the garden door and throwing items both randomly and at the visitors.

Other concerning features

The family may be known to children's social care with repeated attendances for injuries or neglect. The child may disclose abuse, be withdrawn or exhibit other behavioural traits. Carers may appear hostile, unconcerned or demand discharge. However, families who have waited in the emergency department (ED) for many hours may also feel vexed and demand to go home.

Factors Associated with Abuse

Families

Both parents may be involved in physical abuse. Men perpetrate sexual abuse more often whilst mothers more commonly fabricate or induce illness in their offspring.

Whilst personality disorders, depression, anxiety, poverty, adverse social circumstances, drug and alcohol abuse have all been reported to increase susceptibility for abuse, it is known to occur in all layers of society whilst most parents from the above risk groups are caring and loving.

Age
Infants and children under 2 years of age are at greater risk of physical abuse. Death from abuse after the age of one is unusual.

Premature infants and those with Special Needs
Poor bonding between child and carer, an infant's complex medical needs and other stress factors have all been cited as reasons why premature infants are at higher risk for abuse and neglect [10].

Physically handicapped children and those with learning difficulties are at increased risk of abuse for similar reasons. Caring for a handicapped child is often 24/7 with little respite. The physical and emotional demands placed on parents can be onerous [11].

Domestic abuse
Abuse directed towards the mother may start or escalate during pregnancy. Abdominal trauma can injure both mother and foetus. Domestic abuse is associated with alcohol intake and drug misuse with poor antenatal care compounding risks for obstetric complications.

It is estimated that 75% of children living with domestic violence have witnessed such abuse and they themselves are more commonly abused or accidentally injured during an altercation [12]. Children where mothers seek refuge may have limited access to health care and education. In addition, a traumatised mother may neglect her children.

Mental Health Problems
Parental mental illness is recorded in 43% of cases where children are the subject of care proceedings [13]. It is estimated that 50,000 – 200,000 children and young people in the UK care for a parent with a severe mental illness [14]. Whilst mental illness in a carer may affect outcomes for a child, many with such diagnoses love and care for their children without fault.

Substance and alcohol misuse
Alcohol abuse is associated with increased violence within the family and physical abuse of children, whilst parental drug use is more commonly associated with neglect and emotional abuse [15].

Structural damage to the foetus from maternal drug ingestion is more common between 4–12 weeks' gestation. Drugs taken later in pregnancy may inhibit growth or cause neonatal abstinence syndrome. For some drugs, as well as nicotine and alcohol, there is an increased risk of low birth weight, premature delivery, perinatal death and Sudden Infant Death Syndrome (SIDS). Opiates, cocaine and benzodiaz-epines can all cause neonatal withdrawal symptoms.

Alcohol abuse increases the risk of miscarriage and Foetal Alcohol Spectrum Disorder (FASD) where growth failure, visual/hearing defects, poor muscle tone, learning, social and behavioural difficulties may be observed [16].

Parents with Learning Disabilities

Children of parents with intellectual disability are at increased risk of developmental delay, neglect and abuse. Intellectual disability is evidenced by an IQ below 70 with significant limitations before the age of 18 in two or more adaptive behaviours (conceptual, social or practical skills). Adequate parenting remains possible until the IQ falls below 55–60, although at this level promoting language development in a child may present difficulties [17].

Risk of Further Abuse

Repeatedly abused children have an increased risk of physical and mental illness, poor life chances, unhealthy lifestyles and violent behaviour. Child abuse has been shown to have adverse effects on behaviour, development, and psychological well-being.

Sibert et al. (2002) found that 30% of infants who were returned to their families after maltreatment were abused again [18].

Jenny et al. (1999) reviewed the medical records of 173 children presenting with abusive head trauma (AHT). Fifty-four (31.2%) had been seen by a doctor after head trauma with the diagnosis un-recognised. The mean time to correct diagnosis among these children was 7 days (0 – 189 days). Abusive head trauma was more likely to be unrecognised in very young children and those without respiratory difficulties or seizures. Fifteen (27.8%) sustained additional injury after the diagnosis was missed and 22 (40.7%) developed medical complications. The authors conclude that 4 of 5 deaths in the group of unrecognised AHT might have been prevented if abuse had been recognised earlier [19].

Developmental Stage

An understanding of the child's developmental stage is essential when considering whether an account provided of an accident is plausible, particularly in infants and children less than 3 years old (Tables 1.6 and 1.7).

Developmental milestones have an age range for most infants and children but some develop faster and are advanced, others more slowly. It is important to corroborate the developmental history provided with videos, images and a comprehensive developmental assessment of the child.

Four to 5 months is the usual age when an infant rolls over. However, this ability can be acquired from as early as 2½ months to as late as 6 months in normal children. Similarly whilst an ability to stand is usually from 9½ months some infants achieve this from 8 months. From 11 months of age an agile infant can climb on to a sofa and up on the back rest. At that age, balance is poorly developed, there is little sense of danger and an increased susceptibility to accident.

Table 1.6 Cognitive and motor developmental milestones [20, 21]

Age	Cognitive	Motor
0–1 month	Distinguish tastes Briefly watches objects Makes eye contact with carer	Lifts chin when lying on abdomen Hands form a fist and are tightly closed Occasionally brings hands to mouth Wraps fingers around object placed in palm
2–3 months	Follows moving objects from side to side of body	Lifts up to chest when lying on abdomen Sits when supported minimum head bobbing Turns head towards bright colours Makes fists with both hands Reaches out for objects but may miss Briefly grasps objects Pulls at blankets or clothing
4–5 months	Shows visual preference Habituates to a picture or object	Bears weight on forearms while on tummy Rolls over Sits well with support, slightly curved back Actively holds on to toys Rocks on abdomen for pleasure
6–8 months	Picks up blocks briefly Inspects objects at length Looks or goes after dropped item	Sits, reaches for objects and picks up Brings object to mouth Pulls blanket off face Plays with hands in front of their face Holds onto objects for up to 30 s Transfers objects from hand to hand Bangs toys on surface Asymmetric neck reflex disappears (22– 26w)
9–11 months	Fears heights Beginning of intelligence Assigns symbols to events Begins to show persistence	Sits without support Crawls up stairs Pulls to standing, gets down from standing Clasps hands or bangs objects together Uses both hands to play with toys Puts blocks in cup
12–15 months	Drinks from a cup Eats from spoon with help Likes helping around the house Removes clothes Searches for a hidden object Understands 'no'	Crawls on hands and knees Stands erect Develops to walking holding on to one hand Develops to walking well. Reaches for objects that are close by Can make a tower of 2 blocks Finger and thumb to pick up small objects Holds crayon making mark on paper
16-18 months	Feeds self Understands object and use recognises familiar pictures	Walks without help Turns more than one page at a time Builds tower of two cubes Removes lid from toy box to retrieve toy Holds two cubes in one hand Scribbles on paper Removes both socks and shoes

(continued)

Table 1.6 (continued)

Age	Cognitive	Motor
18–24 months	Refers to self by name Invents play with a toy Mental problem-solving Has insight and forethought Control of bladder/bowels (24m)	Jumps up Throws ball overhead Builds tower of 4–6 blocks Draws straight line Turns pages of board book one at a time Places three shapes in a puzzle
25–30 months	Egocentric Symbolic and fantasy play Begins to understand time Uses symbols increasingly Dresses/undresses with help	Runs Can build tower of 6–8 blocks Copies circle Throws ball about 4–5 feet Removes screw on cap from bottle Draws a straight horizontal line Able to turn a door knob
31–36 months	Brushes teeth with little help Washes and dries hand Puts on shirt Names a friend Still engages in fantasy play	Balances on one foot for 2s Runs easily, rides a tricycle Uses a toilet Draws circles, end point ½ inch of beginning Builds tower of 8 cubes Cuts paper with scissors
4 years	Dresses/undresses little help Gives first and last name Draws person with 3 body parts Counts to 5 Numbers and shapes	Balances on one foot for 3–4s Hops, jumps from step Copies a circle and cross Unbuttons large buttons Strings 4–5 beads
5 years	Dresses alone Bathes self Counts up to ten objects Draws a person with 6 parts	Skips using alternate feet Catches large balls Walks backwards toe to heel Copies a drawn square

A child with motor impairment may have decreased or increased muscle tone (hypotonia or hypertonia) delaying motor development. Neglect may impede socio-emotional development. A fearful, emotionless 2–3 year old with otherwise normal development may indicate neglect.

For the first few months of life, an infant is unable to turn or crawl. Nevertheless some neonatal reflexes may permit reflex movement. The asymmetric tonic neck reflex (ATNR) diminishes at 4–5 months. When the infant's head is turned to one side, the arm and leg on that side stretches with bending of the limbs on the other side.

The Bauer reflex is present up to 4 months of age. When pressure is applied to the soles of the feet (lying face-down), with hips and knees bent the infant may move forward with alternating right and left movements.

Table 1.7 Language and social developmental milestones [20, 21]

Age	Language	Social
0–1 month	Makes low throaty noises Responds to voice	Makes eye contact when alert Quietens when picked up
2–3 months	Responds with vocalization Makes cooing sounds	Stops crying when parents approach Smiles back
4-5 months	More vocalisation Responds to voice, head turns	Responds socially with smiles to friendly faces Shows facial expression of emotions
6–8 months	Babbles with consonants Vocalizes pleasures/displeasures	Fear of strangers and excitement to familiar people Holds out arms when wants to be picked up
9–11 months	Da-da, Ma-ma meaningfully Responds to 1–2 words plus name	Discriminates between parents Socially interactive
12–15 months	2–6 words Imitates sounds of animals	Distinguishes self from others Waves bye-bye, plays peek-a-boo
16-18 months	4–6 six words at 15 months 10 or more words at 18 months	Prefers certain people to others Likes to look at pictures
18–24 months	Speech half understandable, pronouns Short sentences with 2–3 words Names 1–2 pictures	Wants to make friends, but unsure how Likes to imitate parents
25–30 months	Gives first and last names Knows body parts Names 4 pictures	Separates easily from parents Notices sex difference Independent in toileting except for wiping
31–36 months	Sentences of about nine words Says sounds a, m, b, p, n, l, w Names 2–4 colours	More friendly Taking turns and sharing Begins to learn meaning of simple rules
4 years	Asks 'What, Where, Who?' Understood by non-family members Says sounds of d, g, f, k, y	Shows many emotions Parallel play with others e.g: board games
5 years	Sentences up to 5–6 words or more	Plays with peer group Likes playing with adults or older children

It is very unusual for an infant under 4 months to turn but very active or hypertonic infants might be able to so. The surface may be uneven, the infant topples and may turn in the process. Hypertonia may lead to awkward jerky movements.

From 4 to 5 years, a child will be able to give an account of an event. Where there is language delay but otherwise normal development the child should be given the opportunity by non-verbal means and the appropriate use of pictures to tell his or her story.

Child Protection Procedures

Definitions

Children in Need
A child is considered to be in need if he or she is unlikely to achieve or maintain a reasonable standard of health or development without the provision of services or is disabled.

Safeguarding
Safeguarding is protecting children from abuse and maltreatment, preventing impairment of health or development, providing safe and effective care and enabling all children to have the best outcomes.

Significant harm
Significant harm is the threshold that justifies compulsory local authority (LA) intervention in the best interests of the child. Harm implies ill-treatment (physical or mental) or developmental impairment (physical, intellectual, emotional, social or behavioural). It includes seeing or hearing the ill-treatment of another.

Referrals to Children's Social Care

A referral is a request from a member of the public or professional raising concerns to the local authority child protection team or police. If the local authority believes there is a significant risk of harm, they may, after efforts to assist the family, commence care proceedings. A pre-proceedings meeting is an attempt to resolve matters prior to Court proceedings.

Children's social care have the responsibility for investigating child protection matters. Health professionals work in partnership with them and the police. If hospital medical staff consider a child to be in need or at risk of significant harm, a referral to children's social care is required and local safeguarding children's board (LSCB) procedures followed. A telephone discussion should be followed by a referral in writing on a standard form.

The police should be involved early, particularly if the paediatrician considers a criminal act has been committed. (e.g: illness induction). They will visit the home and collect forensic information such as medications. Forensic investigations such as DNA analysis of blood or hair should be conducted under their direction.

Meetings

Strategy Discussion
Where there is cause to believe that a child is suffering or is likely to suffer significant harm, the LA will co-ordinate a multi-agency strategy discussion to include paediatricians, GP, nurses, health visitor, legal, police and other representatives. The

purpose of the meeting is to share information, decide whether Section 47 enquiries or a criminal investigation are required, and what action may be needed to ensure the immediate protection of the child including whether or not to initiate an emergency protection order.

In hospital, after the meeting the lead consultant, senior nurse and social worker will inform carers about concerns raised and action planned. If a criminal offence has been committed the police will make such disclosures. Support to both child and carers is required.

Section 47 of the Children Act 1989 places a duty on local authorities to investigate the circumstances of children considered to be at risk of 'significant harm' and to decide what action, if any, is required to safeguard and promote the child's welfare.

Initial child protection conference

Section 47 enquiries initiated by the local authority are followed by a child protection conference bringing together family members and professionals to agree what actions should be undertaken to safeguard.

A child protection plan (CPP) is an inter-agency document setting out what is required to protect a child from further harm, to promote the child's health and development and to support the family as appropriate.

Child protection review conference

This reviews progress against the child protection plan and to consider whether it should continue.

Serious Case Review (SCR)

An SCR is undertaken after a child dies or is seriously harmed and abuse or neglect is thought to be involved. It considers the manner in which organisations and individuals worked together to safeguard and lessons that may be learnt for the future.

Each year, approximately 4,500 children die in England mainly from medical causes. Up to 20% are a result of accidents, homicides, suicides or unexplained. Confidential enquiries into child mortality have revealed that in 26% of deaths, (including those from natural causes) factors including parental care, the environment or provision of healthcare could have been modified or improved [22].

Paediatricians when confronting the sad event of a child dying will be aware of the possibility of abuse and undertake a thorough assessment sharing their findings with the police and social care. At the conclusion of any investigations the paediatrician will offer a post-bereavement interview, if preferred, in the family home, to avoid the emotional trauma of carers having to return to the hospital.

Guidance and Legislation

Statutory guidance for Safeguarding in England

Statutory guidance within 'Working Together to Safeguard Children (2013)' and the United Nations Convention on the Rights of the Child provide details of relevant legislation [23, 24].

Children Act 1989

This legislates for England and Wales. The Children (Northern Ireland) Order 1995 and the Children (Scotland) Act 1995 enshrine the same principles which include the direction that local authorities have a duty to safeguard and promote the welfare of children and make arrangements with others to provide services on their behalf. The Act empowers the police to remove a child (or prevent removal from suitable accommodation) if there is a risk of significant harm [25].

Children Act 2004

This provides further direction on safeguarding to local authorities regarding co-operation, establishing an LSCB for their area and other matters [26].

Care Orders made by the Family Court

Emergency protection order (EPO)

The Court may make an EPO if there are grounds to believe that a child is likely to suffer significant harm if not removed to a different location. An emergency protection order provides authority to remove a child and place him or her under the protection of the local authority.

Supervision order

This places the child under the supervision of the local authority.

Interim care order

Once an interim care order is made, it will last until the final order unless there is a further Court order discharging it before that. In some cases the child will continue living at home with specified conditions.

Full care order

A full care order gives the local authority parental responsibility for the child. A placement order allows a child to be placed with prospective adopters prior to an adoption order.

Adoption order

An adoption order transfers parental responsibility to the adoptive parents. The only criterion for such an order is 'in the best interests of the child'.

Special guardianship order

A special guardianship order is one appointing one or more individuals to be a child's 'special guardian'.

Courts

Family Courts

Private law proceedings are usually between parents and relate to domestic matters such as living arrangements and contact. Public law proceedings are between the local authority seeking an order and the family.

In care proceedings, the Court will determine whether the child has suffered or is likely to suffer significant harm and what order (if any) best supports the child's welfare.

Hearings consist of a 'finding of fact' addressing potential harm suffered with a second hearing to decide what order is required. The standard of proof is on 'the balance of probabllities' with the burden resting with the local authority to demonstrate that the child has suffered or is likely to suffer significant harm.

Paediatricians attend Court to give evidence mainly for Public Law Proceedings either as a professional witness being the treating doctor or as an instructed expert providing an independent opinion within an area of expertise. An experts meeting may take place in advance of Court proceedings [27].

Evidence-based legal practice (like evidence-based medicine) seeks to analyse the current best evidence and clinical expertise to assist Courts in making decisions. In Family Courts, barristers for the LA, the child (represented by a Guardian *ad litem*), mother and father independently test an expert's evidence in what must be considered a robust form of clinical governance. The paediatrician is asked to consider clinical situations from different perspectives, reassess evidence and reconsider conclusions. Courts are concerned with the professionals ability to refer to clinical experience as well as a comprehensive knowledge of the current literature.

Criminal Proceedings

In family proceedings carers may lose parental control of their child. In criminal proceedings they may lose their liberty. The latter are advanced by the Crown Prosecution Service (CPS) in England and Wales, and the Crown Office Procurator Fiscal Service in Scotland. The trial may be held before a judge with or without a jury.

The person charged is presumed innocent unless and until proven guilty. The standard of proof is 'beyond reasonable doubt', with the burden resting with the prosecution to establish that the alleged perpetrator is guilty of the crime. The jury must be *sure* of guilt before they can convict.

As in Family Courts, paediatricians may be ordered to attend either as a professional or expert witness. The prosecution presents evidence-in-chief followed by defence cross-examination then re-examination by the prosecution. Golden rules for evidence in both Family and Criminal Courts apply (Table 1.8).

Table 1.8 Golden rules for evidence

An accurate and comprehensive report
Meticulous review of papers prior to evidence
Identify any errors or changes of opinion prior to evidence
A comprehensive knowledge of the current literature
An ability to draw on clinical experience
A balanced view with accidental, inflicted and medical causes equally considered
Reverence and humility
Remain within your area of expertise
Reconsider an opinion if presented with new evidence or an alternative view
Request time out of Court to read and reflect if required

References

1. Department of Education. National Tables A1 and A2, Children looked after in England including adoption year ending 31st March 2015. 2015.
2. Dept for Education. Main table D4 in Characteristics of Children in Need in England, 2014–15. 2015.
3. Knox G. Characteristics of Children in Need in England' England, 2011–12, Department for Education.
4. May-Chahal C, Cawson P. Measuring child maltreatment in the United Kingdom: a study of the prevalence of child abuse and neglect. Child Abuse Negl. 2005;29(9):969–84.
5. HM Government. Sexual Offences Act. 2003.
6. Royal College of Paediatrics and Child Health. Safeguarding children and young people: roles and competences for health care. 2014.
7. General Medical Council. 'Gillick competency and Fraser Guidelines'. 2012.
8. RCPCH. UK-WHO Growth Charts. http://www.rcpch.ac.uk/Research/UK-WHO-Growth-Charts.
9. Rosenthal PA, Doherty MB. Serious sibling abuse by preschool children. J Am Acad Child Psychiatry. 1984;23(2):186–90.
10. Sameroff A, Abbe L. The consequences of prematurity: understanding and therapy. In: Pick H, editor. Psychology: from research to practice. New York: Plenum; 1978.
11. Frisch L, Rhodes F. Child abuse and neglect in children referred for learning evaluations.J Learn Disability. 1982;15:583–6.
12. Abraham C. The hidden victims: children and domestic violence. London: NCH Action for Children; 1994.
13. Brophy J, Jhutti-Johal J, Owen C. Assessing and documenting child ill-treatment in minority ethnic households. Family Law. 2003;33:756–64.
14. Mental Health Foundation. My Care: the challenges facing young carers of parents with a severe mental illness. 2010.
15. Velleman R. Working with substance misusing parents as part of court proceedings. Representing Children. 2001;14(36):48.
16. Fitzgerald H, Puttler L, Mun E, Zucker R. Prenatal and postnatal exposure to parental alcohol-use and abuse. In: Osofsky J, Fitzgerald H, editors. WAIMH handbook of infant mental health,vol. 4. Infant mental health in groups at high risk. New York: Wiley; 2000.
17. McGaw S, Beckley K, Connolly N, Ball K. Parenting assessment manual. Trecare NHSTrust;1999.

18. Sibert JR, Payne EH, Kemp AM, Barber M, Rolfe K, Morgan RJ, et al. The incidence of severe physical child abuse in Wales. Child Abuse Negl. 2002;26:267–76.
19. Jenny C, Hymel KP, Ritzen A, Reinert SE, Hay TC. Analysis of missed cases of abusive head trauma. JAMA. 1999;282(7):621–6.
20. Illingworth, RS. The development of the infant and young child. Normal and abnormal. 5th ed. Churchill Livingstone. Jan 1974; volume 88, issue 2, page 99.
21. Frankenburg WK, Dodds J, Archer P, et al. The DENVER II: a major revision and re-standardization of the Denver Developmental Screening Test. Pediatrics. 1992;89:91–7.
22. Pearson GE. Why children die: a pilot study 2006; England (North East, South West and WestMidlands), Wales and Northern Ireland. London: CEMACH; 2008.
23. HM Government. Working together to safeguard children. 2013.
24. United Nations. 'Article 3', United Nations Convention on the Rights of the Child 1989. 1989.
25. British Parliament. Children Act 1989. 1989.
26. British Parliament. Children Act 2004. 2004.
27. General Medical Council. Acting as a witness in legal proceedings. 2013.

Bruising in Infants and Children

2

Abstract

Bruises may be accidental, inflicted or the result of an underlying medical disorder. They are commonly accidental but also the commonest manifestation of inflicted injury with 90% of victims sustaining skin injury.

A bruise is the escape of blood from ruptured blood vessels caused by blunt trauma damaging underlying skin and blood vessels. Blood leaks from the capillaries and larger vessels into unbroken skin. Swelling is due to blood or fluid leakage into the bruise.

Clinical Assessment of Bruising

Abstract

The number of accidental bruises increases with mobility. Fewer than 1% of pre-mobile infants have bruising, whilst in those beginning to mobilise (aged 6–12 months) up to 20% can be expected to have some skin injury. At these ages, an injury will usually be associated with a credible history of a memorable event and its aftermath.

In fully ambulant children aged 12 months and above, accidental bruises to the shins and other bony prominences over the front of the body are common. Smaller bruises may not be associated with a history of an accident or aftermath.

Maguire et al. (2005) reviewed 23 studies, 7 of non-abusive bruising, 14 abusive and 2 of both. In pre-mobile infants aged 0–6 months 1% had 1–2 bruises. In those beginning to mobilise aged 6–12 months 17% had 1–6 bruises whilst in walkers aged more than 12 months 53% had 1–27 bruises. The majority in the last group were on the shins [1].

Carpenter (1999) reviewed 177 non-abused infants aged 6–12 months who were sitting, pulling to stand and cruising. Of these, 22 (12%) had bruises related to early mobility. Fifteen had 1 bruise, five had 2, one 3 and one 4. Injuries were circular or rectangular, maximum 1cm in diameter and over bony prominences on the front of the body. Half were on the forehead, the remainder on the head, face and shins [2].

Sheets et al. (2013) reported that minor injuries can precede severe physical abuse in infants. The authors reviewed 401 infants less than 12 months old with definite concern for abuse, intermediate or no concern. A sentinel injury was defined as a previous injury reported in the medical history that was suspicious for abuse. Of 200 definitely abused infants, 27.5% had a previous sentinel injury compared with 8% of the 100 infants with intermediate concern. None of the 101 non-abused infants (controls) had a previous sentinel injury. Sentinel injuries in the abused group were bruising (80%), intra-oral injury (11%), other injury (7%) [3].

Medical Assessment

History and Examination

A comprehensive medical history and examination should be undertaken as described in chapter 1, pages 4–6. Systems enquiries, past medical history, family history, whether Vitamin K was given at birth and reports of abnormal bleeding are relevant. The account of an accident and its aftermath is compared with clinical findings and the developmental stage of the child.

Physical Examination should include observation of parent-child interaction, signs of neglect, assessment of growth and development, systems examination and a careful search for any skin marks or other injuries. Attention should be paid to any skin condition that might be mistaken for injury. Accurate documentation of skin marks on body maps and good quality images with a standard ruler placed against any skin marks should be undertaken by either the hospital's medical photography department or police.

Each mark must be diagnosed where possible and documented in the medical notes and on body diagrams. Injuries should be considered individually and an opinion reached as to whether they are accidental, inflicted or if investigations for a medical diagnosis increasing the child's susceptibility to bruising are required. It is equally important to take an overview of all injuries observed as well as other concerning features including evidence of neglect and emotional abuse.

Haematological Investigations

A careful history and examination will guide the selection of investigations required. Reports by a carer that the child or family members bruise easily should be confirmed prior to more extensive testing. Where investigations are not done, the absence of a past history of bruising, no relevant family history and resolution of injuries in care without recurrence makes an underlying medical disorder highly unlikely. However, transient bleeding disorders, although rare cannot be completely ruled out without testing at the time of injury. Pre-mobile infants with unexplained bruising should always be investigated.

Coagulation (clotting) is the process by which blood changes from a liquid to a blood clot. A bleeding disorder may increase susceptibility to petechiae, bruising and bleeding or accelerate and worsen these following trivial trauma.

Primary haemostasis involves the formation of a platelet plug at the site of injury. Common associated disorders include von-Willebrand disease, idiopathic thrombo-cytopenic purpura and other disorders of platelet function (eg. Glanzmann's thrombasthenia).

Secondary haemostasis occurs at the same time with clotting factors responding in a complex cascade to form fibrin strands strengthening the platelet plug. Disorders include factor deficiencies, ingestion of anticoagulant drugs and vitamin K deficiency. Not all factor deficiencies are associated with bruising and bleeding (e.g.: Factor XII).

Children with congenital bleeding disorders do not have linear bruises unless injured by an object producing them. They tend to bruise in the usual locations for accidental injury and are not immune to abuse [4–6].

There are different approaches to the investigation of the child presenting with abnormal bruising. A suggested method is set out below (Tables 2.1 and 2.2).

Other Investigations

For children under 2 years of age a skeletal survey with repeat imaging after 10–14 days is required. Infants under 1 year of age should have a head CT (up to 2 years if clinically indicated) and ophthalmology examination to exclude retinal haemorrhages.

Table 2.1 First line investigation for abnormal bruising

Full blood count and film	Haemoglobin low in:
	Blood loss, toxins, haemodilution, anaemias
	White cell count:
	Raised in infection, inflammation, trauma, stress response
	Platelet Count:
	Low in platelet disorders, leukaemia, viral infections, some drugs
	High in iron deficiency, bleeding, stress response, viral infections
Prothrombin time (PT)	Tests the integrity of the extrinsic coagulation cascade
	Prolonged in:
	Vitamin K deficiency, Liver disease, DIC, Polycythaemia
	Factor II, V, VII, X deficiencies
Partial thromboplastin time (aPTT)	Tests the integrity of intrinsic coagulation cascade
	Prolonged in:
	Liver disease, heparin treatment, polycythaemia
	Factor VIII, IX, XI, XII deficiencies, Von Willebrand disease
Thrombin Time (TT) or Fibrinogen (Clauss)	Tests the integrity of final common pathway

Table 2.2 Second line investigation for unexplained bruising

Under 24 months:	
Coagulation screen	
Factor VIII	Haemophilia A
Factor XIII	Congenital Factor XIII deficiency
Von Willebrand factor VWF antigen and VWF activity	von Willebrand disease
Platelet function studies	
PFA-100 closure time or Platelet glycoproteins	Preferred investigation in neonates and infants
	Abnormal in inherited platelet function defects
Protein C, protein S	Abnormal anti-coagulation proteins
Over 24 months:	
Coagulation factors	
Factor VIII	Haemophilia A
Factor XIII	Congenital Factor XIII deficiency
Von Willebrand factor VWF antigen and VWF activity	von Willebrands disease
Platelet function studies	
Platelet aggregation and Nucleotide release	Abnormal in:
	Inherited platelet function defects.
	Von willebrands disease.
Alpha 2 antiplasmin	Where there is a positive family history
Other Factor assays that may be considered as part of an extended haematological screen:	
Factor II	Prothrombin deficiency
Factor V	Proaccelerin, Owren's disease
Factor VII	Congenital Factor VII deficiency
Factor IX	Haemophilia B
Factor X	Congenital Factor X deficiency
Factor XI	Haemophilia C
Factor XII	Does not affect clotting but can prolong the APTT

Features of Accidental Versus Inflicted Bruising

Bruises have features that guide the clinician towards a diagnosis of either accidental or inflicted injury. None, however, are diagnostic for the latter, other than those that carry the imprint of an implement used [7].

Accidental Bruises

Accidental bruises tend to be small, single, located over the front of the body over bony prominences most commonly knees and shins in ambulant children. In infants

Table 2.3 Features of accidental bruising

A credible history of a memorable event and its aftermath
Compatible with the child's developmental stage
Features suspicious for inflicted injury are absent (Table 2.4)
Predominantly over bony prominences on the front of the body
In those beginning to mobilise:
'T' shaped distribution across forehead, nose, upper lip and chin
Back of head
In ambulant infants and children:
Shins, knees, elbows and other bony prominences

beginning to mobilise the 'T' shaped distribution of bruises across the forehead, nose, upper lip and chin may result from attempts to move forward or stand where impact against solid objects causes injury. Bruising to the back of the head commonly results from injuries sustained when a child impacts against furniture or the floor on attempting to stand or walk [8] (Table 2.3).

In ambulant infants and children, accidental bruises are observed over bony prominences including the lower back, shins, knees, and elbows.

A diagnosis of accidental injury is suggested by a credible history of a memorable event and its aftermath and injuries compatible with the child's developmental stage. However, for minor injuries in ambulant children a history of accident may not be recalled.

Kemp et al. (2015) prospectively studied 328 infants and children aged less than 6 years old (mean age 19 months) in whom 3523 bruises were recorded from 2570 data collections. Of all bruises 6.7% of 1010 pre-mobile infants had at least one bruise (2.2% of babies who could not roll over and 9.8% in those who could), compared with 45.6% of 478 early mobile and 78.8% of 1082 walkers. The most common site affected in all groups was below the knees, followed by 'facial T' and head in pre-mobile and early mobile infants. The ears, neck, buttocks, genitalia and hands were rarely bruised (<1%). Having a sibling increased the mean number of bruises [9].

Inflicted Bruises

Inflicted bruises are more commonly multiple, clustered and located on soft parts of the body away from bony prominences. In abused children bruises may be few or absent in common accidental locations such as the shins.

The commonest sites for inflicted injuries are cheeks, ears, eyes, head and neck. Other common sites include trunk, buttocks, arms, abdomen, genitals, upper legs, axilla, back, backs of limbs, feet, hands and upper limbs. Defensive bruises occur on the upper arm, on the outside of the thigh, or on the trunk and adjacent extremity. An inflicted bruise may carry the imprint of an implement used. There may be associated petechiae (Fig. 2.1).

Fig. 2.1 An infant was presented for care with a history that he had fallen off a couch and injured his back. Multiple puncture marks are observed over his lower back that carry the imprint of an implement used, most likely human nails (Image courtesy of Dr. Junaid Solebo)

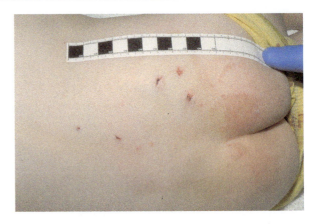

Table 2.4 Features of inflicted bruising

No credible history of a memorable event or its aftermath
Injuries not compatible with the child's developmental stage
Bruises over soft parts of the body away from bony prominences
Multiple bruises from a single reported episode of trauma
Linear or other shapes carrying the imprint of an implement used
Defensive bruises to limbs and trunk
Large bruises
Clusters over the same area or trunk and adjacent limb
Bruises are few/absent in common accidental locations eg. shins
Associated petechiae
Often found with other injury types eg. fractures
Common sites:
Cheeks, ears, eyes, head and neck
Abdomen, buttocks, trunk and arms
Genitals, upper legs, axilla, back, backs of limbs, feet and hands, forearm, upper limb

Factors that raise concerns for abuse (chapter 1, page 7) are a clinical examination that does not match the account of injury, no credible history of a memorable event and its aftermath, discrepant accounts, delays in presentation and a history that does not fit with the child's developmental abilities. The carer may blame a sibling, the family may be known to children's social care with repeated attendances for injuries. There may be other injuries or signs of neglect (Table 2.4).

Kemp et al. (2014) collected data from 506 children under 6 years referred to child protection teams. Physical abuse (PA) was confirmed in 350 (69.2%) and excluded in 156 (30.8%). Children in the PA group were significantly more likely to have bruising than children where PA was excluded (89.4% vs 69.9%) with more sites affected. The difference between the number of bruises and the number of sites affected between walking and earlier developmental stages was significant but not between baby and early mobility. Bruises on the left ear, buttocks, genitalia, cheeks, neck, trunk, head, front of thighs and upper arms were significantly more common in the PA group. Petechiae were reported in 54/350 (15.4%) of the PA children compared with 3/156 (1.9%) of PA excluded.

Linear bruises or bruises with a distinct pattern (slap mark, finger-tip or matching an implement) were observed in 47 (13.4%) PA children and 4 (2.56%) PA excluded. Clusters (defined as at least two bruises in the same location) were more common in the PA group (67.4% at least one cluster) compared with 33.9% of the PA excluded children.

The most common sites for clusters were on the upper arms, cheeks and front and back of the trunk. The mean size of bruises in the two groups was similar, 1.53cm in the PA group and 1.57cm in the PA-excluded group. Of the PA group, 13% were known to social services for previous child abuse concerns compared to 5% PA excluded. Of the PA group 25.2% had additional injuries compared to 10% of PA excluded. Of the PA group the following additional injuries were recorded: inflicted head trauma (8.6%), fractures (14.3%) bruising overlying the fracture (26%). Twenty (5.7%) children had additional soft tissue injuries, bites (7), abrasions (3), burns (4), torn labial frenulum (6), and subconjunctival haemorrhage (1) [10].

Brinkmann et al. (1979) found clusters of skin injuries in 88% of 93 severely abused children (0–16 years) defining these as at least three injuries (bruises, scars, grazes and lacerations). In this study injuries were mainly to the outside front and back of limbs, head, back and buttocks [11].

Pascoe et al. (1979) found that bruises to soft areas on the cheeks, neck, trunk, genitals, and upper legs were observed significantly more often in children suspected of having been abused or neglected [12].

Johnson and Showers (1985) reviewed 616 children suspected of having been abused. Of 775 injuries 80% involved the skin including bruises and haematomas (56%), erythema and marks (9%), burns (8%), abrasions and scratches (7%) [13].

Pierce et al. (2010) reviewed children under 4 years of age admitted to a paediatric intensive care unit (42 with physical abuse and 53 with accidental trauma). Bruises to the ears, neck, right arm, hands, chest, buttocks and genitalia were more common in the abused children than in those with accidental injuries [14].

Nayak et al. (2006) reported that bruising to the head, neck or trunk were more common in children referred for suspected abuse than in those for accidental injuries [15].

Dunstan et al. (2002) reviewed 133 physically abused and 189 control children aged 1–14 years noting differences in the length of bruises more significantly in the head and neck, less so in the limbs. A scoring system was developed that, the authors state, discriminated between abused and non-abused children [16].

Petska et al. (2013) described 3 infants all less than 5 months old presenting with facial bruising which was not investigated. All three re-presented with abusive head trauma (AHT) confirming the view that facial bruising in a pre-mobile infant signals the risk for further abuse [17].

Harper et al. (2014) prospectively reviewed children less than 10 years of age for possible physical abuse. Of 2890 cases, 33.9% (980/2890) were under 6 months and of these 25.9% (254/980) had bruises of which 57.5% were isolated. Skeletal surveys in this group identified injury in 23.3% (34/146), neuroimaging in 27.4% (40/146), with abdominal injury being found in 2.7% (4/146). Overall, 50% (73/146) had at least one additional serious injury. Testing for bleeding disorders was performed in 70.5% (103/146) with none identified [18].

Mechanism, Force Required and the Aftermath of Injury

Mechanism

A direct blow, twisting, squeezing, poking and pinching mechanisms may rupture blood vessels and cause bruising as can impact against a hard surface.

Active children engaging in 'rough and tumble play' sustain bruises mainly to the shins or other bony prominences. Babies often scratch themselves over the face, forehead, arms, sometimes chest and abdomen. They may hit themselves with rattles or other toys over the face and cause a small bruise. The carer will reliably offer a history of an event and its aftermath if he or she was present.

Some mechanisms are highly unlikely to rupture blood vessels and cause bruising. Sleeping on an object produces a skin imprint with some reddening which usually disappears within 30–60 minutes. Bruising from infant car seats and seat belts is possible if an account of excessive restraint is provided eg. driver braking suddenly with the infant showing distress. Bruises do not occur after winding unless excessive force has been applied. Normal or even rough handling does not cause bruising.

Injury after handling by medical or nursing staff during procedures is sometimes proposed as a possible explanation for injuries found. Bruising is often observed after blood testing where a child's hand or foot has been squeezed. Intravenous line placement may also lead to a ruptured blood vessel and skin injury.

Children can sometimes be held firmly during radiographs and other procedures by inexperienced staff. Whilst the possibility of injury cannot be discounted, the author has never encountered this occurrence or received such reports from other medical or nursing staff. A careful history should be taken from anyone present during an investigation where injury is reported to have occurred.

Force Required

Whilst the force required to rupture a blood vessel cannot be measured it is in excess of normal or rough handling. A smack may cause capillary dilatation with reddening of the skin which disappears within 30–60 minutes. Greater force is required to rupture capillaries.

A number of factors determine the size and depth of a bruise including the force of impact, size of blood vessels (capillaries rupture more readily than larger vessels), vascularity of the injured tissue and fragility of the blood vessels involved [19]. The area around the orbit is highly vascularised with blood vessels that may rupture extensively following trauma leading to bruising from a lesser force than required in less vascularised areas.

Aftermath of Injury

Distress

In the aftermath, depending on the force used and extent of injury, an infant will cry out in pain but settle within a few minutes if comforted. A child may seek the comfort of a carer and point out where he or she has been hurt. Distress continues for longer if there is associated soft tissue swelling, additional injuries or fear of further injury.

For infants and young children a credible history of an accidental event and its aftermath is reliably provided if the carer was present. An older child will usually recall an accident and the pain felt. However, some accidental bruises are sustained in play and go unnoticed by the child. Whether or not children differ in their response to pain is a matter of speculation.

Observers

With inflicted injury a perpetrator will recognise that excessive force had been applied and see bruising on exposed and superficial areas within minutes being on 'the look out' for injury. A non-perpetrator in close vicinity will hear or see that the child is distressed and in infants, notice bruising within about an hour over exposed areas and a few hours on clothed areas at general care. In older children skin marks may be overlooked in non-exposed areas until bath or bedtime, sometimes until the following morning.

Non-perpetrators, not being aware that an injury had occurred, may misinterpret a bruise as a rash or infection. A concerned carer will often seek advice from a neighbour or their own parents, before presenting the child for medical care.

Ageing and Resolution of Bruises

The current literature indicates that bruises cannot be aged accurately by colour from clinical assessment or photographs.

Clinical Aspects

The usual colour progression for a bruise is from red/purple to blue then green, yellowish brown prior to resolution. However, time intervals for progression vary, not all bruises pass through the above colour changes, different colours can be seen in a bruise at any one time and bruises sustained at the same time may have a different colour. A carer may reliably report the last time no bruising was observed.

Factors that affect the colour of a bruise include the force of injury, depth of bruising (deep and superficial bruises occurring at the same time may be of different colours), the amount of blood leaked, skin pigmentation (bruises are easier to identify on a light skinned child) and the site of injury. Blood may track to a location from a more distant injury.

Research Evidence

Bariciak et al. (2003) reported variability in observer interpretation and description of bruise colour. Reviewing images yielded a 50% agreement to within 24 hours. In this study yellow bruising was not observed before 24 hours and one child had a blue bruise on the arm and a green/yellow bruise on the leg sustained at the same time [20].

Stephenson and Bialas (1996) noted that different colours appeared in the same bruise at the same time and that not all colours appeared in every bruise. In general, red, blue, purple colours were more commonly observed in bruises less than 48 hours old whilst yellow, brown, green bruises were most often observed in bruises over 7 days old. However, red, blue, purple colours were identified in up to 30% of observations in bruises older than 7 days while yellow, brown or green was observed in up to 23% of bruises less than 48 hours old [21].

Carpenter (1999) reported a wide variation in observer variability when attempting to age bruises. Blue, black, yellow and green colours were observed at various times during resolution of bruising. In this study, yellow appeared only in bruises over 48 hours old [22].

Resolution of Bruising

Superficial bruises generally resolve within 2–3 days and most bruises cannot be identified after 7–10 days. Large deeper bruises may still be evident 10–14 days after injury. In some locations bruises may last longer. Blood that has collected below the inferior margin of the orbit may take several weeks to fully resolve.

Petechiae (blood spots) disappear relatively quickly. McCann et al. (2007) examined accidental and sexually abusive trauma sustained by 239 girls. Petechiae were identified in 50% but not seen after 72 hours [23].

Other Factors

Bruises result from ruptured blood vessels. When these are superficial capillaries, skin discolouration is likely to occur in the minutes after injury. When deeper vessels rupture (eg. following a blow to the thigh) blood may track superficially with bruising observed after hours, sometimes days [24].

Following acute sports injury the first 24 hours is considered the most painful with swelling at its worst a few hours to 2 days after injury. After 72 hours there is less pain and tenderness. Richardson (1994) reported that swelling is common for 2 days until serum is re-absorbed [25]. In clinical practice swelling (oedema), often but not always tender, indicates injury occurring within the previous 72 hours.

Other Methods of Assessment

Wood lamp/ultraviolet imaging

Ultraviolet light involves the use of a high quality digital image that may reveal healed wounds, bite marks, and bruises not seen with conventional photography. The technique relies on the fact that leaked blood absorbs more visible violet light. Facilities for UV imaging exist in some hospitals.

Barsley et al. (1990) and Hempling (1981), reported that ultraviolet imaging has the potential of revealing bruises not visible to the naked eye [26, 27]. UV imaging has also been shown to be valuable in visualising 'tram-track bruising' months after injury, [28].

Haemoglobin

Hughes et al. (2004) reported that the non-invasive measurement of haemoglobin and its degradation products using reflectance spectrophotometry might allow more accurate dating of bruises [29].

Digital photography and plastic overlay

A combination of digital photography and plastic overlay can outline a handprint and assist in identifying a perpetrator [30].

Injuries that Carry the Imprint of an Implement Used

Whilst bruises have features that guide the clinician towards an opinion as to their cause, none are diagnostic for inflicted injury other than those that carry the imprint of an implement used (Fig. 2.2).

Fig. 2.2 Injuries that carry the imprint of an implement used, in the absence of a credible history of an accident and its aftermath strongly suggest an inflicted injury (Image reproduced with permission of the Wellcome Library, London)

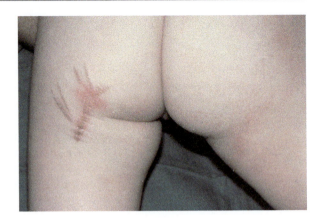

Belt

A belt typically produces a band of bruising, sometimes with a horseshoe shape at one end from the buckle and puncture marks from the tongue of the buckle.

Bite Marks

A 2–4.5cm circular or oval bruise may be observed caused by the two opposing concave arches of the perpetrator's teeth. There may be central bruising or sparing and irregularities within the arc from individual tooth characteristics. Mandibular teeth are more clearly seen than maxillary teeth. Both vertical and horizontal sizes should be measured as well as the distance between the maxillary canines when these are visualised. An intercanine distance of less than 2.5cm is consistent with the teeth of a young child; 2.5–3cm consistent for a child or small adult and 3–4.5cm for an adult [31].

Photo-documentation with a standard ruler is essential if an expert opinion is being sought and the injury matched with the teeth of the perpetrator. Ideally the injury should be swabbed first with a wet swab then a dry one for DNA analysis [32].

Gold et al. (1989) noted that human bites can mimic dermatoses citing the case of a 2-year-old girl with annular lesions mistaken for a dermatophyte infection. After several days, a dermatologist identified the lesions as human bites [33].

Paediatricians will recognise that an injury resembles a bite mark but accurate forensic analysis can be conducted only by a forensic odontologist (www.bafo.org.uk/list.php) (accessed 15.04.17).

Cord/Rope Folded Over

A cord folded over and used to strike a child may cause irregular bruising and petechial loop marks or small abrasions.

Gag Marks

Holding a child's face with force may cause bruising on both cheeks suggesting a grabbing action. If associated with force feeding, gag marks (bruising extending from the mouth) and intra-oral injuries (e.g: torn frenulum) may be observed.

Hair Tourniquet Syndrome

A hair or other fine thread may become tightly tied around a toe or finger constricting blood flow, leading to redness and painful swelling of the affected digit. In infants, hairs or threads may be lost inside socks. The syndrome has been described in both inflicted and accidental injury.

Hair Pulling

Abusive hair pulling leads to traumatic alopecia. A subgaleal haematoma may develop (page 125). Other causes of hair loss must be excluded to include alopecia areata, self-inflicted hair pulling or infections such as tinea capitis.

Ligatures

Children may be restrained with ties leading to part or full circumferential ligature marks on the neck, ankles, wrists, arms or legs. Kornberg (1992) noted that holding a child's limbs during physical abuse may cause ligature marks around the ankles and wrists [34]. In rare cases circumferential hyper-pigmented bands on the lower leg are caused by tight fitting socks (sock line hyperpigmentation) (Fig. 2.3).

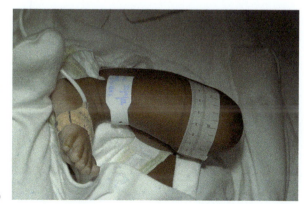

Fig. 2.3 An infant was presented for care with a narrow band of bruising around both calves which had the appearance of a ligature. After full investigation these were considered to be hyper-pigmented bands caused by tight fitting socks (sock line hyper-pigmentation) (Image courtesy of Dr. Junaid Solebo)

Fig. 2.4 A 9-month-old infant was presented with a mark to her leg. Her mother was unable to provide an explanation. A long linear bruise is observed that carries the imprint of an implement used (Image courtesy of Dr. Junaid Solebo)

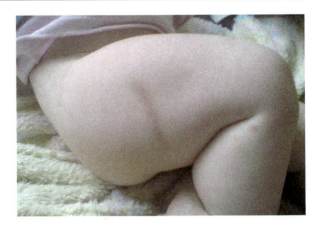

Sticks and Rods

Single or multiple linear bruises of variable width and depth are observed (Fig. 2.4).

Other Injury Patterns

Negative Images from an Adult Hand or Other Blunt Instrument

Blunt force from an adult hand or other object leaves bruising on the skin when sufficient force is used. Blood vessels that are directly impacted may rupture causing a positive image of the object used. However, the imprint may also appear 'negative' with an outline of adult fingers made by petechial bruising between them due to capillary rupture as blood is pushed away from the point of impact [35]. Where another blunt instrument is used, a negative image of the object may be outlined by a fine rim of petechiae caused by capillary rupture at its margins.

Stair Falls

Following stairway falls (page 60), injuries are predominantly to the head, neck and distal extremities. The most severe bruising occurs to the part of the body that lands first. The child then rolls step by step with further bruising less likely due to the short distances involved. Children who present with multiple truncal or proximal extremity injuries who reportedly fell downstairs are more likely to have suffered inflicted injury [36, 37].

Joffe and Ludwig (1988) studied 363 children aged 1 to nearly 19 years, with injuries from a fall downstairs. Ten were being carried by their carer and 24 in a baby walker when they fell. Injuries were recorded as follows: head and neck (73%), extremities (28%), trunk (2%) and fractures (6%). Children who had fallen more than four steps did not sustain more injuries than those who fell fewer than four steps. Joffe and Ludwig noted that a fall downstairs is a series of smaller falls, the first being the longest (height of the child plus the initial number of steps fallen) [38].

Tracking of Blood

Tracking of blood can alter the apparent location of the original injury. An injury to the forehead may result in peri-orbital bruising, one to the scrotal or penile area in a triangular-shaped bruise to the suprapubic area with the apex being at the site of the original injury.

Petechiae

Petechiae (blood spots) are pinpoint bruises on the skin and mucosal surfaces resulting from increased vascular congestion of blood vessels causing capillary rupture. They develop within a few minutes of injury and usually disappear by 72 hours. When found with bruising they increase the likelihood of inflicted injury.

Petechiae are caused by blunt compression, slapping, squeezing, gripping, suction, shaking or impact against a hard surface. They are observed over the head, face and neck after imposed upper airways obstruction or following compression of the chest or abdomen.

Medical causes include coughing, excessive crying or retching. Viral or severe bacterial infections may result in widespread petechiae not usually confined to one area as found following trauma. They are also found in children with platelet abnormalities, leukaemia and other haematological conditions.

Nayak et al. (2006) reported that the presence of petechiae with bruising increased the likelihood of physical abuse identifying them in 21.9% of children less than 17 years old who had suffered abuse [15].

Specific Sites for Bruising

Abdomen and Flank

Soft parts of the body away from bony prominences are more common sites for inflicted injury. Abdominal bruising may be associated with hollow viscus or solid organ damage (chapter 6).

Arms and Shoulders

Bruises to the forearm or upper limb may be 'defensive' where the child has tried to protect him or herself from blows. Clusters of small bruises indicate a squeezing/gripping force from an adult hand or imprints from another implement. The shoulders are unusual areas for accidental injury.

Back and Spine

The back and spine are a common site for inflicted injury. In ambulant children, however, occasional small bruises over the lower back are observed over bony prominences. In infants, a forceful grip around the chest or abdomen may cause bruising over both the front and back of the body.

Buttocks

The buttocks are highly suspect for inflicted injury where there is no account of an accident and its aftermath. Clusters of small bruises suggest application by an adult hand producing a finger-thumb pattern. There may be linear petechial bruising from adult fingers (negative or positive imprints) or patterns from another implement used (Fig. 2.5).

Vertical gluteal cleft bruising (the groove between the buttocks from sacrum to perineum) may be found following a blow horizontally across the lower back above the buttocks with blood tracking vertically along the gluteal cleft or to other anatomical sites.

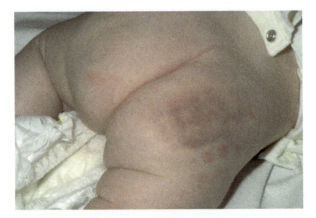

Fig. 2.5 A 4-month-old infant was brought to the hospital by social care after bruising was seen on his buttock. The mother stated he injured himself on the cot bars. A negative imprint can be observed with an outline of adult fingers and bruising between them due to capillary rupture (Image courtesy of Dr. Junaid Solebo)

Calf

The back of the lower leg is an uncommon site for accidental injury although small isolated bruises may be observed in active children.

Chest

Accidental injuries occur more commonly over the front of the body. Small bruises over bony prominences are seen in ambulant children. Bruises over both the front and back of the chest in an infant may indicate a squeezing/gripping mechanism.

Ear

The cartilage of the ear is a common site for inflicted injury. The ear is tucked into the side of the head and relatively protected. In sideways falls, the shoulder lands first, taking much of the impact. High energy contact sports may lead to accidental ear injuries in older children.

In inflicted injury, the upper part of the ear may be pinched, gripped, pulled and twisted. The ear may be slapped or punched. Injury to both sides of the cartilage indicates a gripping action (Fig. 2.6).

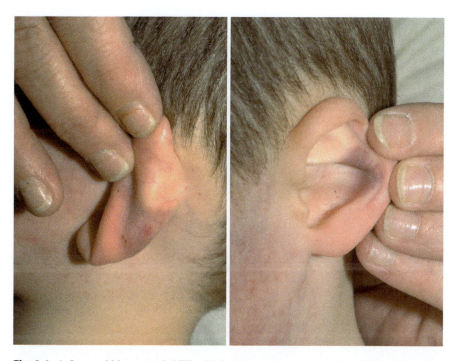

Fig. 2.6 A 5-year-old boy attended ED with bruising to the ear said to have been noticed that morning with no history of trauma. Bruising is observed to both the front and back of the pinna suggesting an inflicted grip (Images courtesy of Dr. Junaid Solebo)

Battle's sign (page 65) is bruising behind the ear over the mastoid process and may indicate a basal skull fracture. It is usually visible hours after injury but may delayed as long as 2–3 days.

Face and Neck

The face is one of the commonest sites for inflicted injury with fewer than 6% of accidental bruises being found on the cheeks and periorbital area. The neck is shielded from injury particularly in infants where there is a small gap between the lower chin and upper chest, with the chin often propped against the chest.

In inflicted injury, clusters of small bruises suggest a finger-thumb application. Holding a child's face with excessive force may cause bruising on both cheeks suggesting a grabbing action. Bruises from direct impact may present as a positive image of the object used or 'negative' with an outline of the fingers made by petechial bruising between them due to capillary rupture as blood is pushed away from the point of impact (Fig. 2.7). If associated with force feeding, gag marks and intra-oral injuries (e.g: torn frenulum) may be observed.

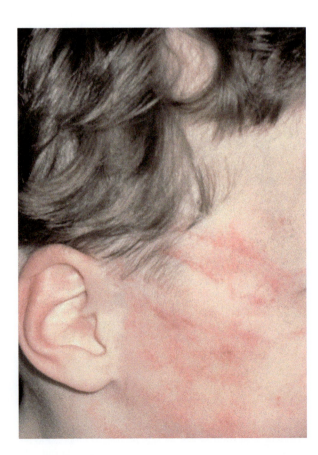

Fig. 2.7 Linear facial bruising with petechiae carrying an imprint of the fingers of an adult hand (Image reproduced with permission of the Wellcome Library, London)

Genital and Inguinal Bruising

Accidental inguinal and genital injuries are reliably associated with a credible history of an event and its aftermath. Straddle injuries whilst riding a bike, sports injuries, falls or injuries from zips in boys are relatively common.

In abuse a child may be punched, kicked, impacted with a blunt instrument or against a hard surface. Penile bruising may be caused by grabbing, squeezing, pulling or twisting actions. A careful assessment for child sexual abuse is required (page 201).

Hobbs and Osman (2007) reviewed 86 boys (average age 62.7 months) with penile or scrotal injuries judged to be inflicted in 63, suspicious in 17 and accidental in 6. Injuries were mainly to the penis and included burns/scars (7), bruises/petechiae (27), wounds, lacerations or scars (39), and other injuries to include fissures, reddening and thickening of perianal tissues (27). Abnormal anal signs were observed in 28 children. In 17 children there were >10 bruises, burns in 12, mouth injuries in 4, brain and retinal haemorrhages in 1 and poor nourishment in 14. There were three fractures thought to be inflicted [39].

Hands and Feet

Bruising found on the sole of the foot or palm of the hand may be the result of normal activities. The back of hands and feet are more commonly associated with inflicted injury.

Head

Infants beginning to mobilise commonly injure their foreheads on furniture or the floor when crawling or attempting to stand. When walking or running, they may fall forward and injure themselves. In so-called 'slips, trips and falls' the commonest sites for bruising are the back of the head and the 'T' shaped distribution of the forehead, nose, upper lip and chin.

Knees and Shins

The knees and shins are common sites for accidental bruising in ambulant children and the majority of walkers will have some shin bruising. However, excessive bruising may represent abuse or lack of supervision. The absence of knee and shin bruising where there is significant injury to other areas raises concerns for abuse.

Orbit

The eye and surroundings structures are common sites for inflicted injury. An orbital haematoma (black eye) may be the result of impact with a blunt instrument or

Fig. 2.8 Orbital haematoma, a common inflicted injury

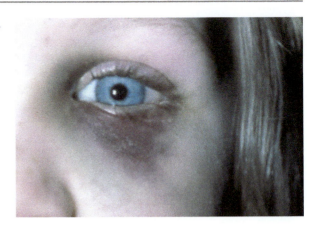

Fig. 2.9 Subconjunctival haemorrhage caused by coughing (Image reproduced with permission of the Wellcome Library, London)

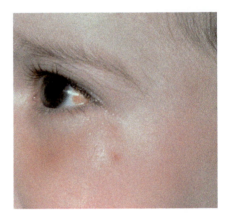

against a hard surface (Fig. 2.8). A significant blow to the forehead may cause a localised haematoma with blood tracking downwards to around the eyes over 24–48 hours giving, a 'black eye' appearance usually on both sides. Shaking injuries may result in orbital bruising.

Racoon Eyes (page 65) are peri-orbital bruises resulting from haemorrhage of the connective tissue around the eyes and are associated with basilar skull fractures. They are usually bilateral, appearing within a few hours but may be delayed as long as 2–3 days. Black eyes are seen shortly after injury with bruising that may spread whilst Racoon Eyes are restricted to the area of the eye.

Subconjunctival haemorrhage (Fig. 2.9) is bleeding underneath the conjunctiva that contains fragile vessels which are easily ruptured. Blood leaks into the space between the conjunctiva and sclera initially appearing bright red, then yellowish/green. Resolution is usually complete by 14 days. Accidental impact, inflicted injury, shaking, smothering, coughing and medical diagnoses are possible causes (Table 2.5).

Table 2.5 Causes of Subconjunctival haemorrhage

Medical:
Hypertension
Clotting disorders and blood dyscrasias
Anticoagulants
Severe choking, coughing, sneezing or vomiting
Scurvy (Vitamin C deficiency)
Acute haemorrhagic conjunctivitis
Accidental and inflicted mechanisms:
Direct accidental or inflicted trauma
Shaking injury
Traumatic asphyxia (smothering)
Severe chest injury
Orbital and zygomatic arch fractures
Strenuous exercise

Pelvis

The bony prominences at the top of the pelvic bone (iliac spines) are often injured accidentally. In abuse, infants and children may be grabbed around the hips/pelvis and buttocks with adult thumbs at the front, fingers at the back. A careful assessment for child sexual abuse is required.

Thigh

The upper thigh is a less usual site for accidental injury. However, ambulant children who commonly injure their knees and shins may also impact the upper leg against furniture and other hard surfaces causing injury. The back of the thigh is more commonly associated with inflicted injury.

Medical Conditions Increasing Susceptibility to Bruising

Blood Disorders (Tables 2.1 and 2.2)

Haemophilia (Factor VIII and IX deficiency)
There may be a history that cord separation at birth or circumcision led to prolonged bleeding. Bruising becomes more pronounced as the child begins to mobilise. It may be nodular from the deep bleeding into soft tissues. The partial thromboplastin time (aPTT) is prolonged with factor assays providing a definitive diagnosis.

Haemorrhagic disease of the newborn
This occurs in infants who have not received Vitamin K at birth. Breast-fed infants born at home are most at risk. Early-onset disease occurs during the first 24 hours

after birth with classic deficiency presenting after 24 hours but within the first week of life. Late onset disease occurs between 2 and 12 weeks but may be delayed for up to 6 months. Some infants present with intracerebral haemorrhage.

Von Willebrand's disease
This disorder results from decreased platelet adhesiveness. There is a mild to moderate bleeding tendency involving mucous membranes in the mouth and elsewhere. Easy bruising, nosebleeds and prolonged bleeding after dental procedures are features. The von Willebrand factor (antigen and activity) is low with mildly prolonged aPTT in approximately 50% of patients secondary to low levels of Factor VIII.

Congenital and acquired vascular abnormalities
Hereditary haemorrhagic telangiectasia is an autosomal dominant condition leading to abnormal blood vessel formation in the skin, mucous membranes, lungs, liver and brain. There may be recurrent nose bleeds or oral bleeding from the upper airways or gastrointestinal tract.

Henoch-Schönlein purpura, (HSP)
This presents in children 1–7 years old with a purpuric rash over the buttocks and lower extremities. The child may have painful joints, arthritis, abdominal pain and renal involvement. Subcutaneous, scrotal, or periorbital oedema may occur. Resolution is usual by 2–6 weeks but 50% of children have recurrences. Investigations are normal.

Idiopathic thrombocytopenic purpura (ITP)
In this condition blood platelets are consumed via an immunological mechanism. It follows a viral illness in approximately 70% of cases. Petechiae (blood spots) and bruising appear 2–4 weeks after the minor illness has resolved. Resolution occurs within 8–12 weeks in more than 75% of cases. Blood platelet counts are low.

Leukaemia
In leukaemia the bone marrow becomes infiltrated with abnormal cells. Bruising may be a prominent feature. The blood film is abnormal and coagulation may be affected.

Anticoagulant and other drug ingestion
Children who ingest anticoagulants, aspirin, other non-steroidal anti-inflammatory drugs (NSAIDs') and some other drugs may have an increased susceptibility to bruising and bleeding.

Infections

Viral and severe bacterial infections may present with petechiae usually widespread over the body, not confined to a small area as more commonly observed following injury. Meningococcal septicaemia causes a widespread non-blanching petechial or purpuric rash with cellulitis creating a bruised appearance. Disseminated Intravascular Coagulation (DIC) may result in abnormalities of clotting with bruising and bleeding.

Collagen Vascular and Nutritional Defects

Ehlers-Danlos Syndrome (EDS)
This is a congenital defect in collagen synthesis that may lead to easy bruising, skin hyperextensibility, joint hypermobility and skin fragility.

Osteogenesis imperfecta (OI)
In some types of OI, as well as fractures, bony deformities, and joint laxity, easy bruising is observed (page 81).

Scurvy
Vitamin C deficiency is rare in the Western world presenting with a sponge like appearance to the gums and bleeding from the mucous membranes.

Folk-Healing Practices

Coining, scraping, spooning (cao gio, quat sha, gua sha)
Warmed oil is applied to the child's skin on the chest or back then rubbed with the edge of a spoon or coin leading to linear bruises and red areas [40].

Cupping
An Asian/Mexican practice where a cup is warmed and placed on the skin creating a vacuum. As the cup cools the skin reddens and a bruise may appear.

Moxibustion
This is a traditional Chinese therapy where burning mugwort (moxa) is placed on points on the body.

Skin Conditions that May Be Mistaken for Bruises

Capillary haemangiomas (strawberry marks)
These birth marks may increase in size over the first 6 months then slowly regress over 2–3 years with 85% fully resolved by 6 years of age.

Congenital melanocytic naevi
These are light brown to black patches that may become thicker and elevated.

Eczema
In this allergic skin condition there are no bruises but skin damage causes reddening with dry areas. Intense itchiness causes the child to scratch and cause injury.

Erythema multiforme
This is an acute hypersensitivity skin condition with red target-like lesions caused by some drugs, foods, immunisations or infections. It may be minor and self-limiting or severe (Stevens-Johnson syndrome) involving mucous membranes with necrosis and sloughing. It is usually symmetrical involving the palms and soles. Lesions are sharply demarcated, round, red or pink and initially flat progressing to raised papules and enlarging to form plaques with a darkened centre. Resolution is usual within 1–3 weeks.

Erythema Nodosum
Red swellings of variable sizes appear on the shins, knees and ankles. Nodules are slightly raised, hot and painful, bright red then fading through the colour changes of a bruise. Throat infections, tuberculosis and inflammatory bowel disease are the main causes in children.

Mongolian blue spots
These are slate grey-blue areas of hyper-pigmentation commonly seen over the lower back and buttocks but also scalp, upper back, knees and feet. They affect about 50% of children of Afro-Caribbean or Asian descent but are occasionally observed in Caucasian infants and children. They usually fade by 5 years of age. Unlike bruises they do not resolve within days or progress through the colour sequence of a bruise.

Phytophoto-dermatitis
When a child's skin is exposed to sunlight after contact with psoralens (chemical compounds found in limes, lemons, parsley, celery, carrots or figs), red marks appear as bruises and, if severe, burns. Lesions resemble drip marks or handprints when a child has been handled by an adult with the juice on his or her hands.

Striae
Striae, or 'stretch marks', are reddish or purple lesions usually on the abdomen. Over time they lose pigmentation and become pale. They are seen in childhood obesity and some endocrine conditions and may appear as bruising.

Tattoos, crayons and felt-tip pens
Rarely but occasionally mistaken for injury.

Others who May Have an Increased Susceptibility to Bruising

Attention Deficit Hyperactivity Disorder (ADHD)

ADHD is characterised by inattention, short attention span and hyperactivity. For diagnosis, behaviours must continue for at least 6 months with symptoms creating real handicap in at least two of the following areas (classroom, playground, home, social settings). Children with ADHD may injure themselves more often than expected and present with excessive bruising.

Autism Spectrum Disorder (ASD) and Learning difficulties

ASD refers to a social communication disorder as defined in the Diagnostic and Statistical Manual of Mental Disorders (DSM-5), May 2013. These are character-ised by abnormalities in social interaction, communication, and by a restricted, stereotyped repertoire of interests and activities.

Studies report that children and young adults with ASD and learning difficulties have higher levels of self-injury. Head banging, arm biting, hair pulling, scratching and self-pinching have been reported [42, 43].

Hyman et al. (1990) reviewed 97 children with self-injurious behaviour. Severe developmental delay was present in 82.5%. Head banging, biting, head/body hit-ting, and scratching were observed. Physical injury was documented in 77% of cases, most commonly excoriations, scars, haematomas, and local infection [44].

Head banging and Body Rocking

Head banging and body rocking involve repetitive movements typically commenc-ing at age 6–9 months and subsiding by 2–3 years. However, 5% of healthy children head bang at age 5. Head banging may occur with the child lying face down or in the upright position where the head is banged repeatedly against a wall, floor or furniture. Body rocking typically involves the entire body. Movements usually stop if the child is distracted or limited by the discomfort caused which also limits any potential injury.

Occasionally, head banging may result in bruising and a credible account such an event and its aftermath cannot be disregarded as a possible cause for injury.

Self-inflicted injuries, dermatitis artefacta

Children may self inflict injuries as part of a more complex psychological illness.

Disability

Disabled children bruise more often over the back of the feet, thighs, arms, hands and trunk, probably as a result of injury during transfer to and from wheelchairs and other aids. Goldberg et al. (2009) studied 50 children and adolescents 4–20 years of age with physical and/or cognitive disabilities. More bruising was observed than in non-disabled children from a comparable study [45].

References

1. Maguire S, Mann MK, Sibert J, Kemp A. Are there patterns of bruising in childhood which are diagnostic or suggestive of abuse? A systematic review. Arch Dis Child. 2005;90(2):182–6.
2. Carpenter RF. The prevalence and distribution of bruising in babies. Arch Dis Child. 1999;80(4):363–6.
3. Sheets LK, Leach ME, Koszewski IJ, Lessmeier AM, Nugent M, Simpson P. Sentinel injuries in infants evaluated for child physical abuse. Pediatrics. 2013;131(4):701–7.
4. Thomas A. The bleeding child: is it NAI. Arch Dis Child. 2004;89(12):1163–7.
5. Bays J. Conditions mistaken for child abuse. In: Reece RM, editor. Child abuse: medical diagnosis and management. Philadelphia: Lea & Febiger; 1994. p. 358–85.
6. O'Hare AE, Eden OB. Bleeding disorders and non-accidental injury. Arch Dis Child. 1984;59(9):860–4.
7. Sussman SH. Skin manifestations of the battered child syndrome. J Pediatr. 1968;72:99–101.
8. Chang LT, Tsai MC. Craniofacial injuries from slip, trip, and fall accidents of children. J Trauma – Inj Infect Crit Care. 2007;63(1):70–4.
9. Kemp AM, Dunstan F, Nuttall D, Hamilton M, Collins P, Maguire S. Patterns of bruising in preschool children. A longitudinal study. Arch Dis Child. 2015;100(5):426–31.
10. Kemp A, Maguire S, Nuttall D, Collins P, Dunstan F. Bruising in children who are assessed for suspected physical abuse. Arch Dis Child. 2014;80(4):363–6.
11. Brinkman B, Puschel K, Matzsch T. Forensic dermatological aspects of the battered child syndrome. Act Dermatolol. 1979;5:217–32.
12. Pascoe JM, Hildebrandt HM, Tarrier A, Murphy M. Patterns of skin injury in non-accidental and accidental injury. Pediatrics. 1979;64:245–7.
13. Johnson CF, Showers J. Injury variables in child abuse. Child Abuse Negl. 1985;9:207–15.
14. Pierce M, Kaczor K, Aldridge S, et al. Bruising characteristics discriminating physical child abuse from accidental trauma. Pediatrics. 2010;125:67–74.
15. Nayak K, Spencer N, Shenoy M, Rubithon J, Coad N, Logan S. How useful is the presence of petechiae in distinguishing non-accidental from accidental injury? Child Abuse Negl. 2006;30(5):549–55.
16. Dunstan FD, Guildea ZE, Kontos K, Kemp AM, Sibert JR. A scoring system for bruise patterns: a tool for identifying abuse. Arch Dis Child. 2002;86(5):330–3.
17. Petska HW, Sheets LK, Knox BL. Facial bruising as a precursor to abusive head trauma. Clin Pediatr (Phila). 2013;52(1):86–8.
18. Harper NS, Feldman KW, Sugar NF, Anderst JD, Lindberg DM. Examining siblings to recognize abuse investigators. Additional injuries in young infants with concern for abuse and apparently isolated bruises. J Pediatr. 2014;165(2):383–388.e1.
19. Ellerstein NS. Cutaneous manifestations of child abuse and neglect. Am J Dis Child. 1979;133:906–9.
20. Bariciak ED, Plint AC, Gaboury I, Bennett S. Dating of bruises in children: an assessment of physician accuracy. Pediatrics. 2003;112(4):804–7.
21. Stephenson T, Bialas Y. Estimation of the age of bruising. Arch Dis Child. 1996;74(1):53–5.
22. Carpenter RF. The prevalence and distribution of bruising in babies. Archives of Disease in Childhood. 1999;80(4):363–366.
23. McCann J, Miyamoto S, Boyle C, Rogers K. Healing of non-hymenal genital injuries in prepubertal and adolescent girls: a descriptive study. Pediatrics. 2007;120(5):1000–11.
24. Johnson CF. Inflicted injury versus accidental injury. Pediatr Clin North Am. 1990;37:791–814.
25. Richardson AC. Cutaneous manifestations of abuse. In: Reece RM, editor. Child abuse: medical diagnosis and management. Philadelphia: Lea & Febiger; 1994. p. 167–84.
26. Barsley RE, West MH, Fair JA. Forensic photography. Ultraviolet imaging of wounds on skin. Am J Forensic Med Pathol. 1990;11(4):300–8.
27. Hempling SM. The applications of ultraviolet photography in clinical forensic medicine. Med Sci Law. 1981;21(3):215–22.

28. Peel M, Hughes J, Payne-James JJ. Post-inflammatory hyperpigmentation following torture. J Clin Forensic Med. 2003;10(3):193–6.
29. Hughes VK, Ellis PS, Burt T, Langlois NE. The practical application of reflectance spectro-photometry for the demonstration of haemoglobin and its degradation in bruises. J Clin Pathol. 2004;57(4):355–9.
30. Patno K, Jenny C. Who slapped that child? Child Maltreat. 2008;13(3):298–300.
31. Kemp A, Maguire SA, Sibert J, Frost R, Adams C, Mann M. Can we identify abusive bites on children? Arch Dis Child. 2006;91:951.
32. Sweet D, Lorente M, Lorente JA, Valenzuela A, Villanueva E. An improved method to recover saliva from human skin: the double swab technique. J Forensic Sci. 1997;42(2):320–2.
33. Gold MH, Roenigk HH, Smith ES, Pierce LJ. Human bite marks. Differential diagnosis. Clin Pediatr (Phila). 1989;28(7):329–31.
34. Kornberg AE. Skin and soft tissue injuries. In: Ludwig S, Kornberg AE, editors. Child abuse: a medical reference. 2nd ed. New York: Churchill Livingstone; 1992. p. 91–104.
35. Reece RM, Ludwig S. Child abuse: medical diagnosis and management. 2nd ed. Philadelphia: Lippincott Williams and Wilkins; 2001.
36. Chiaviello CT, Christoph RA, Bond GR. Stairway-related injuries in children. Pediatrics. 1994;94(5):679–81.
37. Docherty E, Hassan A, Burke D. Things that go bump…bump…bump: an analysis of injuries from falling down stairs in children based at Sheffield Children's Hospital. Emerg Med J. 2010;27(3):207–8.
38. Joffe M, Ludwig S. Stairway injuries in children. Pediatrics. 1988;82(3):457–61.
39. Hobbs CJ, Osman J. Genital injuries in boys and abuse. Arch Dis Child. 2007;92(4):328–31.
40. Yeatman GW, Dang VV. Cao Gío (coin rubbing). Vietnamese attitudes toward health care. JAMA. 1980;244(24):2748–9.
41. Sandler AP, Haynes V. Non-accidental trauma and medical folk belief: a case of cupping. Pediatrics. 1978;61(6):921–2.
42. Clements J, Zarkowska E. Behavioural concerns and autistic spectrum disorders: explanations and strategies for change. London: Jessica Kingsley Publishers; 2000.
43. Minshawi NF, Hurwitz S, Fodstad JC, Biebl S, Morriss DH, McDougle CJ. The association between self-injurious behaviors and autism spectrum disorders. Psychol Res Behav Manag. 2014;7:125–36.
44. Hyman SL, Fisher W, Mercugliano M, Cataldo MF. Children with self-injurious behavior. Pediatrics. 1990;85(3 Pt 2):437–41.
45. Goldberg AP, Tobin J, Daigneau J, Griffith RT, Reinert SE, Jenny C. Bruising frequency and patterns in children with physical disabilities. Pediatrics. 2009;124(2):604–9.

Further Reading

CORE INFO Cardiff Child Protection Systematic Reviews/www.core-info.cardiff.ac.uk/ (accessed 15.04.17).

Fractures

3

Abstract

Up to one third of children sustain a fracture before their sixteenth birthday, most of which are accidental [1]. Landin 1983, reviewed all fractures in 8642 children over 30 years concluding that the chance of sustaining a fracture age 0–16 was 42% for boys and 27% for girls [2].

Most accidental fractures occur in children over 5 years of age [3]. Studies record fractures in up to a third of children suffering abuse with a majority of inflicted injuries occurring in those under 12 months of age. Fractures of ribs, arm and leg accounted for over half of the inflicted bone injuries in young children in one series [4]. McClain et al. (1993) reported that if an abused child is returned to his or her previous environment there is 30–50% chance of further abuse to include fractures [5].

Bone Anatomy and Fracture Types

The bones of children are less mineralized and more elastic than adult bones. Healing is more rapid especially in infants. Growth plates consisting of cartilage are the weakest part of the long bone in a child's skeleton. They are close to joints and vulnerable when the joint is subjected to force, often resulting in metaphyseal corner fractures (classic metaphyseal lesions, CML).

A knowledge of the basic anatomy of the long bone is useful when describing fractures (Fig. 3.1). Fracture types are described in Table 3.1.

© Springer International Publishing Switzerland 2017
D.L. Robinson, *Pediatric Forensic Evidence*, DOI 10.1007/978-3-319-45337-8_3

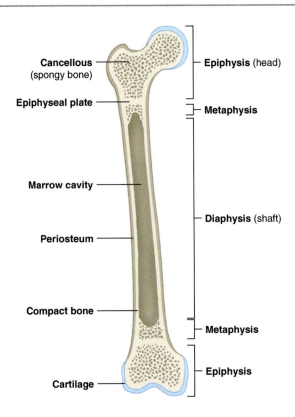

Condyle	Rounded articular (joint) surface at the end of a bone
Diaphysis	Shaft of a long bone
Epiphysis	Part of the long bone developed from a centre of ossification
Epiphyseal plate	A layer of cartilage that separates the epiphysis from the shaft
Metaphysis	Flared end of the bone between epiphyseal plate and diaphysis
Periosteum	Thick, fibrous membrane covering the surface of a bone

Fig. 3.1 Anatomy of the long bone

Clinical Assessment

Medical Assessment

A comprehensive medical history and examination should be undertaken as described in chapter 1 pages 4–6. Systems enquiries, past medical and family history are all relevant. The account of an accident and its aftermath are compared with clinical findings and the developmental stage of the child.

Physical examination should include observation of parent-child interaction, signs of neglect, assessment of growth and development, systems examination and a careful

Table 3.1 Fracture types and mechanisms

Description	Explanation and mechanism
Complete	The fracture line traverses both cortices of the bone
Comminuted	Bone broken into multiple pieces
Compound	Open fracture (through the skin)
Depressed Skull	Skull is inwardly displaced
Diastatic	Separation of bone fragments
Distal	Located further away from the centre of the body
	Nearer the feet or hands
Greenstick	Incomplete fracture
	Compressed side is bowed
Hairline	No displacement of bone fragments
Impacted	Compression fracture
	Involves the entire bone, impacted bone buckles
	Often involves the metaphysis
Incomplete	Bone fragments are still partially joined
	The fracture does not traverse the width of the bone
	Bowing often without fracture
Linear	A break resembling a thin line
Oblique	Angled across the long axis of the bone
Occult	Fracture clinically evident but no radiographic evidence
Pathological	Bone weakened by an underlying disease process
Proximal	Towards the trunk of the body
Spiral	Fracture line encircles a portion of the bone
	Caused by twisting, rotation of an extremity
	May be accidental in ambulant children
Stellate	Fracture lines radiate from a central point
Supracondylar	Above the condyle of a long bone
	Usually refers to humeral fracture
Torus (buckle)	Localized buckling of the cortex of the bone
Transverse	Fracture perpendicular to the long axis of the bone
	Caused by bending or direct trauma

search for any injuries with accurate documentation on body maps and good quality images where relevant.

Routine blood investigations (page 7) should include full blood count and clotting screen, C-reactive protein, renal and liver function tests. Normal vitamin D, calcium, phosphate, alkaline phosphatase and parathyroid hormone (PTH) levels will reliably exclude Vitamin-D deficient rickets in the absence of radiological evidence for the disease.

A multidisciplinary approach, to include paediatricians, paediatric radiologists, orthopaedic surgeons, A&E staff, health visitor, nurses and social worker is required. The police will visit the family home if necessary, interview carers and collect forensic evidence.

If inflicted injury is suspected, a referral to children's social care is required and local safeguarding children's board (LSCB) procedures followed. A telephone discussion should be followed by a referral in writing on a standard form (page 16).

Radiological Investigations

Skeletal survey
The skeletal survey should be undertaken to the technical standards recommended by the Royal College of Radiologists, Royal College of Paediatrics and Child Health radiological guidance (2008) [6]. A full skeletal survey is required in all children less than 2 years of age where physical abuse is suspected.

A skeletal survey should also be considered in severe inflicted injury at any age, where there has been previous inflicted skeletal trauma, unexplained neurological presentation or suspected abusive head trauma (AHT), a child dying in suspicious circumstances and in a sibling (age under 2 years) of a child with inflicted injury. Older children with a disability and suspected physical abuse should also be considered for a skeletal survey.

Repeat radiographs between 10–14 days may reveal additional fractures and follow-up imaging should include antero-posterior and left and right oblique chest radiographs. This has been shown to provide additional information in 46–61% of cases, often rib and metaphyseal fractures [7]. Ingram et al. (2000) reported that a repeat study increases the sensitivity of detection of rib fractures by 17% and specificity by 7% [8]. Karmazyn et al. (2011) evaluated the prevalence and site of fractures detected on skeletal surveys performed for suspected child abuse in children under 2 years. A total of 930 children (515 boys and 415 girls) with a median age of 6 months were studied. Fractures were detected in 317 children (34%), of whom 166 (18%) had multiple fractures. The most common sites were the long bones (21%), ribs (10%), skull (7%), and clavicle (2%). There were 3 spinal, 1 pelvic, 6 hand and 2 foot fractures [9].

Maguire et al. (2013) reviewed 23 studies addressing radiological investigations and 9 studies addressing fractures indicative of abuse concluding that single investigation will miss inflicted fractures (in 8.4–37.6% of cases). A meta-analysis of femoral and humeral fractures by age highlighted that children younger than 18 months are significantly more likely to have sustained their fracture as a consequence of abuse [10].

Computed Tomography
CT is valuable in the assessment of vertebral fractures to establish stability. A head CT is indicated for suspected abusive head trauma (AHT). If CT with 3D reconstruction on bony windows has not been performed skull radiographs are required to exclude fractures. Infants under 1 year of age require a head CT (up to 2 years if clinically indicated) and ophthalmology examination. Chest, abdominal and pelvic

CT (including 3D reconstructions) are useful in assessing organ and visceral injuries and may also identify metaphyseal and rib fractures.

Nucleotide Bone Scan/Bone Scintigraphy

A bone scan at the time of first skeletal survey may detect rib fractures less than 7–10 days old, diaphyseal fractures and early periosteal elevation. It is not sensitive for the detection of skull fractures and does not provide accurate dating of injuries. The radiation dose is relatively high and nuclear medicine scans for the investigation of suspected abuse are now performed in only a very few centres.

Features of Inflicted and Accidental Fractures

Concerning features

Following accidental injury, medical attention is usually sought promptly. In abuse a delay in seeking care is more common. Other factors that raise concerns are a clinical examination that does not match the account of injury, no credible history of a memorable event and its aftermath, discrepant accounts and a history that does not fit with the child's developmental abilities. The carer may blame a sibling, the family may be known to children's social care. There may have been repeated medical attendances for injuries, other injuries or signs of neglect (pages 7–12).

Multiple fractures

Multiple fractures in various stages of healing are a hallmark for inflicted injury in the absence of an underlying condition increasing the child's susceptibility to fractures [11].

Age

Pre-mobile infants are at increased risk of sustaining inflicted fractures. Studies record fractures in up to a third of children suffering abuse with a majority of inflicted fractures occurring in children under 12 months of age.

Pandya et al. (2009) reviewed 500 cases of inflicted trauma (birth to 4 years) comparing these with 985 cases of accidental trauma. For those under 48 months the odds of rib (14.4 times), tibia/fibula (6.3 times), radius/ulna (5.8 times), and clavicular fractures (4.4 times) were higher in the inflicted vs accidental group. For those under 18 months of age, the odds of rib (23.7 times), tibia/fibula (12.8 times), humeral (2.3 times), and femoral fractures (1.8 times) were higher in the child abuse group. In the over 18 months age group, the risk of humeral (3.4 times) and femoral fractures (3.3 times) was higher in the accidental trauma group. The authors noted that below 18 months, fractures of the rib, tibia/fibula, humerus and femur were more likely to be inflicted. Beyond 18 months, long bone fractures were more likely to be accidental [12].

In children aged 1–4 accidental fractures of the arms and clavicles are common mainly following falls. In children over 10 years old, road traffic accidents result in more fractures than in younger children.

Occult fractures
Inflicted fractures may be occult (not evident clinically) particularly rib, metaphyseal and vertebral. At the time of injury an infant may cry out in pain but settle fairly quickly if comforted. A perpetrator will be aware that excessive force had been applied whilst a non-observer may be faced with a fractious, crying infant with poor feeding put down to colic or a mild viral illness. In many instances occult fractures are discovered only on routine radiographs.

Fracture types
Metaphyseal corner fractures (classic metaphyseal lesions, CML), rib (particularly posterior), scapular, spinous processes and sternal fractures are highly specific for inflicted injury. Epiphyseal separation, vertebral body, digital and complex skull fractures as well as periosteal new-bone formation all raise suspicions for abuse. A humeral fracture in a pre-mobile infant is more likely to be inflicted particularly if spiral [13]. The same applies to any long bone fracture in a non-ambulant child.

Farnsworth et al. (1998) reported that supracondylar fractures in ambulant children are more likely to be accidental [14]. Typical fractures around the growth plates (Salter-Harris) are rare in the context of abuse.

Loder et al. (1991) reviewed 75 children with inflicted fractures. The average age was 16 months. Of 154 fractures, 77% were acute and 23% old. The most common fracture occurred in the skull (32%), the most common long bone fracture in the tibia (16%). Of all long bone fractures 41% were transverse and 28% corner fractures [15].

Bruising and Haematomas

Studies have reported bruising in approximately 10% of children who sustain fractures whether accidental or inflicted. Where deeper vessels are injured and rupture, blood may track superficially with bruising seen up to 48 hours later (page 33). If blood is resorbed at a deeper level there may be no bruising.

Peters et al. (2008) reviewed 192 children with inflicted fractures. No bruising was found in 111 (57.8%). Forty patients (20.8%) had bruising near the site of at least one fracture, most commonly skull. Bruising for lower limb fractures was observed as follows: tibia 3.8% (2), fibula 16.7% (1). Rib fractures were uncommonly associated with bruising [16].

Mathew et al. (1998) reviewed 93 fractures in 88 children. Eight (9%) had haematomas at presentation with 25 (28%) after 1 week [17]. Starling et al. 2007 found fracture-related haematomas in fewer than 10% of children after skull fractures were excluded [18].

Fracture Dating

Healing passes through a number of stages, which merge into one another. There is a continuum rather than distinct stages. The dating of fractures is imprecise but most accurate the closer the radiograph is taken to the date of injury.

Soft Tissue Swelling
Immediately following injury, there is bleeding and soft tissue swelling leading to oedema that may be observed on radiographs as blurring of the soft tissue planes. This generally persists for a few days but may last longer if the injury was severe. Fractures with no visible soft tissue swelling are usually less than 24 hours or more than 10–14 days old.

Sub Periosteal New Bone Formation (SPNBF)
The periosteum (fibrous covering of the bone) is elevated by bleeding beneath it which stimulates this membrane to produce new bone as part of the healing process known as SPNBF, which may be visible as early as day 7 but is invariably present by day 11 following injury. At this stage, whilst swelling may have subsided, the limb remains tender with pain on movement. It should be noted that SPNBF can occur in the absence of a fracture when the periosteum is stripped off the underlying bone by gripping/twisting forces.

Callus
SPNBF thickens as more bone is formed leading to callus formation. More mature bone bridges the fracture. Callus is first visible between 10–14 days following injury, but may be delayed up to 21 days. Up to this stage the limb remains tender on pressure with likely pain on movement and a reluctance to use the limb. Most fractures are splinted during this period.

Remodelling
The original shape of the bone is restored in a process that may occur over a number of months to years. Some fractures are unrecognisable on radiographs within months due to complete healing and remodelling.

Exceptions
The process outlined above applies mainly to shaft fractures of long bones and ribs. Metaphyseal, costochondral and skull fractures do not heal by this process. Both metaphyseal and costochondral fracture fragments become gradually incorporated into the underlying bone in a process that takes up to 4 weeks. Soft tissue scalp swelling found clinically or radiologically helps to differentiate recent (less than 14 days) from older skull fractures. An uncomplicated linear skull fracture, sustained during birth, is no longer distinct after 2 months with complete resolution by 6 months.

Falls and Fractures

The force required to cause a fracture cannot be measured. However, an understanding of the type of injuries sustained following simple and complex falls provides some guidance as to what force may be required to cause bony injury.

Short Falls

Accidental falls probably result in a larger number of fractures (particularly skull) than diagnosed, as many children do not have radiographs. Present research, as set out below, indicates that although fractures from short falls are less usual they have been clearly recorded in some research studies. In addition, there are case reports of serious injuries including fatalities after relatively short falls.

Warrington and Wright (Avon Study of Parents and Children 2001) reviewed 3357 falls in in 2554 pre-mobile infants in the first 6 months of life based on 11,466 parental responses to a mailed questionnaire. Of the total number of falls 53% fell from a bed or settee and 12% from carers arms or when the person carrying them fell down. In 21 falls (<1%) concussion or fracture resulted. Skull fracture was diagnosed in three children but not observed after a fall from a bed or settee. No child suffered intracranial injuries. Visible injuries were reported in 14% of which 56% were haematomas. The authors conclude that falls from beds and settees did not result in skull fractures [19].

Tarantino et al. (1999) reviewed 167 infants, mean age 5.2 months, who fell less than 1.25 metres. Of the total, 55% rolled off a bed, 20% were dropped from a carer's arms, 16% rolled off a couch and 10% fell from other objects. Minor or no injury was recorded in 85% whilst 15% had significant injuries including 16 with a head injury (12 skull fractures and 2 intracranial bleeds, the latter confirmed as child abuse) and 7 long bone fractures. After excluding suspected abuse, being dropped by a carer was the only mechanism associated with significant injury [20].

Lyons and Oates (1993) reviewed 207 children under 6 years of age. There were 124 falls from cots and 83 from beds. Heights ranged from 65cm (bed rail down) to 110cm (rail up) in falls from a cot, and from 50–85cm (including bed rail) in falls from a bed. There were 29 superficial injuries (contusions or minor lacerations), one simple skull fracture (age 10 months, fall from cot) and one fractured clavicle (21 months, fall from cot, bed rail up) [21].

Johnson et al. (2005) reviewed 72 infants and aged 4 months to 4 years 9 months who sustained a head injury following a reported accidental fall. The heights of falls were less than 50cm to over 3 metres. Forty-nine were on to a hard surface and 23 were on to a soft surface. In 52, the fall resulted in a visible injury to the head (35 on hard surface, 17 on soft surface). Clinically visible skull injuries were observed in all children who had fallen over 1.5 metres and in 95% of children that had fallen over 1 metre. Thirty-two children (44%) had skull radiographs. Four had fractures. Of 3 linear parietal fractures 2 were sustained by falls of just over 100cm and 1 by a fall of 80–90cm on to the hard-edged surface of a stone fire surround. A fourth sustained a basilar fracture in a fall of over 3 metres from a first floor window. Johnson concluded that skull fractures probably occur in fewer than 5% of children and require a fall of at least 1 metre or on to an object that results in a 'small-area impact' [22].

Hughes et al. (2015) studied infants and children aged ≤48 months attending hospital following a reported fall from less than 3 metres (10ft). Forty-seven sustained a skull fracture or intra-cranial injury (ICI) with 416 having minor head injuries. No skull fracture/ICI was recorded in children who fell <0.6 metres (2 ft) based on the height of the head centre of gravity. Skull fractures/ICI were more common in infants aged ≤12 months, from impact to the temporal/parietal/occipital region or impact onto wood and falls from a carer's arms particularly when on the stairs [23].

Ibrahim et al. (2011) retrospectively reviewed 285 infants and children up to 48 months with accidental head injury from a fall either ≤3 ft, more than 3ft and less than 10ft, high falls ≥10 ft and stair falls. Of those falling ≤3 ft, 23% of toddlers (1–4 years) and 73% of infants (<1 year) sustained a skull fracture. For those falling >3ft but <10 ft, 49% of toddlers and 69% of infants sustained a skull fracture. For stair falls 33% of toddlers and 73% of infants sustained a skull fracture. Only hospitalised patients were included all of whom underwent neuro-imaging [24].

Thomas et al (2013) reviewed 149 cranial CT scans in patients 0–2 years with accidental head trauma, reporting 29 (19.5%) skull fractures where the fall was 0.5m–3.6m (mean 1.4 metres). Intracranial haemorrhage was found in 23 (15.4%) where the fall was 0.5m–4.5m (mean 1.5 metres) [25].

Monson et al. (2008) reviewed 14 neonates from 88,774 births following a fall. Seven fell to the floor with the mother lying on the bed or seated in a chair. Four fell in the delivery room, two out of a cot and one from an infant swing. One infant had a large haematoma on the forehead and another sustained a depressed skull fracture from a fall of 50–70cm following delivery [26].

Wheeler and Shope (1997) reported a 7-month-old who fell, sustaining a ping-pong (depressed) fracture of the right parietal bone. The height of the fall was approx 60cm on to a metal toy car and was unwitnessed [27].

Denton et al. (2003) described a 9-month-old who struck his head on a concrete floor after a fall from a bed. He appeared well for 72 hours but was then sadly died. Post mortem showed a skull fracture, cerebral oedema and subgaleal haematoma. No child protection concerns were raised after investigation [28].

Chiaviello et al. (1994) studied 65 patients aged 3–17 months who sustained infant walker related injuries to include a fall down the stairs 46 (71%), tipping over 14 (21%), fall from the porch 2 (3%) and burn injury 3 (5%). Injuries were found on the head and face (97%), extremities (6%), trunk (3%). Nineteen patients suffered severe injuries: skull fracture 10 (15%), concussion 8 (12%), intracranial haemorrhage 5 (8%) full thickness burns 2 (3%) and a fracture of the cervical spine 1 (2%). One child died having sustained a skull fracture, subdural haemorrhage and a fracture of a cervical vertebra. When burn patients were excluded, severe injuries were observed only in children who fell down the stairs [29].

High level falls

High level falls remain a major cause of serious injury and death in children.

However, many children, a majority of whom are under 6 years of age, survive and fully recover. Injuries sustained are mainly to the head and neck [30].

A 14-month-old girl was found on the concrete driveway two floors below the family flat. The mother could not confirm whether she had secured the window from which she fell. She sustained soft tissue injuries to the head and neck, a fractured skull but no intracranial injury. The bedroom from which she had fallen had a child's bed (her sister's) six inches from the wall and just below the window. Developmentally she was considered capable of climbing on to the bed, navigating the short gap to the window and exploring further. Injuries were found to be accidental.

Barlow et al. (1983) reviewed 61 children under 16 years of age. All children falling from less than three storeys survived whilst 50% died following a fall from the fifth or sixth floor. Of all deaths 78% were from head injury to include skull fractures, contusions and brain lacerations [31].

Williams (1991) reported on 398 children of whom 106 under 3 years were evaluated. In this group there was an independent eye witness to a fall. Williams also evaluated 53 children where there was no independent observer. In the latter group two children died after a fall reported to be less than 1.5 metres. In the group with an independent witness, 44 children fell less than 3 metres and three who fell against a sharp edge sustained a small depressed fracture. One death was recorded in a child who fell over 20 metres [32].

Wang et al. (2001) reported that fractures of the extremities, lung contusion and pneumothorax were more common in falls of more than 4–5 metres and that abdominal injuries (liver lacerations, visceral and spleen injuries) were more frequently observed in falls of less than 4–5 metres [33].

Stair falls

Following stairway falls (page 36), injuries are predominantly to the head, neck and distal extremities.

Joffe and Ludwig (1988), prospectively studied 363 children and young adults aged 1–18 (54 under 1 year) with injuries resulting from a fall downstairs. Ten were being carried by their carer and 24 in a baby walker when they fell. Injuries were recorded as follows: head and neck (73%), extremities (28%), trunk (2%) and fractures (6%). Sixteen children sustained a fracture of an extremity and six children a skull fracture. Those who had fallen more than four steps did not sustain more injuries than children who had fallen less than four steps. There were no intracranial haemorrhages, brain contusions or deaths.

Joffe and Ludwig noted that a fall downstairs is a series of smaller falls, the first being the longest (height of the child plus the number of steps intially fallen) and that such falls are less serious than a free fall from the same height. Multiple or severe injuries associated with a history of stair fall raise concerns for inflicted injury [34].

Pierce et al. (2005) reported that following stairway falls injuries are observed predominantly to the head and neck (70%) and distal extremities (30%). Truncal injuries were found in only 2–3%. Injuries to more than one body part occurred in 3–6%. Bruises, abrasions, or lacerations predominated with fractures mainly to a distal limb [35].

Chiaviello et al. (1994) reviewed 69 children less than 5 years of age with injuries resulting from a fall downstairs including three children who had fallen together with their carer. Accidents with baby walkers and abuse were excluded. Head and neck injuries were observed in 90%, extremity in 6% and truncal injuries in 4%. Injury to more than one body area did not occur. Eleven sustained concussion (16%), five skull fractures (7%), two cerebral contusions (3%), one subdural haemorrhages (1%) and one fracture of the second cervical vertebra (1%). Children who had been carried by a carer who fell on them against the stairs sustained the most serious injuries [36].

Bunk Bed

Whilst falls from bunk beds usually cause only soft tissue injuries, fractures, concussion and other serious injuries have all been recorded.

Selbst et al. (1990) compared 68 children with injuries resulting from a fall from a bunk bed with 54 children who had presented for other reasons, but slept in a bunk bed.

Seventy percent of the injury group and 48% of the control group were less than 6 years old. Injuries were sustained by a fall from the upper bed (58%), the ladder (11%) or lower bed (12%). Injuries were located as follows: head (52%), facial (12%), lower extremities (13%) and upper extremities (10%). Specific injuries were lacerations (40%) contusions (19%), concussion (12%) and fractures (10%). There were no life-threatening injuries or deaths [37].

Mayr et al. (2000) reviewed 218 bunk-bed accidents in children, 23.8% of whom were under 3 years of age. In 23.2% there was a fall down the ladder. Serious injuries were found in 91 children (41.7%) including 3 multiple injuries, 7 skull fractures, 44 with concussion, 33 fractures of long bones, 2 metatarsal dislocations and 2 lacerations of the spleen. There were 89 contusions and sprains [38].

Other Short Domestic Falls

Smith et al. (1995) reviewed 62 children aged 4 months to 10 years presenting with *shopping-trolley-related injuries*. Most injuries were sustained by falling out of the trolley (58%). Forty-nine (79%) sustained head injuries. Eleven fractures were identified, skull (5), femoral (2), metatarsal (1), clavicular (1), radius (1) and ulna (1). Nine (14%) sustained lacerations and 30 (48%) suffered superficial injuries. There were no intra-cranial injuries [39].

Watson and Ozanne (1993) reported the death of two children, one after falling from a *pram*, the other from a *high chair* [40]. Arnholz et al. (1998) reported bilateral skull fractures and scalp haematoma in a 6-week-old who fell from a *pram* (90cm) on to the top of his head on concrete steps [41].

Wickham and Abrahamson (2002) reported on 17 infants (average age 6.9 months) who fell from a *bouncy chair* which was placed on a table or other high surface. Fourteen fell on to a solid surface with one sustaining a skull fracture [42].

Claydon (1996) reported the death of a 5-month-old who fell from a *baby bouncer* landing on to thick carpet after two other children had rocked him. His head was no more than 60cm from the floor. The infant cried but over the next 5 hours became drowsy. On arrival at hospital a CT demonstrated epidural haemorrhage. Claydon suggests that pivoting about the central point of the bouncer seat increased the momentum of the head before it struck the ground [43].

After a fall from a *baby walker* the majority of injuries to the head or face are minor. However, skull fractures, intracranial haemorrhage and deaths have all been reported [44].

Rieder et al. (1986) studied baby walker-related injuries in 139 children aged 4–15 months of whom 123 fell down the stairs (89%). As well as soft tissue injuries, the following fractures were found: skull (93), lower arm (3), clavicle (2). One child suffered a fracture of the nasal septum. Other injuries included: lacerations (6), abrasions (3), burns (3) and dental injuries (6). The most serious injuries (fractures and closed head injury) were sustained where there were, in addition, stair falls [45].

Powell et al. (2002) reviewed injuries in children up to 3 years old from *high chair falls* (40,650 falls, average age 10 months). The following injuries were reported: head (44%), facial (39%), contusions and abrasions (36%), lacerations (25%), intracranial injuries (21%) and fractures (8%). There were no reported deaths [46].

Skull Fractures

Skull fractures occur with equal frequency in both accidental and inflicted injuries in infants under 1 year of age. Leventhal et al. (1993) reported that up to 88% of inflicted skull fractures occur under 1 year but that this was also the commonest age for accidental skull fractures. [11]. In children over 18 months they are more commonly the result of accident. The parietal bone, followed by occipital, frontal and temporal bones are most commonly affected (Fig. 3.2). From 1 to 4 years accidental falls are the most prevalent cause. In children between 4 and 14 years of age, road traffic accidents predominate.

Stewart et al. (1993) reviewed records of 111 infants under 3 months of age at presentation and 1 year later. Injury was due to abuse or neglect in 28%. Falls were the most common accidental injury (67%). The percentage of infants with skull fractures was greater in the abuse/neglect group than in the accidental group (7/31 vs 7/80) with more diastatic and multiple skull fractures (6/7 vs 2/7) as well as intracranial hemorrhages (3/7 vs 0/7). More infants in the abuse/neglect group had extremity fractures (4/31 vs 2/80). A greater number of subsequent traumatic injuries were found in the abuse/neglect group [47]. Reece (2000) reported that 80% of skull fractures sustained through child abuse occurred in infants less than 1 year of age [48].

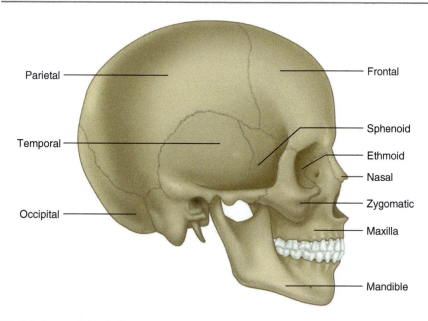

Fig. 3.2 Bones of the skull

Mechanism and Force Required

Skull fractures are due to direct impact from a blunt instrument or impact against a hard immoveable surface. Rapid impact may result in a fracture and superficial scalp injury whilst compression results in single or multiple fractures. Intracranial injury may result from either mechanism. Whilst the force required to cause a fracture cannot be measured, an understanding of those sustained after falls provides some guidance (page 58).

A fall of at least 60–90cm (see literature review page 58–59), is usually required to cause a skull fracture depending on the child's age, point of impact and the surface impacted. Typical accidents include a fall from a carer's arms, road traffic accident or a child swung in play and accidentally impacted against a wall or floor. In abuse, the child may be dropped from a significant height, impacted against a hard surface or hit with a blunt instrument. Short household falls can result in linear parietal skull fractures. Higher forces are generally required to produce depressed, diastatic (>3mm), multiple, stellate fractures, those that cross suture lines or involve the occipital bone/ base of the skull [49].

Hobbs (1984) reviewed 89 children with skull fractures under 2 years of age of which 29 (33%) were considered inflicted, 60 accidental. There were 20 deaths including 19 among the abused children. Radiological features in the abuse group included multiple, complex, depressed or growing fractures, a maximum width of greater than 3mm, involvement of more than one cranial bone, non-parietal fractures, occipital location and those associated with intracranial injury. Accidental injury usually resulted in single, narrow, linear fractures most commonly of the parietal bone with no associated intracranial injury [50] (Table 3.2).

Table 3.2 Features suspicious for inflicted skull fracture	Age under 1 year
	Bilateral, multiple, complex, depressed or growing fractures
	Maximum width of greater than 3mm
	More than one cranial bone involved
	Non-parietal fractures particularly occipital location
	Those associated with intracranial injury
	Where the fall reported was less than 60–90cm

Aftermath and Observers

Following accidental injury, a history of a memorable event and its aftermath is usually provided. In the aftermath, an infant will cry out or scream in a manner not previously heard by a carer who may comment on this. Thereafter there will be distress for 5–10min but, if comforted and fed, an infant may settle so long as there are no complications to include intra-cranial injury, superficial haematoma, other injuries or fear of further injury.

Simple skull fractures may be asymptomatic or present with fractiousness in an infant or headache in an older child. Physical examination may reveal a scalp swelling. Where there has been intracranial injury a child may present with encephalopathy or in a collapsed state (chapter 5).

The perpetrator or observer will immediately be aware that excessive force had been applied. A non-observer may see a fractious infant and scalp haematoma within hours, although the latter observation may be delayed for up to 24 hours particularly in infants with thick hair.

> A 3-month-old infant was presented for care with a swelling on the left side of his head (cephalhaematoma). The father stated he had hit his head on the door frame as he was being carried. A head CT showed skull fractures with bilateral subdural haematomas considered to be inflicted. The account provided was inconsistent with the injuries sustained.

Types of Skull Fracture

Simple Linear
Simple linear parietal skull fractures are equally common in both accidental and inflicted head injuries. They account for a majority of all skull fractures in children resulting from impact. Cephalhaematomas are commonly found.

Symmetrical linear fractures
Crush injury leads to symmetrical linear fractures on either side of the skull with fractures radiating out from the highest point of pressure or impact. They have been reported when an infant's head was shut in a car door or stamped on by an

adult. Bi-parietal skull fractures may also occur following a single midline cranial impact.

Duhaime et al. (1992) reviewed 7 children aged 15 months to 6 years with crush injuries. All patients sustained basilar fractures and 6 had multiple and often extensive fractures of the skull. Four were victims of road traffic accidents, the other three serious crush injuries with a heavy object [51].

Depressed Fractures

In depressed fractures, parts of the outer surface of the skull bone are displaced inwards. In one third, the dura is damaged whilst in a quarter, there is damage to the cerebral cortex. Post-traumatic seizures may occur [52]. Kleinman (1987) noted that depressed fractures of the occipital bone are suspect for child abuse [53].

Growing fractures

A growing fracture is more common if the original fracture had a separation of more than 4mm. Clinical symptoms develop gradually. Pezzotta et al. (1985), reviewed 132 children with a growing fracture. Initial clinical symptoms were seizures (40%), focal neurological deficits (43%) and/or unconsciousness (38%) [54].

Basilar Fractures

Trauma to the back of the head may lead to a basilar fracture with vomiting, unconsciousness, seizures, Battle's sign and Racoon Eyes. There may be blood behind the tympanic membrane or leakage of cerebrospinal fluid from the ear and nose.

Battle's sign (page 40) presents as bruising behind the ear over the mastoid process and may indicate a basal skull fracture. It is usually visible hours after injury but may be delayed for as long as 2–3 days.

Racoon Eyes (page 42) are peri-orbital bruises resulting from haemorrhage of the connective tissue around the eyes and associated with a basilar skull fracture. They are usually bilateral appearing within a few hours but may be delayed by as long as 2–3 days. Orbital haematomas (black eyes) are seen shortly after injury with bruising that may spread whilst Racoon eyes are restricted to the area of the eye [55].

Orbit and Zygomatic Arch

Blunt trauma to the eye may cause raised intra-orbital pressure and a so-called 'blow-out' fracture. The orbital floor fractures, resulting in herniation of intra-orbital tissues and bleeding into the orbit. There may be associated nasal bleeding [56].

Facial Fractures and Dental Damage

Damage to teeth is found in both accident and inflicted injury. Over 45% of children suffering abuse have oro-facial injuries [57, 58]. Haematomas, contusions, bites, lacerations, dental injuries and fractures have all been recorded.

Cameron et al. (1978) reviewed 29 cases of fatal child abuse. Of the children examined (average age 14.5 months), 50% had abrasions and bruising on the head, face and neck. Injuries described on the jaw and neck were fingertip-like abnormalities [59].

Associated Injuries

Scalp Swellings, Cephalhaematoma

Soft tissue swelling is commonly found with skull fractures clinically or on radiographs. A traumatic cephalhaematoma (page 122) follows direct impact of the skull by a blunt instrument or against a hard surface. King et al. (1988) reported that 54% of infants with inflicted head injury had no bruising at initial presentation [60].

Kleinman and Spevak (1992) examined the CT scans of 35 children aged 3 months to 8 years with recent skull fractures. At least 4mm of soft tissue swelling was found in all cases [61].

Ruddick et al. (2010) reviewed 11 newborn infants who sustained falls on to a hard surface whilst still in hospital. Skull fractures were found in 4 of 6 who had radiographs whilst scalp swelling was present in only 3 of 11 infants. Two of these had radiographs and both had fractures [62].

Scalp swellings that are caused by impact mostly appear within minutes but may be overlooked for up to 24 hours (usually by a non-observer/perpetrator who is not on the "look out" for injuries) particularly where an infant has thick hair. They may increase in size in the 2–3 days after head injury. Some are tender to palpation for up to 72 hours and most resolve clinically by 1–2 weeks.

Brain and Spinal injury

Skull fractures may be associated with both brain and spinal injuries (chapter 5). Harwood-Nash (1971) reported that skull fractures were more often seen with subdural haemorrhages in older children than in infants [63]. In a fracture of the temporal bone, the middle meningeal artery may be damaged leading to epidural haemorrhage which is often accidental. In a fracture of the occipital bone, the venous sinus may be damaged leading to a venous epidural haemorrhage in the posterior cranial fossa.

Mogby et al. (1998) reviewed 87 children under 2 years with a skull fracture. In 67 with no neurological deficit, 32 underwent CT. Six (19%) had small focal haemorrhages around the fracture. Of 20 children with acute neurological deficit, CT showed abnormalities in 16 (3 minor and 13 serious pathologies) [64].

Skull Fractures in Utero and Birth Trauma

The highest risk during pregnancy is during the third trimester, when the skull has descended into the pelvis. Trauma sustained *in-utero* may be associated with intracranial injury resulting from maternal injuries where the skull is impacted against the sacrum.

Skull fractures occurring during delivery are usually linear parietal following a difficult or instrumental delivery. They have also been described after a normal vaginal birth [65]. Complex fractures have been reported after instrumentation and depressed fractures after manipulation during a Caesarean section or vacuum extraction [66].

Rubin (1964) reviewed 15,435 births finding one skull fracture [67]. Alexander et al. (2006) reviewed 418 infants with injuries from 37,110 Caesarean sections. Six had a skull fracture due to factors prior to operation such as attempts at vaginal delivery [68].

Rib Fractures

In the absence of underlying bone disease or a history of major accidental trauma, rib fractures (particularly posterior) are highly suspect for inflicted injury in pre-mobile infants. Ninety percent occur under 2 years of age.

Many may be undiagnosed if radiographs are not performed when an infant is presented for care or follow-up radiographs omitted. Kleinman et al. (1988) reported that up to 50% of recent rib fractures are not evident on a radiograph even when straight and oblique views are obtained. It is therefore recommended that follow-up images are performed between 10–14 days [69].

Mechanism and Force Required

Rib fractures follow compression of the thorax with distortion of the rib cage often during squeezing/shaking episodes in infants. As such, they are associated with abusive head trauma (chapter 5). Squeezing generates force on both the back and front of the chest resulting in fractures from stress in the rib and leverage around the vertebra. Where the mechanism is shaking, bruising is seldom observed [70].

It is generally accepted that posterior rib fractures require the posterior end of the rib to be levered over the transverse process of the spine. This cannot occur when the child is lying on his or her back because the posterior ribs rest against a surface and are relatively fixed. However, when the child is gripped with a force pushing the spine forwards and the posterior end of the ribs backwards posterior fractures may occur.

Kleinman et al. (1992) from postmortem studies found that the location and healing patterns of rib fractures suggested they occured as the rib was levered over the transverse process of the adjacent vertebral body [71].

Rib fractures also result from direct impact, accidentally following road traffic accidents and significant falls or from inflicted injury. Bruising may then be found at the point of impact.

Aftermath and Observers

In the aftermath of injury, an infant will scream out in a manner not heard previously by a carer, who may comment on this unusual cry and recognise that excessive and inappropriate force had been applied. Crying and screaming may continue for some minutes after injury which is followed by discomfort or pain during handling.

There may be a clicking noise due to fractured ends of ribs moving against one another. A non-perpetrator is unlikely to recognise that the ribs have been injured but will find the infant fractious particularly on handling with possible breathing difficulties to include a raised respiratory rate and grunting.

Symptoms may be reduced if pain relief is given or the infant comforted and held still. However, irritability and crying during handling may last for up to 72 hours.

Rare complications include rupture of intercostal vessels, haemothorax, pneumothorax or subcutaneous emphysema. Lower rib fractures may damage the spleen, stomach or bowel. When several ribs are fractured at different locations a 'flail chest' may result. At inspiration the chest wall moves in and at expiration it moves out. Gipson and Tobias (2006) described a 21-day-old infant with a flail chest resulting from inflicted injury [72].

Inflicted vs Accidental Rib Fractures

Inflicted rib fractures may be single but are commonly multiple, occurring at the same location on adjacent ribs. Posterior fractures are more specific for abuse (Table 3.3) [73].

Barsness et al. (2003) reviewed 62 children under 3 years with a total 316 rib fractures. In 51 (82%) fractures were the result of abuse. In those under 3 years old the positive predictive value of a rib fracture as indicator of child abuse was 95%. Multiple fractures were more common in abuse as were posterior and lateral fractures [74].

Chest compression may impede respirations and oxygen uptake. At postmortem where other signs of asphyxiation are absent, rib fractures may indicate an asphyxial episode. Boos (2000) reported the case of a father who confessed to pushing several times on the chest of a child and pushing the child's legs against his chest. In a further incident he wrapped the child in a sheet impeding respirations. At postmortem there were 14 rib fractures of different ages as well as face and scalp haematomas [75].

Table 3.3 Radiological features suspect for inflicted injury

No underlying bone disease
Multiple, bilateral fractures
Fractures of different ages
Posterior and lateral fractures

Carty & Pearce (2002) reviewed 467 children referred with a suspected diagnosis of inflicted injury. There were 154 rib fractures with a single fracture in 31 (20%) [76].

Kemp et al. (2008) reviewed 32 publications comparing accidental with inflicted fractures in childhood concluding that rib fractures, regardless of type, are highly specific for abuse. After excluding children who were involved in a road traffic accident, violent trauma and post-surgical cases the probability of abuse for a rib fracture was 0.71 [77].

Other Causes

Birth Trauma

The true incidence of rib fractures following birth is unknown since there is usually no clinical indication for a chest radiograph. There are, however, occasional case reports of them in new-born infants. Rubin (1964) in a prospective study of 15,435 births, found no rib fractures. There were 43 clavicular fractures, 7 humeral fractures and one skull fracture [67]. van Rijn, Bilo and Robben (2008) described 3 cases of birth-related posterior rib fractures associated with large infants and difficult deliveries. More than 50% had shoulder dystocia [78].

Cardiopulmonary Resuscitation (CPR)

CPR involves significant force applied to the rib cage to achieve adequate cardiac output. The hand is placed across the sternum and depressed repeatedly. In infants the thumbs are placed on the sternum, fingers over the spine and compressions applied.

In adults, rib fractures frequently occur with CPR. In infants and young children the thorax is more compliant with fractures only rarely described. Some are discovered at autopsy where previous radiographs were normal.

Spevak et al. (1994) reviewed postmortem data of 91 infants under a year resuscitated for other reasons than child abuse. No rib fractures were found [79].

Dolinak (2007) performed autopsies in 70 infants between 2 weeks and 8 months of age who had been resuscitated. After removing the pleura from the ribs of eight children, he found anterolateral rib fractures. Seven of the infants had more than one fracture. Five had bilateral rib fractures [80].

Clouse and Lantz (2008) reported four infants (1 day to 3 months) with posterior rib fractures who died following CPR attempts by thumbs placed on the sternum, fingers over the spine. Child abuse was ruled out. Three had recent rib fractures related to resuscitation attempts prior to death. A fourth had older rib fractures with callus formation from previous resuscitation attempts [81].

Maguire et al. (2006) reported 3 children with rib fractures (2 under 6 months, one, 5 years of age) following CPR out of 923 cases. Resuscitation was carried out for different periods of time by trained and non-trained staff. All rib fractures were multiple and anterior. Two had mid-clavicular fractures and one had bilateral fractures at the sterno–chondral junction. No posterior rib fractures were identified [82].

Betz and Liebhart (1994) reviewed 233 postmortems (ages 5 days - 7 years). Of these, 190 deaths were described as non-traumatic, 43 traumatic. In 94 of 190 deaths due to natural causes, resuscitation was attempted and in 2 cases, fractures of the ribs were found on both sides in the midclavicular line. In 15 of 43 traumatic deaths, fractures mainly of the posterior ends of the ribs occurred [83].

Matshes and Lew (2010) reported five infants where multiple acute anterolateral rib fractures followed two handed CPR delivered by trained medical personnel [84].

Reyes et al. (2011) reviewed 571 infants who had CPR performed prior to death between 1997 and 2008. There were 19 infants (3.3%) with resuscitation related rib fractures, 14 of whom died between 2006–2008. The authors noted an increased number of infants with rib fractures at autopsy after revision of paediatric CPR guidelines [85].

Accidental Injury

Rib fractures are caused by direct impact during a road traffic accident, severe falls or other serious accidents.

Bulloch et al. (2000) reviewed 39 infants under 1 year of age with rib fractures. Thirty-two were caused by child abuse, 1 from birth trauma, 3 due to bone fragility and a further 3 from accidental trauma. Of the latter, the first case was an infant restrained in an unsecured car seat. The infant was thrown forward sustaining 5 rib fractures (lateral and mid-posterior) and a liver laceration. The second infant presented to the emergency department (ED) with wheezing. A chest radiograph showed 5 healing rib fractures (4th–8th left mid-posterior). The mother stated that a 5-year-old had fallen on the infant 1 month earlier. She had sought medical attention at that time reporting that the infant's chest felt 'crackly'. No radiographs had been obtained. The third infant was injured during a fall down a flight of stairs. His father said he had landed on top of him. Radiographs showed a fractured anterior 7th rib on the right, a transverse fracture of the left femur, linear skull fractures and a laceration of the spleen. Child protection teams for cases 2 and 3 accepted explanations provided, even though both were unwitnessed [86].

Cadzow and Armstrong (2000), reviewed infants aged 2 years or younger with rib fractures. Child abuse was diagnosed in 15 of 18 cases. The initial presentation most often included intracranial injury and limb fractures. Three of the infants with inflicted rib injuries were discharged home with one re-presenting with significant further injury [87].

Physiotherapy

Gorincour et al. (2004) prospectively studied infants and children who had received physiotherapy for bronchiolitis. Six under 2 years of age had lateral rib fractures with 12 of 14 abnormalities from the 4th to 7th ribs [88].

Chalumet et al. (2002), reported five infants and children (average age 3 months) who sustained rib fractures after physiotherapy for pneumonia (1) or bronchiolitis (4). The average number of fractures was four. One was posterior [89].

Premature Infants

Premature infants particularly those born at less than 30 weeks weighing less than 1000 grams have an increased susceptibility to fractures due to osteopenia of prematurity.

Bishop et al. (2007) reported that metabolic bone disease of prematurity was seen in the UK mainly in infants born at <28 weeks gestation with fractures typically occurring at 10 weeks of age and usually ceasing before of 6 months [90].

Cosway et al. (2015) described 61 infants and children under 2 years of age with rib fractures. There were 20 cases of physical abuse (PA), 11 post-surgical and 3 of accidental trauma. Two cases had fractures following CPR, 18 had metabolic bone disease of prematurity (MBDP) and one, another metabolic bone disease. In six the cause was undetermined. The number and distribution of rib fractures and the age of infants did not discriminate between MBDP and PA. Fractures were predominantly posterior, postero-lateral or lateral. All cases of MBDP were born at 31 weeks gestation or less, birth weight < 1.25kg. Each child with MBDP had at least one additional risk factor; chronic lung disease (7), prolonged total parenteral nutrition (10), steroid use (4), frusemide (8) or necrotising enterocolitis (3). All PA cases had other injuries or signs of neglect [91].

Coughing Fits

Rib fractures have been described in adolescents and adults with severe coughing. The youngest child reported with a 1st rib fracture due to whooping cough was 11 years old [92].

Clavicular Fractures

Clavicular injuries are the commonest birth-related fractures. In older children direct impact or falling on to an outstretched arm are common accidental causes. Fractures of the middle third (the shaft) are most prevalent (76–85%), distal third 10–21%, and medial third 3–5% [93]. In pre-school ambulant children accidental clavicular fractures account for 8–15% of all fractures [94]. They may co-exist with injuries to the proximal humerus.

Mechanism and Clinical Presentations

Accidental Causes

Fractures of the middle third of the clavicle in ambulant children result from a fall onto the shoulder/outstretched arm or direct impact from a blunt instrument. Reported accidental causes in infants include a child or adult falling on to the baby or following shaking/squeezing in attempts to resuscitate an infant who has stopped breathing.

Inficted injury

Of all inflicted fractures, 2–7% are clavicular [94]. In those under 18 months, apart from birth injury, such fractures are suspect for abuse in the absence of a credible history of an injury and its aftermath. The CORE information website (see further reading) reports that in a child of less than 4 years with a clavicular fracture an inflicted cause is 4.4 times more likely (range 1.9–10.2).

Inflicted causes include excessive squeezing from an adult grip around the chest and shoulders with direct pressure on the clavicle, a direct blow or impact against a hard immovable surface. Violent shaking or twisting of the arm has been associated with fractures of the ends of the clavicle. A direct blow causes a mid-shaft fracture, traction to the arm typically a lateral fracture.

Merton et al. (1983) noted that inflicted clavicular fractures were usually associated with other skeletal injuries [95].

Birth Injury

Most clavicular fractures from birth injury occur during passage through the vaginal canal during a normal vaginal delivery. Rubin (1964) in a prospective study of 15,435 births, found 43 clavicular fractures of 51 infants who had sustained a fracture [67].

Aftermath and Observers

In the aftermath of injury an infant will scream out in a manner not heard previously by a carer who may comment on this. Crying and screaming may continue for some minutes which is followed by discomfort or pain during handling for up to 72 hours. If the infant is comforted and kept still he or she may settle.

A perpetrator or observer will recognise that excessive force had been applied. A non-observer is unlikely to recognise the clavicle had been injured in a pre-mobile infant but be faced with a fractious baby with often limitation of movement of the arm on the affected side.

Children complain of pain around the fracture and may be reluctant to use the arm on the affected side. They may 'look' towards the side of the fracture to relax the sternocleidomastoid muscle and avoid it pulling at the broken bone. In the early stages there may be pain from haematoma or fluid collection.

Joseph and Rosenfeld (1990) reported that following birth injury, most newborns showed no symptoms, with 40% of fractures found only after repeated examination. A swelling on the clavicle due to new bone formation may be a chance finding by a carer as healing progresses [96].

Sternal Fractures

These are rare in children and highly suspect for inflicted injury in the absence of a credible history of significant accident. They are caused by a direct blow or forceful compression to the chest.

DeFriend and Franklin (2001) reported two children who sustained a sternal fracture from a fall off a swing [97]. Ferguson et al. 2003, reviewed all children who had a plain radiograph of the sternum, or CT thorax after trauma. Twelve of 33 children (aged 5–12 years) had radiological evidence of sternal fracture. Seven fractures resulted from direct blows to the anterior chest, five from hyperflexion injury of the thoracic spine. None resulted from a road traffic accident [98].

Scapular Fractures

Scapular fractures are rare due to the protected anatomical position of the bone within muscle and connective tissue. High energy impact may be responsible and pulmonary complications may co-exist. In older children a fall on to the shoulder may cause a scapula fracture. In the absence of a reported accident they have a high specificity for child abuse [53]. A shaking injury may lead to avulsion fractures of the acromion and other parts of the scapula.

Long Bone Fractures

Accidental trauma accounts for most long bone fractures in ambulant children. Inflicted trauma is more common in pre-mobile infants regardless of type or site of fracture.

Mechanism and Clinical Presentations

A direct blow, compression, bowing, twisting or a combination of forces are seen in both accidental and inflicted injury. In a transverse fracture, the fracture line is perpendicular to the long axis of the bone, whilst in an oblique fracture, the line is at an angle usually around 30–40 degrees. A spiral fracture line encircles a portion of the bone.

In accidental injury there is direct or indirect impact if for example a child falls from significant height or is involved in a road traffic accident. Spiral tibial/fibular (less commonly femoral, rarely humeral) fractures may occur accidentally when a carer grabs the limb to prevent an infant from falling and applies a gripping/twisting force.

In inflicted injury a blow or kick to a limb, a violent grab, twisting, levering or impact against a hard surface may all be responsible for long bone fractures.

Worlock (1986) reported on 35 children under the age of 5 with inflicted fractures. Injuries to the long bones were spiral or oblique with spiral fractures of the humerus shaft being more common. Tibia and fibula fractures were found only in children under 18months and 7 of 12 inflicted tibial fractures were metaphyseal [3].

Leventhal et al. (2008) reviewed 253 long bone fractures in 215 children with the following findings: abuse (24.2%), unintentional (67.4%), unknown (8.4%).

Features of inflicted fractures included carers reporting only a change in behaviour, no accident or a minor fall, fractures of the radius/ulna, tibia/fibula, or femur in under one year and mid shaft/metaphyseal fractures of the humerus [4].

Aftermath and Observers

Symptoms and healing are affected by the severity of injury, degree of displacement, immobilisation and any underlying disorder.

Whether infants and children differ in their response to pain is a matter of speculation. In the aftermath of an injury sufficient to cause a long bone fracture, a child will scream out often in a manner not heard previously by a carer who may comment on the unusual cry. A crack or 'give' may be heard or felt as the bone fractures.

Farrell et al. (2012) reported on 206 children of whom 69% had accidental upper extremity fractures (mean age 3.7 ± 1.6 years). The median time to medical evaluation was 1 hour with 21% seen at more than 8 hours. Carers reported crying at injury (91%) and irritability for more than 30 min. (83%). Parents observed no external sign of injury in 15% and 12% were reported to use the limb normally. All noticed at least one sign or symptom. Although some children did not manifest all expected responses, no child with an accidental fracture was asymptomatic. Delay in seeking care was associated with more subtle signs of injury [99].

Crying and distress may continue for some minutes, longer if the fracture is displaced when movement usually causes agonising pain. If comforted and kept still with no pressure placed on the fracture, pain may be controlled whilst any movement of the affected limb exacerbates discomfort for at least 72 hours depending on severity. During this period the infant will be reluctant to use the limb which is often held limply ('pseudoparalysis'). Symptoms may be reduced if pain relief is given.

A perpetrator or observer will be aware that excessive force had been applied and be on the 'look out' for injury. A child's distress and reluctance to use the limb in the aftermath will also be appreciated.

Depending on location and severity, there is pain on pressure for 10–14 days. Orthopaedic surgeons use the latter as a guide as to when to remove splints. For more complex fractures symptoms may last longer.

Tender swelling is an unreliable sign but when present suggests an injury within the previous 72 hours. Bruising is an inconsistent finding whilst abnormal alignment may be found in some long bone fractures.

Clinical assessment may be difficult. Pre-mobile infants have limited normal movements so that an injury may not always be obvious to a non-perpetrator. Infants cry when they are hungry and uncomfortable and it may be difficult to distinguish this from the anguish of an injured baby. Presentation for care following inflicted injury may be delayed during which time symptoms may lessen and function improve. By the time the infant or child is presented for care, signs may be minimal.

Femoral Fractures

Fewer than 2% of all fractures involve the femoral shaft. Road traffic accidents, significant falls and inflicted injury are the main causes. Under the age of 15 months, a spiral fracture is the commonest inflicted femoral fracture [100]. For mechanism and aftermath see pages 73–74.

Thomas et al. (1991) reported that 60% of femoral shaft fractures diagnosed in children under a year and 20% in those aged 2–3 years were due to abuse [101].

Baldwin et al. (2011) identified 70 patients with inflicted femoral fractures comparing them with 139 patients with accidental femoral fractures. Risk factors included a history suspicious of abuse, physical or radiographic evidence of prior injury and age younger than 18 months. The risk of inflicted injury was as follows: no risk factors (4%), one risk factor (29%), two risk factors (87%) all three risk factors 92% [102].

Hui et al. (2008) reviewed infants and children under 3 years of age who were diagnosed with a femoral fracture. The overall percentage of inflicted injury was 11% (14/127) and 17% (10/60) in infants under 12 months. Age younger than 12 months, delayed presentation, an unwitnessed injury, inconsistent accounts and other associated injuries were significant risk factors for inflicted injury [103].

Schwend et al. (2000) reviewed 139 children under 4 years of age with an isolated fracture of the shaft of one or both femurs. A total of 126 children (91%) of average age 2.3 years sustained a fracture most likely as a result of accident. Being non-ambulant was the strongest predictor of abuse [104].

Femoral fractures as a result of birth trauma are rare. Morris et al. (2002) found seven neonates with a total of eight femoral fractures in 55,296 live births. Two were diagnosed at birth, the remainder between 2–21 days. Spiral fractures of the proximal part of the femur were most commonly observed and have been reported in breech and forceps delivery, twin and premature births as well as Caesarean sections [105].

Tibia and Fibula Fractures

In pre-mobile infants or those beginning to mobilise, transverse fractures of the tibial shaft are suspect for inflicted injury resulting from direct impact. A grabbing/twisting force is associated with both spiral and oblique fractures. For aftermath see pages 73–74.

A tibial toddler fracture is a common accidental hairline spiral fracture in children aged 1–3 years. If a child slips and falls whilst running, the foot may become fixed under furniture and rotation occurs. The knee and hip are stationary whilst the lower leg twists. Other activities such as slipping or sliding with a brisk landing may involve rapid limb rotation [106]. Similar fractures may occur accidentally when a carer grabs the leg to prevent an infant from falling and applies a gripping/twisting force.

Fractures of both tibia and fibula have been reported where a child's foot was caught between a bicycle frame and the spokes of the wheel with the child seated on a backseat [107].

Coffey et al. (2005) reported that among trauma patients the incidence of abuse was 104 (2%) of 4942 children 18 months or older and 175 (32%) of 555 infants and children younger than 18 months. There were 1252 (23%) patients with lower extremity injuries and 66 of these were younger than 18 months. In the extremity trauma group, for those 18 months or older, 16 (1%) of 1186 were abused compared with 44 (67%) of 66 patients younger than 18 months. Among all trauma patients younger than 18 months, 41/55 lower extremity fractures were linked to abuse as were 134/500 other injuries. Among the 41 abuse-related fractures, femoral was the most common (22), followed by a tibial fracture (14) [108].

Humeral Fractures

Fewer than 10% of all childhood fractures are humeral with spiral and oblique fractures more commonly associated with inflicted injury particularly in those under 3 years of age. They are most frequently mid-shaft or metaphyseal. Direct impact results in transverse fractures, twisting forces in spiral or oblique fractures. For aftermath see pages 73–74.

Leventhal et al. (1993) reported that fractures of the radius, ulna, tibia, fibula, femur and mid-shaft or metaphyseal fractures of the humerus in children of less than 1 year old were usually the result of child abuse [11]. Humeral fractures have also been described in infants being turned from front to back or rolling over (page 81).

In older children the most frequent cause of a humeral fracture is accidental trauma either direct impact, blunt force against the shoulder, a fall on the back of the shoulder or backwards on to the extended arm. Spiral or oblique fractures are due to rotation of the body on to an outstretched arm seen following a fall whilst running.

Supracondylar fractures in older children occur accidentally following a fall on to the elbow or outstretched hand or direct impact on a bent elbow joint. Strait et al. (1995) found that in 20% of children under 15 months a supracondylar fracture was a result of child abuse [13]. Fractures of the distal epiphysis in children commonly indicate inflicted injury (excluding birth trauma).

Thomas et al. (1991) reviewed the medical records and radiographs of 215 children younger than 3 years of age with fractures. Of these, 14 had humeral fractures, 11 considered to be inflicted. Humeral fractures other than supracondylar were all found to be due to abuse. There were 25 femoral fractures of which 9 were found to be inflicted, 14 from accidents, and 2 unknown. Sixty percent of femoral fractures in infants younger than 1 year of age were considered inflicted. The authors noted however, that femoral fractures in ambulant children were often accidental and associated with trips and falls [101].

In birth trauma proximal humeral fractures result from hyperextension of the arm during passage through the birth canal particularly in breech deliveries. Epiphyseal fractures most commonly involve the proximal humerus and are also associated with difficult deliveries.

Radius and Ulna Fractures

Forearm fractures account for 42% of all fractures in children with a peak incidence being over 5 years of age [109]. The distal part of the radius and ulna are most usually affected with mid-shaft fractures being observed more frequently in young children [110].

In accidental injury a fall on an outstretched hand is the most common cause. Of all inflicted bone injuries approximately 10–20% are shaft fractures of the radius and ulna, usually transverse. For aftermath see pages 73–74.

Pulled elbow syndrome (nursemaid's elbow) is subluxation of the head of the radius due to arm pulling observed more commonly in children aged 2–3 years. Arm pulling may be accidental or inflicted.

Hands and Feet

Fractures of the hands and feet are common in older children but suspicious for abuse in infants and toddlers. Foot fractures occur from objects being dropped on to the foot, falls, or twisting movements. They may be painful with a reluctance to stand or asymptomatic. Fractures of the fingers are due to direct trauma or a bending, twisting force. Pain, swelling and a reluctance to move the affected finger may be found although many are reported to be asymptomatic. Whilst the perpetrator in inflicted injury will know that excessive force had been applied an non-observer may not know that an injury had occurred.

Valencia et al. (2005) reported that at age 1–2 years distal phalangeal fractures were more common whilst at age 12 years proximal phalangeal fractures predominated [111].

Nimkin et al. (1997) reviewed 11 fractures of the hands and feet in infants under 10 months of age. Fractures of the metacarpals or proximal phalanges of the hands and those of the first metatarsals of the feet were more commonly seen. Buckle fractures of the proximal phalanx were considered to be the result of forced hyperextension of the fingers [112].

Barber et al. (2015) reviewed skeletal surveys performed for suspected abuse in 567 infants. In 313 (55%), 1029 fractures were found including long-bone, skull, ribs, clavicle, spine, scapula, hands, feet and pelvis. Of the 425 infants who underwent neuroimaging, 154 (36%) had intracranial injury. The mean age of fractures to the hands or feet was 5 months (1–10 months) [113].

Lindberg et al. (2013) collected data for all children younger than 10 years of age where there were concerns for abuse. Initial skeletal survey showed that 471/2049

(23.0%) had at least 1 previously undiagnosed fracture including 49 (10.4%) to the hands, feet, spine, or pelvis. In 10 cases, radiographs identified at least 1 fracture of the hands, feet, spine, or pelvis when no other fractures were identified [114].

Kleinman et al. (2013) reviewed skeletal surveys of all children younger than 2 years with suspected abuse. Sixty-two percent (225/365) had positive findings, with 44% (98/225) having more than one fracture. Of all positive skeletal surveys, 8.9% (20/225) had fractures involving the spine, hands, or feet. Of all patients with more than one fracture on skeletal survey, 20.4% (20/98) had fractures involving these areas [115].

Stress fractures are tiny cracks in a bone of the foot caused by the repetitive application of force such as repeated jumping up and down or running long distances.

Spinal Fractures

Inflicted injury to the spine may result in vertebral compression fractures, usually thoracolumbar from forceful slamming on to the buttocks or feet. Dislocations and subluxations have been described. Hyperflexion or extension of the torso (as seen in shaking injuries) may cause fractures predominantly to the lower thoracic and higher lumbar vertebrae [116]. Co-existent abusive head trauma (AHT) particularly in those under 1 year of age is common. This has prompted a move towards routine spinal MRI for AHT.

Accidental spinal fractures in older children are the result of significant falls, road traffic accidents or sports injuries. There are case reports of falls less than 1.5 metres causing cervical spinal fractures [117] as well as birth injury being responsible [118].

Often clinical signs are minimal with neurological abnormalities present only if there is vertebral dislocation or subluxation. In young children, damage to the spinal cord occurs more frequently without a fracture (spinal cord injury without radiological abnormality - SCIWORA).

For cervical injury, children may present with respiratory difficulties or neurological deficit. For thoraco-lumbar injuries, visible swelling or deformity, neurological deficit below the level of injury and associated intracranial haemorrhages have been described (page 126). In the aftermath of injury a child will cry out in pain but settle so long as there are no neurological complications. There may be pain on spinal movement.

Cirak et al. (2004) reviewed 406 children with traumatic injuries of the spinal column and cord. Road traffic accidents were commonest up to 2 years, falls more common between 2–9 years and sports injuries predominated between 10–14 years of age. Most fractures were in the upper cervical spine. The incidence of SCIWORA was 6%. Traumatic brain injury was present in 37% [119].

Oral et al. (2006) reported a 4-year-old who sustained an avulsion fracture of the second cervical vertebra after the babysitter had thrown the child on to a bed from 1–2 feet. [120]. Ogden (1990), described multiple fractures of the spinous processes of the thoracic and lumbar spine due to shaking [121].

Barber et al. (2013) reviewed skeletal surveys and neuroimaging of 751 children (ages 0–4 years) with suspected inflicted injuries. Of those with a positive skeletal survey, 9.7% (14/145) had spinal fractures. Further imaging confirmed the fractures in 13 of 14 children with 12 additional spinal fractures identified. In five cases, spinal fractures were the only positive skeletal findings. In 71% spinal fractures were associated with intracranial injury [122].

Choudhary et al. (2012) reviewed 252 children aged 0–2 years with AHT. A second group of 70 children aged 0–2 years were treated for accidental trauma. In the AHT group 67/252 (26.5%) had spinal imaging. Of these, 38/67 (56%) had thoracolumbar imaging, with 24 (63%) having thoracolumbar subdural haemorrhage a finding that was rare in those with accidental trauma [123].

Pelvic Fractures

Pelvic fractures generally occur in association with other serious injuries. They are due to direct trauma from falls, road traffic accidents and crush injuries. Bruising to the perineum, buttocks and thighs raises concerns for child sexual abuse (CSA) [124].

Johnson et al. (2004) reported three children all of whom were victims of CSA. A 3-year-old girl suffered extensive injuries to the soft tissue of the arms, legs and perineum with fractures of both pubic arches and sacro-iliac joint. A 5-year-old girl sustained rectal rupture from sexual abuse with an old healed fracture of the pubic arch being found on radiographs. A 5-month-old sustained a tear of the hymen and a fracture of the femoral shaft [125].

Other Clinical and Radiological Considerations

Metaphyseal Corner Fractures (CML)

Metaphyseal fractures (classic metaphyseal lesions, CML) are highly suspicious for inflicted injuries in infants under 1 year of age and rarely, if ever observed in osteogenesis imperfecta or other skeletal dysplasias. Only Astley (1979) has reported metaphyseal fractures in OI [135]. In the neonatal period, metaphyseal fractures have been reported following birth injury, physiotherapy or casting for talipes.

CMLs are difficult to detect or date on radiographs due to an absence of periosteal elevation and haemorrhage. They do not typically result in significant swelling or bruising and may not be recognised by a carer or clinician. At the point of injury the infant is likely to scream out in pain but settle quickly. Most heal by 4 weeks without the need for immobilisation.

Metaphyseal fractures are predominantly found in infants and children of less than 2 years of age, most frequently at the distal femur (above the knee), proximal and distal tibia (above the ankle) and the proximal humerus (below the shoulder). They are less frequently observed at the elbow, wrist and proximal femur. CMLs may be multiple and bilateral and often found in children under 2 years where a skeletal survey has been performed for suspected abuse.

Pulling, twisting, gripping and shearing forces to an extremity are established causes. Hymel and Spivak (2001) reported that violent shaking may lead to metaphyseal fractures of the distal femur and proximal and distal tibia being associated with posterior rib fractures and abusive head trauma [126].

Kleinman et al. (2011) reviewed the prevalence of the classic metaphyseal lesion (CML) in infants at low and high risk for inflicted injury. Low-risk infants met the following criteria: skull fracture without significant intracranial injury, history of a fall and no other social risk factors. High-risk infants: significant intracranial injury, retinal haemorrhages and skeletal injuries (excluding classic metaphyseal lesions and skull fractures). There were 42 low-risk infants (mean age, 4.4 months) and 18 high-risk infants (mean age, 4.6 months). At least one CML was identified in 9 infants in the high-risk category. None were identified in the low-risk group. The authors noted that the CML was a high-specificity indicator of infant abuse [127].

O'Connell and Donohue (2007) reported on three cases of CML of the distal femur after Caesarean section over a 22-year period. [128]. Grayev et al. (2001), reported that CMLs have been described following the treatment of club feet in children. However, one child in the series had been abused with skeletal survey showing 24 rib fractures [129, 130].

Sub-Periosteal New Bone Formation (SPNBF)

Subperiosteal new bone formation follows stripping of the periosteum by friction or blunt trauma with underlying haematoma but no associated fracture. A double contour on radiographs is observed due to lifting of the periosteum.

SBNBF must be distinguished from periosteal thickening of the long bones in neonates and infants between 1 and 4–6 months of age and from a pathological periosteal reaction resulting from infantile cortical hyperostosis, osteomyelitis, vitamin C deficiency (scurvy), vitamin A intoxication, leukaemia and congenital syphilis. Periosteal reaction is also a feature of healing fractures.

Normal Variations

Both normal metaphyseal variants or 'spurs' can be mistaken for metaphyseal fractures. Cortical irregularity observed in the tibia, accessory growth centres or skull sutures may all be mistaken for fractures.

Growth-Retardation/Arrest Lines

These are radiopaque lines across the metaphyses. They have been reported in childhood diseases where growth is delayed or has halted including malnourishment, infections, some endocrine conditions, chronic juvenile arthritis, chemotherapy treatment and prolonged immobilisation.

Daily Care and Medical Procedures

Fractures rarely occur during normal or even rough handling of an infant or child. Some children with underlying medical conditions are more prone to fractures during normal care.

Hymel and Jenny (1996) reported mid-shaft humeral fractures in two infants. In patient 1, a two year old sister turned a 5-month-old infant from back to front whist he had his arms extended. The episode was co-incidentally videotaped. In patient 2, the father of a 3-month-old girl reconstructed on video an episode where he turned her from back to front [130]. Somers et al. (2014) described seven infants aged 4–7 months in whom a humeral fracture was the only injury and where the carer described the fracture occurring when the child rolled over, trapping the dependent arm, without the intervention of a carer. A credible history of an event an its aftermath was provided in all cases [131].

Pickett et al. (1982) described an infant born at 33 weeks gestation with contractures who received physiotherapy. Multiple radiological abnormalities to both legs were found at age 4 weeks of age including periosteal reactions and metaphyseal fractures of the medial proximal part of both femurs only in areas treated by a physiotherapist [132]. Simonian and Stahel (1995) reported fractures around the knee joint following passive exercises for contractures around the joint [133].

Intraosseus needles are placed in the tibia and used for fluids and drug administration when intravenous access cannot be achieved. Radiographic findings following insertion may be similar to a healing fracture. Bowley (2003) reported a 2-year-old who sustained a tibial fracture after the use of an intra-osseous needle [134].

Conditions that Increase Susceptibility to Fractures

Osteogenesis Imperfecta (OI, Brittle Bone Disease)

Osteogenesis imperfecta is a rare (1 in 10,000 births), inherited disorder of connective tissue that results from an abnormal quantity or quality of type I collagen leading to osteoporosis and increased bone fragility. The disease is equally distributed between boys and girls, and is often seen in other family members, although spontaneous mutations do occur.

Type I accounts for 80% of cases having an autosomal dominant inheritance. Collagen is of normal quality but produced in insufficient quantities. Fractures usually begin during preschool years. Features are blue sclera, hearing impairment, easy bruising, joint hypermobility, growth deficiency, dentinogenesis imperfecta and short stature.

Type II is the perinatal lethal form of the disease presenting with severe skeletal deformities, intrauterine growth retardation, short bowed legs and arms and multiple fractures with deficient skull ossification at birth. There is insufficient quality and quantity of collagen. Most infants die in early infancy.

Type III is the progressive deforming type, inherited either as autosomal dominant or a new dominant mutation. Bone fragility and osteopenia are more severe and fractures at birth are present in two-thirds. Growth retardation and skeletal abnormalities are common. Sclerae may be blue or grey. Dentinogenesis imperfecta and ligamentous laxity occur in 50% with easy bruising in 25%.

Type IV is the rare autosomal dominant variant ranging from mild to severe. It is the most difficult to distinguish from inflicted injury. Collagen quantity is sufficient but of insufficient quality. Fractures are common but deformities milder. Bones may appear normal on radiographs at the time of the first fracture. Blue sclera, abnormal hearing and easy bruising are uncommon. Dentinogenesis imperfecta and osteopenia are found.

Types V – VIII are moderately to severely deforming. Type V is autosomal dominant, Types VI – VIII recessive.

Other clinical features

Radiological features may include multiple Wormian bones, osteopenia, bowing of the long bones, slender ribs and vertebral compression fractures. Gahagan et al. (1991) noted that recurrent fractures often occurred in different settings helping to distinguish osteogenesis imperfecta (OI) from abuse [136].

OI is a clinical diagnosis made on the basis of family history, repeated fractures, clinical examination, radiology and biochemistry. In patients with clinical features or a strong family history, further investigations are warranted. Where the sclera are normal with no positive family history and no Wormian bones or radiographic changes, the diagnosis becomes less likely.

Investigations

DNA analysis

Molecular testing for the genes COL1A1/1A2 and IFITM5 can be performed with more than 90% of mutations causing the dominant form of OI and alterations of type I collagen being detected [137].

Skin Biopsy

Biochemical testing of collagen from cultured fibroblasts can extend to sequencing of genes. Despite this, some mutations will be overlooked.

Dual Energy X-ray Absorptiometry (DEXA)

DEXA provides information about bone quantity and is used to assess bone mineral density (BMD) particularly in adults with osteoporosis. Its use in children is limited. Bone mineral density may be low or normal in children with OI and there is no reliable published reference data.

Zionts et al. (1995) used DEXA scanning to compare the BMD of nine children aged 2–13 years with mild OI detecting significant differences compared with controls. The mean BMD in the children with OI was 76.7% of normal in the lumbar spine and 71.2% of normal in the femoral neck [138].

Bone Biopsy

Biopsy of the iliac bone can identify OI. A child must weigh at least 10 kilograms for the procedure which is rarely undertaken.

'Temporary Brittle-Bone Disease' – a non-diagnosis

Temporary brittle bone disease (TBBD) does not exist as a clinical entity and is included for completeness as the 'diagnosis' is often raised in child care proceedings. Patterson et al. (1993) described 39 children who presented with symptoms that they described as a variant of osteogenesis imperfecta, a temporary condition where fractures after minimal trauma were limited to the first year of life. Both radiological and clinical features were reported. However, a child with inflicted injury was excluded from the report. In 2001 the evidence of an expert witness was deemed inadmissible with the judge ruling that the study was unreliable and unproven [139]. Present evidence and opinion indicate there is no scientific basis on which TBBD can be accepted as a disease entity.

Vitamin D Deficient Rickets

Physiology

Osteopenia (osteopathy/metabolic bone disease) refers to decreased bone mineral density, the commonest cause in newborns being is Vitamin D deficiency where decreased amounts of calcium and phosphorus may weaken the bone, increasing an infant's susceptibility to fractures, skeletal deformities, poor growth and muscle weakness.

In the last trimester of pregnancy, calcium and phosphorus are transferred from the mother to the foetus to enable bone growth. A premature infant may not receive adequate amounts of these substances and have a bone mineral content 40–50% less than the full-term infant. Horsman et al. (1989) reported that the deficit at birth between preterm and full-term infants resolves by 50 weeks postconception [140].

In premature infants, liver and renal immaturity may exacerbate calcium deficiency due to an inability to metabolise Vitamin D and promote calcium and phosphate absorption. Calcium is required to sustain cardiac and other vital functions. If present in insufficient quantities, it is liberated from bones resulting in demineralisation and vitamin D deficient rickets.

Vulnerable Infants and Children

Infants born before 30 weeks gestation weighing less than 1.25kg often have a degree of biochemical rickets on blood testing. As this progresses metabolic bone disease can result with characteristic radiolographic changes and pathological fractures. Additional risk factors include, conjugated hyperbilirubinaemia, necrotising enterocolitis, gut resection and prolonged diuretic or steroid therapy.

Fifty percent of infants weighing less than 1000g may develop a degree of metabolic bone disease of prematurity usually between 6–12 weeks of age. Amir et al. (1998) found that of 973 premature infants, 1.2% at more than 6 months had fractures [141]. Other studies have reported fractures in up to 27% of high risk infants [142]. However, since this research, there have been significant improvements in nutritional management and neonatal care.

Dahlenberg et al. (1989) compared children with fractures to those with accidental injury without fractures finding no difference between them in the incidence of prematurity suggesting that an increased risk of fracture does not persist into childhood [143].

Vitamin D deficiency is also associated with vegetarian diets, prolonged breast-feeding without vitamin D supplementation and lack of exposure to sunlight. Other vulnerable patients include infants of vitamin D deficient mothers, children with neuro-disability and some ethnic groups including children born to parents of South East Asian (Bangladeshi, Indian and Pakistani), Middle-Eastern and Afro-Caribbean origin.

Medical conditions associated with vitamin D deficiency include malabsorption, renal, liver disease, pancreatic insufficiency, some syndromes and inborn errors of metabolism.

Children with Vitamin D deficient rickets present with tender swollen wrists, delayed eruption of teeth, muscle weakness, costochondral swelling, frontal bossing, soft skull (craniotabes), skeletal deformities and delayed growth. Rickets from whatever cause can result in pathological fractures.

Vitamin D intake

The recommended daily intake of vitamin D for infants and young children is 7µg – 8.5µg (280–340 IU) daily (Letter of UK Chief Medical Officers, 2012). Bagnoli et al (2013) investigated 73 healthy full-term infants at 3 months demonstrating impaired bone mineralisation on ultrasound and concluding that exclusively breast-fed infants required at least 400 IU of vitamin D daily [144]. Since artificial formulae are fortified with vitamin D, these infants do not require supplementation.

Biochemical Features

Biochemical features of vitamin D deficiency rickets include an elevated alkaline phosphatase level, low Vitamin D, low or normal calcium, low phosphate and raised parathyroid hormone levels (Table 3.4).

There is no evidence that low vitamin D levels (a common finding in infants and children), in the absence of biochemical and radiological evidence for rickets, increases susceptibility to fractures.

The British Paediatric and Adolescent Bone Group (BPABG) (2012) advised that where there are unexplained fractures in infancy the level of 25 hydroxyvitamin D is not relevant unless there is both radiological and biochemical evidence of rickets.

Table 3.4 Biochemical features of Vitamin D deficiency rickets osteopaenia	Elevated alkaline phosphatase levels, usually in excess of 1000iu/l
	Low levels of vitamin D (usually less than 12.5nmol/l)
	Low phosphate
	Calcium levels are often variable (lower end of normal or low)
	Raised serum parathyroid hormone (PTH)

Vitamin D deficiency is evidenced by a plasma level of 25 hydroxyvitamin D of less than 25nmol/l (10ng/ml), insufficiency between 25-50nmol/l (10–20ng/ml) and sufficiency as a level greater than 50nmol/l [145, 146].

Gordon et al. (2008) prospectively studied 365 infants and toddlers aged 8–24 months attending for a routine health visit. The prevalence of vitamin D deficiency (20ng/mL or less) was 12% (44/365) with 7 having severe deficiency. Of the 365 infants, 146 (40.0%) had levels below an accepted normal value (30ng/mL or less). In the deficiency/severe deficiency group, 7.5% (3) exhibited rachitic changes on radiographs and 32.5% (13) had evidence of demineralisation. Breastfeeding without supplementation among infants and lower milk intake among toddlers were predictors of vitamin D deficiency [147].

Radiological Features
Some bone mineral content has to be lost from the skeleton before metabolic bone disease becomes apparent on radiographs although research in this area is sparse. Healing rickets may have normal biochemistry. Widening, splaying and fraying of the metaphysis, pseudofractures, periosteal reactions and new bone formation may be observed. When fractures occur, radiographic features of rickets are apparent.

Perez-Rossello et al. (2012) identified 40 children with vitamin D deficiency (25-hydroxyvitamin D $\leq$ 20ng/mL) aged 8 to 24 months. Radiographs were scored by three readers with use of the 10-point Thacher score for rachitic changes and a five-point scale for demineralization. Rachitic changes were identified in two patients (5%) and demineralization in two patients (5%). No fractures were identified [148].

Rickets and Child Abuse
The presence of rickets does not exclude child abuse. Duncan and Chandry (1993) reported an infant aged 3 months with multiple fractures and rickets. She died at the age 5 months but child abuse, although suspected could not be confirmed. Three years later, abuse was confirmed in another child of the same family [149].

Other Conditions

The following conditions have distinct clinical features to include either an increased susceptibility to fractures or radiographic features that may be mistaken for them. They are included for completeness but are unlikely to be confused with inflicted injury.

Metabolic and Nutritional
Copper Deficiency
This occurs in both premature infants and in diseases with intestinal copper transport abnormalities. Chapman (1987) reported that radiographic features included osteopenia, subperiosteal new bone formation, metaphyseal abnormalities and zones of calcification [150].

Hypophosphatasia
Vitamin D resistant hypophosphataemic rickets leads to decreased mineralisation with wide sutures progressing to craniosynostosis and pseudo-fractures of the long bones. Perinatal and infantile forms are autosomal recessive, the milder forms autosomal recessive or dominant.

Kinky Hair Syndrome
Kinky hair syndrome (Menkes syndrome) presents with hypotonia, convulsions, failure to thrive, hypopigmentation, developmental delay and hair that is kinky, coarse, and hypopigmented. It is a progressive neurodegenerative disease the result of a congenital, X-linked recessive defect in copper metabolism. Radiographic findings may be indistinguishable from fractures. Wormian bones are a feature [151].

Osteoporosis/Ehlers-Danlos Syndrome (EDS)
In osteoporosis there is low bone mass and regression of bone tissue resulting from chronic disease, malnutrition, immobilisation and genetic defects. Idiopathic osteoporosis is a self-limiting condition seen in the second decade of life. Familial osteoporosis is associated with defects of LRP5 gene. Yen et al. 2006 reported osteoporosis in 11 patients with EDS (13 months – 36 years) evaluated with a bone mineral density study (Journal of the Formosan Medical Assoc).

Vitamin C Deficiency
Scurvy presents with fractures, subperiosteal and soft tissue haemorrhages. The diagnosis is rare under 6 months of age. Clinical signs include swelling of the ends of the long bones, a shiny, livid (blue-black) overlying skin with bleeding/swollen gums.

Congenital Conditions and Syndromes
Alagille Syndrome
This is an autosomal dominant syndrome affecting the liver, heart, kidneys, eyes and skeleton.

Congenital Pseudoarthrosis
A rare disorder associated with neurofibromatosis type 1 (NF1) causing bowing of the tibia and fibula increasing the risk of fractures.

Skeletal Dysplasias
Spondylometaphyseal dysplasias are characterised by flattened vertebrae with hip and knee metaphyseal lesions. Severe hip deformity (coxa vara) may result.

Other
Cole Carpenter syndrome (eye abnormalities, hydrocephalus and osteopenia), Bruck syndrome (joint contractures and bone fragility), McCune Albright syndrome (skin pigmentation and hormonal imbalance) and Cytomegalovirus infections may all increase susceptibility to fractures.

Neurological Conditions
Duchenne Muscular Dystrophy
This inherited disorder leads to progressive proximal muscular dystrophy and pseu-dohypertrophy of the calf muscles. McDonald et al. (2002) reported 378 patients (average age 12 years), of whom 79 (20.9%) had sustained a fracture [152].

Epilepsy and Cerebral Palsy
Children with epilepsy and cerebral palsy are at increased risk of fractures particu-larly of the lower extremities. Accidental trauma during a seizure, decreased bone density due to inactivity, anticonvulsant drugs, increased muscular tone with con-tractures and decreased muscle mass are all potential causes. Phenobarbitone, Phenytoin, Carbamazepine and Sodium Valproate have been associated with a reduction in bone density.

Sheth et al. (2006) reported that fracture rates for epileptic patients were three times more common than in the general population [153]. Lingam et al. (1994) reported 5 patients with cerebral palsy (aged 10–19 years) with five femoral and one other fracture without identifiable accident [154].

Pain Insensitivity and Immobilisation
In spina bifida there may be insensitivity to pain in the lower extremities with some children developing immobilisation-related osteoporosis increasing susceptibility to fractures.

Long-term immobilisation is associated with decreased bone mass, osteopenia and osteoporosis increasing a child's propensity to fractures. Duncan (1998) reported that tube fed, pre-mobile children with cerebral palsy may develop osteo-penia and fractures without trauma [155].

Congenital insensitivity to pain is an autosomal recessive condition predisposing affected individuals to injuries.

Other Medical Conditions
Caffey's disease
Infantile cortical hyperostosis is a presumed inflammatory disease leading to peri-osteal reactions during infancy. It predominantly affects the long bones, but may be seen in the mandibles, ribs, scapulae and clavicles. By the age of 3 years, clinical and radiological abnormalities have disappeared.

Reports suggest that patients present with swollen and painful extremities, fever, raised inflammatory markers and a high alkaline phosphatase. Proposed causes are inherited, immunological or infectious. Radiographs show sub-perios-teal new-bone formation and sub-periosteal haemorrhages leading to new-bone formation which is also be found in inflicted injury. However, in abuse, periosteal reactions involve both shafts and metaphyses whereas in Caffey's disease the metaphyses are spared [156].

Although many dispute the existence of Caffey's as a clinical entity, case reports continue to appear in the recent literature eg: Rodriguez et al. 2016.

Congenital syphilis
Congenital syphilis may mimic metaphyseal fractures and periosteal new bone formation. Solomon and Rosen (1975) reviewed 112 children with congenital syphilis, the commonest abnormalities being metaphyseal osteomyelitis and periosteal reactions [158].

Leukaemia
Radiographs may show osteopenia, metaphyseal/periosteal abnormalities and pathological fractures.

Osteomyelitis and Septic Arthritis
In osteomyelitis pathological fractures may occur. Taylor et al. (2008) described a 7-month-old infant presenting with a humeral fracture. Follow-up examination revealed a pathological fracture and biopsy a Staphyloccus aureus infection [157].

Sickle cell anaemia
Sickle cell anaemia results in sickle-shaped red blood cells which may occlude small vessels leading to pain and infection. Radiographic findings include periostitis, radiolucencies and sclerosis resembling a healing fracture.

Medications

Anti-Convulsants
Phenobarbitone, Phenytoin, Carbamazepine and Sodium Valproate may all affect bone density.

Anti-Coagulants
Heparin is a blood thinner. When used for a short period of time, the effect on the skeleton is minimal, but with long-term use it may reduce bone density.

Bisphosphonates
Bisphosphonates are used in osteogenesis imperfecta, juvenile arthritis and in some other conditions. When given intravenously growth-retardation lines may be observed.

Diuretics
Frusemide is a diuretic commonly used in premature infants and those with cardiac disease. Side effects include dehydration, low potassium, sodium, magnesium and calcium. The drug increases calcium excretion with the potential for metabolic bone disease and an increased propensity to fractures.

Methotrexate
Methotrexate, if used in high dosages, may cause osteopenia.

Prostaglandins
Prostaglandins used in newborns with congenital heart disease have been found to cause periosteal reactions. Letts et al. (1994) described five infants with reactions evident after 14 days of prostaglandin infusion [159]. Faye-Petersen et al. (1996) compared postmortem bone findings for infants not on Prostaglandins and term infants after 4, 27, and 56 days of treatment. Bone architecture was not significantly different from controls after 4 days. Radiographs were negative after 27 days but bone pathology showed femoral periosteal osteoblast proliferation. At 56 days, there was radiologically apparent neo-cortex formation in rib and scapular bones. Pathologically, there was thickened periosteum and fibrocartilage-like tissue in the femoral shaft [160].

Synthetic Glucocorticoids (Corticosteroids)
Synthetic glucocorticoids, particularly Prednisolone, are widely used in a variety of chronic childhood conditions such as asthma, rheumatoid arthritis and inflammatory bowel disease. They are used long-term following organ transplantation. High levels of glucocorticoids may result in bone loss leading to osteoporosis and an increased risk of fractures.

Vitamin A
Vitamin A can be bought over the counter and if taken in excessive quantities may lead to hypervitaminosis A with radiological periostitis that may be mistaken for trauma.

References

1. Lyons RA, Delahunty AM, Kraus D, Heaven M, McCabe M, Allen H, et al. Children's fractures: a population based study. Inj Prev. 1999;5(2):129–32.
2. Landin LA. Fracture patterns in children. Analysis of 8,682 fractures with special reference to incidence, etiology and secular changes in a Swedish urban population 1950–1979. Acta Orthop Scand Suppl. 1983;54 Suppl 202:1–109.
3. Worlock P, Stower M, Barbor P. Patterns of fractures in accidental and non-accidental injury in children: a comparative study. Br Med J. 1986;293(6539):100–2.
4. Leventhal JM, Martin KD, Asnes AG. Incidence of fractures attributable to abuse in young hospitalized children: results from analysis of a United States database. Pediatrics. 2008;122:599–604.
5. McClain PW, Sacks JJ, Froehlke RG, et al. Estimates of fatal child abuse and neglect, United States, 1979-1988. Pediatrics. 1993;91(2):338–43.
6. Royal College of Radiologists, Royal College of Paediatrics and Child Health. Standards for radiological investigations of suspected non-accidental injury. 2008.
7. Kemp AM, Butler A, Morris S, Mann M, Kemp KW, Rolfe K, et al. Which radiological investigations should be performed to identify fractures in suspected child abuse? Clin Radiol. 2006;61(9):723–36.

8. Ingram JD, Connell J, Hay TC. Oblique radiographs of the chest in non-accidental trauma. Emerg Radiol. 2000;7(1):42–6.

9. Karmazyn B, Lewis ME, Jennings SG, Hibbard RA, Hicks RA. The prevalence of uncommon fractures on skeletal surveys performed to evaluate for suspected abuse in 930 children: should practice guidelines change? AJR Am J Roentgenol. 2011;197(1):W159–63. doi:10.2214/AJR.10.5733.

10. Maguire S, Cowley L, Mann M, Kemp A. What does the recent literature add to the identification and investigation of fractures in child abuse: an overview of review updates 2005–2013. Evid Based Child Health Cochrane Rev J. 2013;8:2044–57.

11. Leventhal JM, Thomas SA, Rosenfield NS, Markowitz RI. Fractures in young children: distinguishing child abuse from unintentional injuries. Am J Dis Child. 1993;147(1):87–92.

12. Pandya NK, Baldwin K, Wolfgruber H, Christian CW, Drummond DS, Hosalkar HS. Child abuse and orthopaedic injury patterns: analysis at a level I pediatric trauma center. J Pediatr Orthop. 2009;29(6):618–25.

13. Strait RT, Seigel RM, Shapiro RA. Humeral fractures without obvious etiologies in children less than 3 years. When is it abuse? Pediatrics. 1995;96(4):667–71.

14. Farnsworth CL, Silva PD, Mubarak SJ. Etiology of supracondylar humerus fractures. J Pediatr Orthop. 1998;18(1):38–42.

15. Loder RT, Bookout C. Fracture patterns in battered children. J Orthop Trauma. 1991;5(4): 428–33.

16. Peters ML, Starling SP, Barnes-Eley ML, Heisler KW. The presence of bruising associated with fractures. Arch Pediatr Adolesc Med. 2008;162(9):877–81.

17. Mathew MO, Ramamohan N, Bennet GC. Importance of bruising associated with paediatric fractures: prospective observational study. Br Med J. 1998;317:1117–8.

18. Starling SP, Sirotnak AP, Heisler KW, et al. Inflicted skeletal trauma: the relationship of perpetrators to their victims. Child Abuse Negl. 2007;31(9):993.

19. Warrington SA, Wright CM. Accidents and resulting injuries in pre-mobile infants: data from the ALSPAC study. Arch Dis Child. 2001;85(2):104–7.

20. Tarantino CA, Dowd D, Murdock TC. Short vertical falls in infants. Pediatr Emerg Care. 1999;15(1):5–8.

21. Lyons TJ, Oates RK. Falling out of bed: a relatively benign occurrence. Pediatrics. 1993;92(1):125–7.

22. Johnson K, Fischer T, Chapman S, et al. Accidental head injuries in children under 5 years of age. Clin Radiol. 2005;60(4):464–8.

23. Hughes J, Maguire S, Jones M, Kemp A. Biomechanical characteristics of head injuries from falls in children younger than 48 months. Arch Dis Child. 2016;101(4):310–5.

24. Ibrahim NG, Wood J, Margulies SS, Christian CW. Influence of age and fall type on head injuries in infants and toddlers. Int J Dev Neurosci. 2012;30(3):201–6.

25. Thomas AG, Hegde SV, Dineen RA, Jaspan T. Patterns of accidental craniocerebral injury occurring in early childhood. Arch Dis Child. 2013;98(10):787–92.

26. Monson SA, Henry E, Lambert DK, et al. In-hospital falls of newborn infants: data from a multi-hospital health care system. Pediatrics. 2008;122(2):e277–80.

27. Wheeler DS, Shope TR. Depressed skull fracture in a 7-monthold who fell from bed. Pediatrics. 1997;100(6):1033–4.

28. Denton S, Mileusnic D. Delayed sudden death in an infant following an accidental fall: a case report with review of the literature. Am J Forensic Med Pathol. 2003;24:371–6.

29. Chiaviello CT, Christoph RA, Bond GR. Infant walker related injuries: a prospective study of severity and incidence. Pediatrics. 1994;93(6 Pt 1):974–6.

30. Lallier M, Bouchard S, St-Vil D, et al. Falls from heights among children: a retrospective review. J Pediatr Surg. 1999;34(7):1060–3.

31. Barlow B, Niemirska M, Ghandi RP, Leblanc W. Ten years' experience of falls from a height in children. J Pediatr Surg. 1983;18:509–11.

32. Williams RA. Injuries in infants and small children resulting from witnessed and corroborated free falls. J Trauma. 1991;31(10):1350–2.

33. Wang MY, Kim KA, Griffith PM, et al. Injuries from falls in the pediatric population: an analysis of 729 cases. J Pediatr Surg. 2001;36(10):1528–34.
34. Joffe M, Ludwig S. Stairway injuries in children. Pediatrics. 1988;82(3 Pt 2):457–61.
35. Pierce MC, Bertocci GE, Janosky JE, Aguel F, Deemer E, Moreland M, et al. Femur fractures resulting from stair falls among children: an injury plausibility model. Pediatrics. 2005;115(6):1712–22.
36. Chiaviello CT, Christoph RA, Bond GR. Stairway-related injuries in children. Pediatrics. 1994;94(5):679–81.
37. Selbst SM, Baker MD, Shames M. Bunk bed injuries. Am J Dis Child. 1990;144(6):721–3.
38. Mayr JM, Seebacher U, Lawrenz K, et al. Bunk beds–a still underestimated risk for accidents in childhood? Eur J Pediatr. 2000;159(6):440–3.
39. Smith GA, Dietrich AM, Garcia CT, et al. Epidemiology of shopping cart-related injuries to children. An analysis of national data for 1990 to 1992. Arch Pediatr Adolesc Med. 1995;149(11):1207–10.
40. Watson WL, Ozanne-Smith J. The use of child safety restraints with nursery furniture. J Paediatr Child Health. 1993;29(3):228–32.
41. Arnholz D, Hymel KP, Hay TC, et al. Bilateral pediatric skull fractures: accident or abuse? J Trauma. 1998;45(1):172–4.
42. Wickham T, Abrahamson E. Head injuries in infants: the risks of bouncy chairs and car seats. Arch Dis Child. 2002;86(3):168–9.
43. Claydon SM. Fatal extradural hemorrhage following a fall from a baby bouncer. Pediatr Emerg Care. 1996;12(6):432–4.
44. American Academy of Pediatrics, Committee on Injury and Poison Prevention. Injuries associated with infantwalkers. Pediatrics. 2001;108(3):790–2.
45. Rieder MJ, Schwartz C, Newman J. Patterns of walker use and walker injury. Pediatrics. 1986;78(3):488–93.
46. Powell EC, Jovtis E, Tanz RR. Incidence and description of high chair-related injuries to children. Ambul Pediatr. 2002;2(4):276–8.
47. Stewart G, Meert K, Rosenberg N. Trauma in infants less than three months of age. Pediatr Emerg Care. 1993;9(4):199–201.
48. Reece RM, Sege R. Childhood head injuries: accidental or inflicted? Arch Pediatr Adolesc Med. 2000;154(1):11–5.
49. Schutzman SA, Greenes DS. Infants with isolated skull fracture: what are their clinical characteristics and do they require hospitalisation? Ann Emerg Med. 1997;30:253–9.
50. Hobbs CJ. Skull fracture and the diagnosis of abuse. Arch Dis Child. 1984;59(3):246–52.
51. Duhaime AC, Eppley M, Margulies S. Crush injuries to the head in children. Neurosurgery. 1995;37(3):401–6.
52. Stock A, Singer L. Head trauma. eMed J. 2001;2(9):18.
53. Kleinman PK. Diagnostic imaging of child abuse. Williams and Wilkins; 1987. p. 162–8.
54. Pezzotta S, Silvani V, Gaetani P, et al. Growing skull fractures of childhood. Case report and review of 132 cases. J Neurosurg Sci. 1985;29(2):129–35.
55. Kaldewaij P, Vos PE. Racoon eyes as a sign of anterior basilar fracture. Ned Tijdschr Geneeskd. 2002;5(1):11–2.
56. Hatton MP, Watkins LM, Rubin PA. Orbital fractures in children. Ophthal Plast Reconstr Surg. 2001;17(3):174–9.
57. da Fonseca MA, Feigal FJ, ten Bensel RW. Dental aspects of 1248 cases of child maltreatment on file at a major county hospital. Pediatr Dent. 1992;14(3):152–7.
58. Vadiakas G, Roberts MW, Dilley DCH. Child abuse and neglect: ethical and legal issues for dentistry. J Mass Dent Soc. 1991;40(1):13–5.
59. Cameron JM. Radiological pathological aspects of the battered child syndrome. In: Smith SM, editor. The maltreatment of children. Baltimore: University Park Press; 1978. p. 69–81.
60. King J, Diefendorf D, Apthorp J, et al. Analysis of 429 fractures in 189 battered children. J Pediatr Orthop. 1988;8(5):585–9.

61. Kleinman PK, Spevak MR. Soft tissue swelling and acute skull fractures. J Pediatr. 1992;121(5 Pt 1):737–9.
62. Ruddick C, et al. Head trauma outcomes of verifiable falls in newborn babies. Arch Dis Child Fetal Neonatal Ed. 2010;95:F144–5.
63. Harwood-Nash DC, Hendrick EB, Hudson AR. The significance of skull fracture in children. A study of 1,187 patients. Radiology. 1971;101(1):151–6.
64. Mogby KI, Slovis TL, Canady AI, et al. Appropriate imaging in children with skull fractures and suspicion of abuse. Radiology. 1998;208(2):521–4.
65. Heise RH, Srivatsa PJ, Karsell PR. Spontaneous intrauterine linear skull fracture: a rare complication of spontaneous vaginal delivery. Obstet Gynecol. 1996;87(5 Pt 2):851–4.
66. Nadas S, Gudinchet F, Capasso P, et al. Predisposing factors in obstetrical fractures. Skeletal Radiol. 1993;22(3):195–8. 1990;79(2):232–3.
67. Rubin A. Birth injuries: incidence, mechanisms, and end results. J Obstet Gynecol. 1964;23:218–21.
68. Alexander JM, Leveno KJ, Hauth J, et al. Fetal injury associated with cesarean delivery. Obstet Gynecol. 2006;108(4):885–90.
69. Kleinman PK, et al. Factors affecting visualization of posterior rib fractures in abused infants. Am J Roentgenol. 1988;150:635–8.
70. Lancon JA, Haines DE, Parent AD. Anatomy of the shaken baby syndrome. Anat Rec. 1998;253(1):13–8.
71. Kleinman PK, Marks Jr SC. Vertebral body fractures in child abuse. Radiologic-histopathologic correlates. Invest Radiol. 1992;27:715–22.
72. Gipson CL, Tobias JD. Flail chest in a neonate resulting from non-accidental trauma. South Med J. 2006;99(5):536–8.
73. Feldman KW, Brewer DK. Child abuse, cardiopulmonary resuscitation, and rib fractures. Pediatrics. 1984;73(3):339–342.
74. Barsness KA, Cha ES, Bensard DD, Calkins CM, Partrick DA, Karrer FM, et al. The positive predictive value of rib fractures as an indicator of non-accidental trauma in children. J Trauma. 2003;54(6):1107–10.
75. Boos SC. Constrictive asphyxia: a recognizable form of fatal child abuse. Child Abuse Negl. 2000;24(11):1503–7.
76. Carty H, Pierce A. Non-accidental injury: a retrospective analysis of a large cohort. Eur Radiol. 2002;12:2919–25.
77. Kemp AM, et al. Patterns of skeletal fractures in child abuse: systematic review. Br Med J. 2008;337:1518.
78. van Rijn RR, Bilo RA, Robben SG. Birth-related mid-posterior rib fractures in neonates: a report of three cases (and a possible fourth case) and a review of the literature. Pediatr Radiol. 2008;39:30–4.
79. Spevak MR, Kleinman PK, Belanger PL, et al. Cardiopulmonary resuscitation and rib fractures in infants. A postmortem radiologic-pathologic study. JAMA. 1994;272(8):617–8.
80. Dolinak D. Rib fractures in infants due to cardiopulmonary resuscitation efforts. Am J Forensic Med Pathol. 2007;28(2):107–10.
81. Clouse JR, Lantz PE. Posterior rib fractures in infants associated with cardiopulmonary resuscitation. Abstract. American Academy of Forensic Sciences, annual meeting; 2008.
82. Maguire S, Mann M, John N, et al. Does cardiopulmonary resuscitation cause rib fractures in children? A systematic review. Child Abuse Negl. 2006;30(7):739–51.
83. Betz P, Liebhardt E. Rib fractures in children–resuscitation or child abuse? Int J Leg Med. 1994;106(4):215–8.
84. Matshes EW, Lew EO. Two-handed cardio-pulmonary resuscitation can cause rib fractures in infants. Am J Forensic Med Pathol. 2010;31:303–7.
85. Reyes JA, Somers GR, Taylor GP, Chiasson DA. Increased incidence of CPR-related rib fractures in infants–is it related to changes in CPR technique? Resuscitation. 2011;82(5):545–8.
86. Bulloch B, Schubert CJ, Brophy PD, et al. Cause and clinical characteristics of rib fractures in infants. Pediatrics. 2000;105(4):E48.

87. Cadzow SP, Armstrong KL. Rib fractures in infants: red alert! The clinical features, investigations and child protection outcomes. J Paediatr Child Health. 2000;36(4):322–6.

88. Gorincour G, Dubus JC, Petit P, et al. Rib periosteal reaction: did you think about chest physical therapy? Arch Dis Child. 2004;89(11):1078–9.

89. Chalumeau M, Foix-L'Helias L, Scheinmann P, et al. Rib fractures after chest physiotherapy for bronchiolitis or pneumonia in infants. Pediatr Radiol. 2002;32(9):644–7.

90. Bishop N, Sprigg A, Dalton A. Unexplained fractures in infancy: looking for fragile bones. Arch Dis Child. 2007;92(3):251–6.

91. Cosway B, Mathura N, Mott A, Bredow M, Fraser J, Rawlinson A, Wei C, Thyagarajan MS, Harrison S, Kemp A. Occult rib fractures: defining the cause. Child Abuse Rev. 2015;24(1):6–15.

92. Prasad S, Baur LA. Fracture of the first rib as a consequence of pertussis infection. J Paediatr Child Health. 2001;37(1):91–3.

93. Rowe CR. An atlas of anatomy and treatment of mid-clavicular fractures. Clin Orthop Relat Res. 1968;58:29–42.

94. Nordqvist A, Petersson C. The incidence of fractures of the clavicle. Clin Orthop Relat Res. 1994;300:127–32.

95. Merten DF, Radkowski MA, Leonidas JC. The abused child: a radiological reappraisal. Radiology. 1983;146:377–81.

96. Joseph PR, Rosenfeld W. Clavicular fractures in neonates. Am J Dis Child. 1990;144(2):165–7.

97. DeFriend DE, Franklin K. Isolated sternal fracture–a swing related injury in two children. Pediatr Radiol. 2001;31(3):200–2.

98. Ferguson LP, Wilkinson AG, Beattie TF. Fracture of the sternum in children. Emerg Med J. 2003;20(6):518.

99. Farrell C, Rubin DM, Downes K, Dormans J, Christian CW. Symptoms and time to medical care in children with accidental extremity fractures. Pediatrics. 2012;129(1):e128–33.

100. Dalton HJ, Slovis T, Helfer RE, Comstock J, Scheurer S, Riolo S. Undiagnosed abuse in children younger than 3 years with femoral fracture. Am J Dis Child. 1990;144(8):875–8.

101. Thomas SA, Rosenfeld NS, Leventhal JM, et al. Long-bone fractures in young children: distinguishing accidental injuries from child abuse. Pediatrics. 1991;88(3):471–6.

102. Baldwin K, Pandya NK, Wolfgruber H, Drummond DS, Hosalkar HS. Femur fractures in the pediatric population: abuse or accidental trauma? Clin Orthop Relat Res. 2011;469(3): 798–804.

103. Hui C, Joughin E, Goldstein S, Cooper N, Harder J, Kiefer G, Parsons D, Howard J. Femoral fractures in children younger than three years: the role of non-accidental injury. J Pediatr Orthop. 2008;28(3):297–302.

104. Schwend RM, Werth C, Johnston A. Femur shaft fractures in toddlers and young children: rarely from child abuse. J Pediatr Orthop. 2000;20(4):475–81.

105. Morris S, Cassidy N, Stephens M, et al. Birth-associated femoral fractures: incidence and outcome. J Pediatr Orthop. 2002;22(1):27–30.

106. Mellick LB, Reesor K. Spiral tibial fractures of children: a commonly accidental spiral long bone fracture. Am J Emerg Med. 1990;8(3):234–7.

107. Roffman M, Moshel M, Mendes DG. Bicycle spoke fracture. Clin Orthop Relat Res. 1979;(144):230–2.

108. Coffey C, Haley K, Hayes J, Groner JI. The risk of child abuse in infants and toddlers with lower extremity injuries. J Pediatr Surg. 2005;40(1):120–3.

109. Rodriguez-Merchan EC. Pediatric fractures of the forearm. Clin Orthop Relat Res. 2005;(432):65–72.

110. Tredwell SJ, Van Peteghem K, Clough M. Pattern of forearm fractures in children. J Pediatr Orthop. 1984;4(5):604–8.

111. Valencia J, Leyva F, Gomez-Bajo GJ. Pediatric hand trauma. Clin Orthop Relat Res. 2005;(432):77–86.

112. Nimkin K, Spevak MR, Kleinman PK. Fractures of the hands and feet in child abuse: imaging and pathological features. Radiology. 1997;203(1):233–6.
113. Barber I, Perez-Rossello JM, Wilson CR, Kleinman PK. The yield of high-detail radiographic skeletal surveys in suspected infant abuse. Pediatr Radiol. 2015;45(1):69–80.
114. Lindberg DM, Harper NS, Laskey AL, Berger RP, ExSTRA Investigators. Prevalence of abusive fractures of the hands, feet, spine, or pelvis on skeletal survey: perhaps "uncommon" is more common than suggested. Pediatr Emerg Care. 2013;29(1):26–9.
115. Kleinman PK, Morris NB, Makris J, Moles RL, Kleinman PL. Yield of radiographic skeletal surveys for detection of hand, foot, and spine fractures in suspected child abuse. AJR Am J Roentgenol. 2013;200(3):641–4.
116. Swischuk LE. Spine and spinal cord trauma in the battered child syndrome. Radiology. 1969;92(4):733–8.
117. Schwartz GR, Wright SW, Fein JA, et al. Pediatric cervical spine injury sustained in falls from low heights. Ann Emerg Med. 1997;30(3):249–52.
118. Shulman ST, Madden JD, Esterly JR, et al. Transection of the spinal cord. A rare obstetrical complication of cephalic delivery. Arch Dis Child. 1971;46(247):291–4.
119. Cirak B, Ziegfeld S, Knight VM, et al. Spinal injuries in children. J Pediatr Surg. 2004;39(4):607–12.
120. Oral R, Rahhal R, Elshershari H, et al. Intentional avulsion fracture of the second cervical vertebra in a hypotonic child. Pediatr Emerg Care. 2006;22(5):352–4.
121. Ogden JA. Skeletal injury in the child. 2nd ed. New York: Saunders; 1990.
122. Barber I, Perez-Rossello JM, Wilson CR, Silvera MV, Kleinman PK. Prevalence and relevance of pediatric spinal fractures in suspected child abuse. Pediatr Radiol. 2013;43(11): 1507–15.
123. Choudhary AK, Bradford RK, Dias MS, Moore GJ, Boal DK. Spinal subdural hemorrhage in abusive head trauma: a retrospective study. Radiology. 2012;262(1):216–23.
124. Ablin DS, Greenspan A, Reinhart MA. Pelvic injuries in child abuse. Pediatr Radiol. 1992;22(6):454–7.
125. Johnson K, Chapman S, Hall CM. Skeletal injuries associated with sexual abuse. Pediatr Radiol. 2004;34(8):620–3.
126. Hymel KP, Spivack BS. The biomechanics of physical injury. In: Reece RM, Ludwig S, editors. Child abuse–medical diagnosis and management. 2nd ed. Philadelphia: Lippincott Williams Wilkins; 2001. p. 1–22.
127. Kleinman PK, Perez-Rossello JM, Newton AW, Feldman HA, Kleinman PL. Prevalence of the classic metaphyseal lesion in infants at low versus high risk for abuse. Am J Roentgenol. 2011;197(4):1005–8. doi:10.2214/AJR.11.6540.
128. O'Connell A, Donoghue VB. Can classic metaphyseal lesions follow uncomplicated cesarian section? Pediatr Radiol. 2007;37(5):488–91.
129. Grayev AM, Boal DK, Wallach DM, Segal LS. Metaphyseal fractures mimicking abuse during treatment for clubfoot. Pediatr Radiol. 2001;31(8):559–63.
130. Hymel KP, Jenny C. Abusive spiral fractures of the humerus: a videotape exception. Arch Pediatr Adolec Med. 1996;150(2):226–8.
131. Somers JM, Halliday KE, Chapman S. Pediatr Radiol. 2014;44(10):1219–23.
132. Pickett WJ, Johnson JF, Enzenauer RW. Case report. Neonatal fractures mimicking abuse secondary to physical therapy. Skeletal Radiol. 1982;8(1):85–6.
133. Simonian PT, Staheli LT. Peri-articular fractures after manipulation for knee contractures in children. J Pediatr Orthop. 1995;15(3):288–91.
134. Bowley DMG, Loveland J, Pitcher GJJ. Tibial fracture as a complication of intra-osseous infusion during pediatric resuscitation. J Trauma. 2003;55(4):786–7.
135. Astley R. Metaphyseal fractures in osteogenesis imperfecta. Br J Radiol. 1979;52:441–3.
136. Gahagan S, Rimsza ME. Child abuse or osteogenesis imperfecta: how can we tell? Pediatrics. 1991;88:987–92.

137. Wenstrup RJ, Willing MC, Starman BJ, Byers PH. Distinct biochemical phenotypes predict clinical severity in non-lethal variants of osteogenesis imperfecta. Am J Hum Genet. 1990;46:975–82.
138. Zionts LE, Nash JP, Rude R, Ross T, Stott NS. Bone mineral density in children with mild osteogenesis imperfecta. J Bone Joint Surg Br. 1995;77(1):143–7.
139. Singer P. Non-accidental injury: expert evidence [2001] 2 FLR 1, 27. Royal Courts of Justice, Family Division.
140. Horsman A, Ryan SW, Congdon PJ, Truscott JG, James JR. Osteopenia in extremely low birth weight infants. Arch Dis Child. 1989;64:485–8.
141. Amir J, Katz K, Grunebaum M, Yosipovich Z, Wielunsky E, Reisner SH. Fractures in premature infants. J Pediat Orthop. 1988;8:41–4.
142. Dabezies EJ, Warren PD. Fractures in very low birth weight infants with rickets. Clin Orthop Relat Res. 1997;(335):233–9.
143. Dahlenberg SL, Bishop NJ, Lucas A. Are preterm infants at risk for subsequent fractures? Arch Dis Child. 1989;64:1384–93.
144. Bagnoli F, Casucci M, Toti S, Cecchi S, Iurato C, Coriolani G, Tiezzi M, Vispi L. Is vitamin D supplementation necessary in healthy full-term breastfed infants? A follow-up study of bone mineralization in healthy full-term infants with and without supplemental vitamin D. Minerva Pediatr. 2013;65:253–60.
145. British Paediatric Adolescent Bone Group. Vitamin D deficiency and fractures. 2012.
146. Royal College of Paediatrics and Child Health. Position statement: vitamin D. 2012.
147. Gordon CM, Feldman HA, Sinclair L, Williams AL, Kleinman PK, Perez-Rossello J, et al. Prevalence of vitamin D deficiency among healthy infants and toddlers. Arch Pediatr Adolesc Med. 2008;162:505–12.
148. Perez-Rossello JM, Feldman HA, Kleinman PK, Connolly SA, Fair RA, Myers RM, Gordon CM. Rachitic changes, demineralization, and fracture risk in healthy infants and toddlers with vitamin D deficiency. Radiology. 2012;262(1):234–41.
149. Duncan AA, Chandy J. Case report: multiple neonatal fractures–dietary or deliberate? Clin Radiol. 1993;48(2):137–9.
150. Chapman S. Child abuse or copper deficiency? A radiological view. Br Med J (Clin Res Ed). 1987;294:1370.
151. Menkes JH, Alter M, Steigleder GK, et al. A sex-linked recessive disorder with retardation of growth, peculiar hair and focal cerebral and cerebellar degeneration. Pediatrics. 1962;29:764–79.
152. McDonald DG, Kinali M, Gallagher AC, et al. Fracture prevalence in Duchenne muscular dystrophy. Dev Med Child Neurol. 2002;44(10):695–8.
153. Sheth RD, Gidal BE, Hermann BP. Pathological fractures in epilepsy. Epilepsy Behav. 2006;9(4):601–5.
154. Lingam S, Joester J. Spontaneous fractures in children and adolescents with cerebral palsy. Br Med J. 1994;309(6949):265.
155. Duncan B. Dietary considerations in osteopenia in tube fed non-ambulatory children with cerebral palsy. Clin Pediatr (Phila). 1999;38(3):133–7.
156. Saul RA, Lee WH, Stevenson RE. Caffey's disease revisited. Further evidence for autosomal dominant inheritance with incomplete penetrance. Am J Dis Child. 1982;136(1):55–60.
157. Taylor MN, Chaudhuri R, Davis J, et al. Childhood osteomyelitis presenting as a pathological fracture. Clin Radiol. 2008;63(3):348–51.
158. Solomon A, Rosen E. The aspect of trauma in the bone changes of congenital lues. Pediatr Radiol. 1975;3(3):176–8.
159. Letts M, Pang E, Simons J. Perostaglandin-induced neonatal periostitis. J Pediatr Orthop. 1994;14(6):809–13.

160. Faye-Petersen OM, Johnson Jr WH, Carlo WA, Hedlund GL, Pacifico AD, Blair HC. Prostaglandin E1-induced hyperostosis: clinic-pathologic correlations and possible pathogenetic mechanisms. Pediatr Pathol Lab Med. 1996;16(3):489–507.

Further Reading

Bilo RAC, Robben SGF, van Rijn RR. Forensic aspects of pediatric fractures: differentiating accidental trauma from child abuse. Berlin/London: Springer; 2010.

CORE INFO Cardiff Child Protection Systematic Reviews/www.core-info.cardiff.ac.uk/ (accessed 15.04.17).

Offiah A, van Rijn RR, Perez-Rossello JM, Kleinman PK. Skeletal imaging of child abuse (non-accidental injury). Pediatr Radiol. 2009;39(5):461–70.

Burns

4

Abstract

A majority of burns are accidental with 70% of these occurring in infants and children under three years of age. Inflicted burns constitute 6–20% of all child abuse cases [1].

Eighty percent of all burn injuries occur in the home as a result of accident, poor supervision, inadequate safety measures or neglect, with up to 25% considered inflicted [2]. Whilst inflicted burns can occur anywhere on the body, the face, head, perineum, buttocks, genitalia, palms, soles of feet and legs are common sites. When the genitalia or perineum are affected, a careful CSA assessment is required. Second or third-degree burns, especially if multiple or symmetrical, are suspicious for abuse in the absence of a credible account of injury.

Purdue et al. (1988) found the mortality rate for accidental burns was 2% compared to 30% for inflicted burns [3].

In addition to the objects referred to in this chapter, inflicted burns have been recorded from cigarette lighters, grease and oil, a stun gun, stove, light bulb, melted plastic, car bonnet, burning cloth, electric water heater and glowing knife.

Medical Assessment

A comprehensive medical history and examination should be undertaken as described in chapter 1 pages 4–6. Systems enquiries, past medical and family history are all relevant. The account of an accident and its aftermath is compared with clinical findings and the developmental stage of the child.

There is a significant association between inflicted burns and other abusive injuries. It is therefore important to have the same meticulous approach to these patients as for other children with suspected abuse (Table 4.1).

© Springer International Publishing Switzerland 2017

D.L. Robinson, *Pediatric Forensic Evidence*, DOI 10.1007/978-3-319-45337-8_4

Table 4.1 Assessment for burns patients

History of events
If witnessed, what accidental event occurred and its aftermath
The temperature of water, fluid or other hot object
For how long was the child in contact with the burning agent
Was the skin covered with clothing
What action was taken
Was the liquid standing or running
The child's explanation for the injury
Examination
Clinical examination including growth and development
Detailed body maps with measurements
Description of each injury including depth
Document whether first, second, third or fourth degree burns
Skin sparing (e.g. buttocks in immersion injury)
The body surface area involved
Any medical condition that might be mistaken for burns
Home and appliances (police and social services)
Heights of surfaces, water depths
Temperature of tap water in the home
Examination of materials alleged to have caused the injury
Photographs of the home and any appliances
Clothing worn should be retained for forensic analysis
Investigations and referrals
Routine blood investigations as indicated (page 7)
Children aged 2 and younger require a full skeletal survey
Those under 12 months neuroimaging and ophthalmological assessment
Photo-documentation
Good quality images with a standard ruler against any injuries (Hospital's medical photography or police)

Physical Examination should include observation of the parent-child interaction, evidence of neglect, assessment of growth and development, systems examination and a careful search for any skin marks or other injuries. It is also important to check for signs of infection either localised to the burn itself or septicaemia. Accurate documentation of the burn or scald marks on body maps with good quality images is essential. All notes must be signed and and date stamped.

The individual injury should be described and diagnosed with careful consideration of other causes for skin lesions that may appear as burns. If a burn or scald is confidently diagnosed, each injury should be considered individually and an opinion reached as to whether it is accidental or inflicted. It is equally important to take an overview of all injuries observed, as well as other concerning features including evidence for neglect and emotional abuse.

Table 4.2 Additional factors that raise concerns for inflicted burns

Does the pattern differ from the history provided
Are burns older than disclosed in history
Do the burns appear to be of different ages
Burns on back of hands, feet, legs, genitalia or buttocks
Recognisable patterns (e.g. stocking and glove demarcation)
Pattern of burns that suggest restraint during injury
Is the injury and account compatible with the child's age and developmental stage
Other injuries or signs of neglect

Factors that raise concern for abuse and those associated with abuse are discussed on pages 7–12. Following accidental injury, medical attention is usually sought promptly. In abuse, a delay in seeking care is more common. Other factors that raise concerns are a clinical examination that does not match the account of injury, no credible history of a memorable event and its aftermath, discrepant accounts and a history that does not fit with the child's developmental abilities. The carer may blame a sibling, the family may be known to children's social care with repeated medical attendances for injuries. There may be other injuries on the child or signs of neglect (Table 4.2).

Pawlik et al. (2016) reviewed 215 children with suspicious burns from a total of 2890 cases referred (7%). Physical abuse was considered likely in 40.9% (88) and unlikely in 59.1% (127). Scalds accounted for 52.6% (113) and contact burns for 27.6% (60). Characteristics associated with abuse included hot water as agent, immersion scald, bilateral/symmetric burn pattern, total body surface area ≥10%, full thickness burns and co-existent injuries [4].

In other published studies, intentional burns were most commonly found on the back, shoulders and buttocks. In some cases they had sharply demarcated edges that could be matched to an implement.

A multidisciplinary approach is required to include paediatrician, plastic surgeon, GP, ED staff, nurses, health visitor and social worker. The police will visit the family home, interview carers and collect forensic evidence. In many cases, patients should be cared for in a regional burns unit.

Pathophysiology

Burns result from thermal energy damaging the skin and subcutaneous tissues. Thermal damage is classified according to whether the injury is caused by dry heat (burning) or by hot liquids (scalding). The extent of a burn depends on the temperature applied, whether the skin and heat source were wet or dry, skin thickness and duration of contact.

Human skin is composed of three layers (Fig. 4.1). The epidermis constitutes the uppermost layer. The dermis is deeper and contains hair follicles, sweat glands, and nerve endings. Beneath the dermis, subcutaneous tissue consisting of fibrous tissue

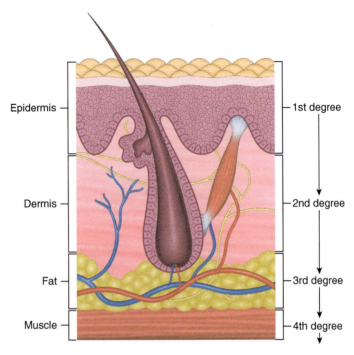

Fig. 4.1 Histology of skin and classification of burns

and fat provide a support structure. The deepest cells in the dermis (the basal layer) replenish skin cells as they are removed naturally or from injury. Burns occur when heat absorbed by the skin leads to tissue damage. If extensive, clinical shock and infection may be fatal if untreated.

Classification by the Skin Depth

First-degree or superficial
First-degree burns constitute minor scalds. The uppermost layers of the epidermis are affected leading to reddened, tender skin sometimes with swelling but no blistering. Injured skin separates and sloughs off within a few days with new cells arising from the underlying tissue. Healing is usually complete without scarring although mild hyper-pigmentation may be seen. Brief contact with hot water or minor sunburn typically cause first degree burns.

Second-degree or partial thickness
Second-degree burns involve the superficial dermis. The skin has a red appearance and blistering occurs which is acutely painful as nerve endings are exposed. A superficial partial thickness burn involves the dermis minimally and heals in about 2 weeks without scarring. A deep partial thickness burn extends deeper into the

dermis taking 3–4 weeks to heal and may scar. If treatment is inadequate extension to a full thickness burn involving the basal layer may occur. Contact with very hot liquids or a hot domestic iron are typical causes.

Third/fourth-degree or full thickness

These injuries extend to the subcutaneous tissue (third-degree) or muscle and bone (fourth-degree). The skin has a white appearance and is painless as blood vessels and nerve endings are destroyed. Healing with scarring occurs by inward growth of skin from tissues surrounding the wound or following skin grafts. Charring of the skin may occur when for example the child is close to an explosion [5] or cigarette ends are applied for a prolonged time [6].

Scar formation depends on the size and depth of the injury, the age of the child and any superimposed infection. Keloids are hypertrophic scars more commonly seen in those of Afro-Caribbean descent. If they are numerous or located where accidental trauma is unlikely, concerns for inflicted injury are raised.

Assessment by Size and Thickness

The size of a burn is calculated as a percentage of body surface area involved. The Lund and Browder chart is considered the most accurate in measuring this percentage (Hettiaratchy S. July 2004).

Minor Burns

Minor burns involve less than 10% of the body surface area and are less than 2% full thickness. Hospitalisation is required for children under 2 years of age, burns on the face, hands, feet, perineum or if abuse is suspected. Management includes cooling with water, cleansing with sterile saline, leaving blisters intact, wound dressings, tetanus prophylaxis and pain control. Circumferential burns of the extremities and chest may require emergency surgery to release constrictions (escharotomy).

Major Burn

Major burns involve more than 10% of the body surface area or are at least 2% full thickness. Children may present in clinical shock from fluid loss and require urgent resuscitation to include management of the airways, breathing and circulation. For the latter fluid resuscitation or urgent blood transfusion may be required. Antibiotics, pain relief, wound debridement, dressings and tetanus prophylaxis are needed.

Critical Burn

This includes a full-thickness burn of > 10% or partial thickness burn of >30% of the child's body surface area. Management includes all the measures described for a major burn and many of these patients require intensive care with assisted ventilation.

Hathaway et al. (1993) reported that when burns involve more than 40% of the body surface area, the mortality rate approached 90% with a larger number of survivors suffering serious long-term disability [7].

Types of Burns and Patterns of Injury

Scalds

Water temperatures
Scalding follows contact from a hot liquid with the child's skin. First-degree burns with reddened skin or second-degree with blistering and skin peeling commonly occur. These are commonly accidental but also the commonest inflicted burn injuries for children admitted to hospital [8].

A comfortable water temperature for bathing infants is between 37°C (98.6F) and 38°C (100.4°F), Normal hot water shower temperature is 43°C (110°F).

Research indicates that an adult's skin in water at 53°C (127°F) would sustain a full thickness burn in about 30–60 seconds at 54.5°C (130°F) in 30 seconds, 65.5°C (150°F) in 2 seconds. It is estimated that a child's skin burns in a quarter of the time of an adults. Dressler and Hozid (2001) reported that at 60°C (140°F) it took one second for a child to sustain a full thickness burn [9].

Spills and Splash Burns
Spills and splash burns are commonly accidental and are the most frequent cause of thermal injury in children. Boiling water, tea, coffee or other fluids may spill or be accidentally poured over a child. Accidental scalds typically occur in the kitchen when an infant beginning to mobilise looks upwards, reaches out for objects and pulls at a container with hot liquid from a kitchen unit or table. Other accidents include scalding water from a tap or the accidental over-heating of food or liquids in a microwave when burns involve the lips, mouth, or throat.

Accidental scalds are typically seen on the face, lower neck (the upper neck is protected by the chin), cheek, shoulder upper chest and upper arms. Splash burns occurring in other areas should be regarded as suspicious for inflicted injury.

As hot liquid runs down the body, it cools rapidly leaving less severe injuries more distant from the initial point of contact. This leaves a pattern of accidental injury giving a clue as to the position of the child when the liquid first made contact with the skin. Splash marks seen as droplets away from the area of maximal contact may be observed. Clothing retains hot liquid increasing contact with the skin and burn severity. A pattern of the child's clothes may be observed delineated on the skin.

In inflicted injury, the pattern may differ. If hot liquids are poured or thrown at the child, maximum injury will be at the point of contact but not necessarily over the upper areas or diminishing lower down over the body as for accidental injuries. Burns over the back are inconsistent with a child pulling a container of hot liquid over him or herself as are uniform burns over the head, abdomen and legs. Inflicted scalds frequently involve the buttocks and legs, are bilateral and symmetrical.

Immersion

In accidental immersion, drip or splash marks are widespread as the child thrashes around unrestrained in an attempt to withdraw from the heat source. Absence of splash marks may therefore indicate restraint.

Inflicted injuries may follow forced immersion and involve the extremities and buttocks or both. Immersion burns occur when the child's body is immersed in a hot liquid. They tend to be of even depth and have a uniform distribution over the areas in contact with the hot liquid. Maguire et al. (2008) reported that such burns were frequently symmetrical with clear upper margins [10]. Scalding from accidentally falling into a hot bath leaves an irregular scald with splash marks.

In forced immersion there may be evidence of both immersion and restraint. If a child is held vertically by the arms or chest then immersed in water, the feet come into contact first with the hot water. The child may retract with legs held out, after which the perpetrator may plunge the child into the water again with genitals and buttocks making contact first. A pattern of burns to the feet, lower legs, buttocks and genitals with few splash marks is highly suspicious for abuse (Fig. 4.2).

In forced immersion, the buttocks may be pressed against the cooler bath base sparing the skin at that point and leading to a so-called 'hole in the doughnut' pattern. In the groin, buttock creases, back of a flexed knee, front of elbow, and where the hip flexes, skin creases may be spared from injury as hot liquid is unable to fully penetrate into these areas. If the lower trunk is forced into flexion during immersion with the child in a seated position, protected skin creases may be observed on the front of the lower abdomen (Table 4.3).

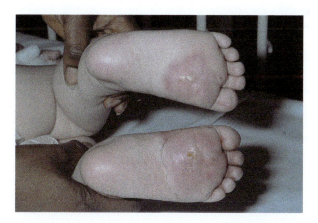

Fig. 4.2 A one year old was presented for care with a fever and what appeared to be immersion burns to both feet. Features of inflicted injury included a lower limb location, clear margins, symmetrical/bilateral involvement with no splash marks. After full investigation, the father admitted to placing both feet in his mouth and sucking with force in order to reduce the child's fever in keeping with a traditional folk-healing practice (Image courtesy of Dr Junaid Solebo)

Table 4.3 Features of accidental and inflicted scalds

Accidental	Inflicted
Head, neck and trunk	Lower limbs, buttocks, perineum
No glove or stocking distribution	Glove or stocking distribution
Irregular margin	Clear margins
Irregular burn depth	Uniform scald depth
Asymmetric involvement	Often symmetrical
Mainly anterior	May be posterior
Unilateral	Bilateral
	Lower extremities may be unilateral
In immersion, splash marks seen	In forced immersion, no splash marks
	Patterns of skin sparing eg: skin creases

"Stocking and glove" burns are circumferential over the arms and legs and may indicate forced immersion particularly if symmetrical. A demarcation line separating the burned from the non-burned area is observed. Palms and soles may be less severely affected because of thicker skin in those areas.

A sharp demarcation line on the lower back may indicate that a child was held still in hot water. The waterline on the child's torso also indicates the depth of the water.

Contact Burns

In accidental injury, the child's skin comes into contact with an iron, hair tongs or other hot domestic item. The resulting injury of universal depth and carries an imprint of the implement. Such burns are often unilateral, on the hands and superficial as the child will withdraw rapidly from the heat source [11].

However, although deep burns from prolonged contact raise concerns for abuse, when for example a child grabs at an electric fire bar, the palm may adhere leading to prolonged contact. In addition, iron burns, whether accidental or inflicted may result in large injuries.

Inflicted burns are commonly over the back of the hand compared to accidental burns where the palm is more usually affected. However, a child's hand or foot may be held against a hot cooker ring burning the palms or soles (Fig. 4.3). The most frequent sites for inflicted contact burns are the leg, trunk, upper arm, thigh, back of the hand and areas that the child is unable to reach (Fig. 4.4).

Inflicted contact burns are often multiple, bilateral and deep. Burns may take on the shape of the offending object more obviously than in accident where a glancing brief contact is more usual. If the pattern left suggests an object not associated with a domestic appliance, further concerns will be raised (Table 4.4).

Inflicted hairdryer burns have been found on the buttocks, face, soles of feet, back and abdomen. In published studies, these had clear demarcation lines and in some cases the imprint of the grid on the face of the dryer was observed.

Fig. 4.3 Burns following contact with a hot cooker plate, a common accidental injury (Image reproduced with permission of the Wellcome Library, London)

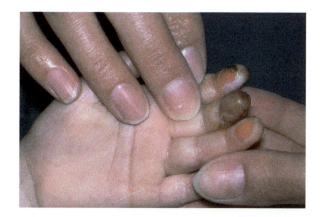

Fig. 4.4 Contact burns with features of inflicted injury being over the buttock and with linear imprints of the implement used (Image courtesy of Dr Morgan Keane)

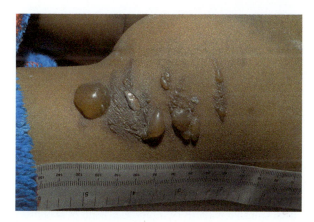

Table 4.4 Features of accidental and inflicted contact burns

Accidental	Inflicted
May carry an imprint of the implement	Imprint may be more pronounced
Single	Multiple
Unilateral	Often bilateral
Superficial	Deep
Front of hand or foot	Back of the hand or foot
Credible history of an accident and its aftermath	Vague, implausible or absent history

Cigarette Burns

Cigarette burns are commonly inflicted. When a child accidentally brushes up against a lit cigarette, there is brief contact, the child retracts and an irregularly shaped, oval or round superficial burn results which may 'tail' if the cigarette was brushed against, or hot ash dropped on to the skin.

In inflicted injury, the tip of the cigarette is pushed into child's skin and held, leaving a deep circular punched out injury of uniform depth and a diameter

Fig. 4.5 A two year old was presented with large clearly demarcated circular/oval burns to the front of both feet. Each had a deep central crater, and, after investigation were considered to be inflicted cigarette burns (Image courtesy of Dr. Junaid Solebo)

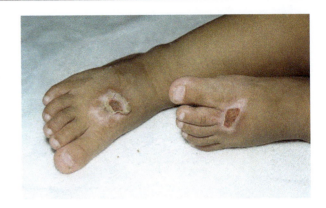

of approximately 10mm. [12]. Localised erythema, blistering or a clearly demarcated circular burn with a deep central crater are suspicious features. Healing leads to small circular scars. In inflicted injury, tail marks may be absent and injuries are often multiple covering small areas (Fig. 4.5).

In published studies, inflicted cigarette burns have been found on the fingers, base of thumb, hand and back and trunk.

Other Patterns of Injury

Chemical Burns

Most accidental chemical burns are splash marks from corrosive household products. Unusual patterns of injury as a result of acid making contact with the skin raise concerns. Upper airways and oesophageal injuries may result from a child swallowing a corrosive product or it being forcibly instilled. Kini et al. (1997) described injury resulting from deliberate caustic instillation into the ear of a child [13].

Electrical Burns

Accidental burns are observed in toddlers and older children who have come into contact with electric cables. They are generally small sometimes with entry and exit points. Unprotected electrical sockets or bare wires suggest supervisional neglect. Showers and Bandman (1986) reported that electrical cords used to inflict burns typically led to curved scars [14].

Zubair et al. (1997) reviewed 127 children with electrical injuries. These included biting an electrical cord (oral injury/48), placing an object into an electrical socket (outlet injury/33), contacting a low-voltage wire or appliance indoors (low-voltage/25), contacting a high-voltage wire outdoors (high-voltage/18), or being struck by lightning (3). Most children with low-voltage electrical injuries could have been cared for on an outpatient basis. Almost all patients with high-voltage injury required admission [15].

Flame

Accidental flame injuries are typically caused by fires and matches. Bonfires, barbeques, fireworks, aerosols and lighters have all been implicated. Inflicted flame injuries are uncommon. They are characterised by extreme depth and are relatively well defined when compared with accidental flame burns.

Friction

Friction burns typically occur when a child is dragged across a carpeted floor. The bony prominences of the elbows, wrists, pelvis, knees, ankles and back are most commonly affected. Friction burns can occur accidentally from slides, skids on carpets and other similar injuries.

Microwave Burns

In microwave burns, the temperature cannot be accurately predicted. Variables include the strength of radiation, duration of exposure, and moisture content of surface tissues.

Alexander et al. (1987) reported that infants placed in microwave ovens sustained life-threatening burns to the skin and muscle with sparing of the subcutaneous fat layer between them [16]. Sharply defined burns are seen closest to the microwave emitting device [17].

Radiant Burns

Radiant heat from a fire or sunlight can cause superficial or deeper injuries. Children may be forced to stand in front of a fire whilst severe sunburn may indicate poor supervision or neglect. Older children are sometimes seen with sunbed related burns.

Further Research Evidence

Fagen et al. (2015) reviewed 112 children with burns aged 1 to 110 months. Forty-five (40%) were inflicted, 36 (32%) indeterminate and 31 (28%) accidental. The most common cause was scalding, the most common location was the perineum and lower extremity in all three diagnostic categories. Associated injuries were fractures in 15/45 (33%) in the inflicted group; 2/36 (6%) in the indeterminate group, and 0/29 (0%) in the accidental group [18].

Kemp et al. (2014) reviewed 1215 children with unintentional burns. Of these 58% (709) had scalds, 32% (390) contact burns and 116 burns from other causes. A minority, 17.6% (214/1215) were admitted to hospital with the remainder treated at home, ED or a burns assessment unit. Of the 1215 cases 72% (878) were under 5 years of age with a peak prevalence at 12 months. The commonest agent in the under 5s was a cup of hot beverage 55% (305/554) and the commonest mechanism being a pull-down injury. In 5–16 year olds, scalds were from hot water in 50% (78/155) and spill injuries 76% (118/155). Scalds affected the front of the body in

96% (680/709) mainly to the face, arms and upper trunk in those under 5 years of age. Older children had scalds to the lower trunk, legs and hands. Contact burns in the under 5s were from touching hot items in the home 81% (224/277). These included hair straighteners and irons 42% and oven hobs 27%. Children 5 years and older sustained more outdoor injuries, 46% (52/113). Of all contact burns 67% (262/390) affected the hands [19].

Kemp et al. (2013) reviewed 20 studies representing 73 children with intentional non-scald burns. The majority were contact burns from household items. Agents included cigarettes (18), irons (9), electric fires/heaters/radiators (10), cigarette lighters (2), hairdryers (7), curling tongs (3), chemicals (3), microwaves (2) flame burns (7), miscellaneous (7) and burns of unknown cause (5). The majority of children were older than 3 years. Characteristic features were clearly demarcated contact burns or scars in shapes that suggested the implement used. Injuries were predominantly recorded on the limbs, trunks and the backs of hands, frequently multiple with other signs of abuse [20].

Maguire et al. (2008) reviewed 26 studies finding that intentional scalds were commonly immersion injuries, caused by hot tap water and affected the extremities, buttocks or perineum or both. They were symmetrical with clear upper margins, and associated with old fractures and unrelated injuries. Unintentional scalds more commonly affected the upper body with irregular margins and depth [10].

Hobbs (1986) reviewed 195 children up to 6 years of age with burns and scalds (30 inflicted, 165 accidental). Scalds accounted for 81% of accidents and 25% of inflicted injuries. Burns accounted for 17% and 44% respectively. Scalds usually followed a spill from kitchen containers in accidents. Forced tap water immersion predominated in inflicted injury. Both accidental and inflicted injuries resulted from contact with various household appliances. The author noted that the back of the hand was an important site for inflicted injury as well as the legs, buttocks, and feet [21].

Ojo et al. (2007) reviewed 155 children less than 6 years of age admitted to a burns unit. Six cases (3.8%) were confirmed as inflicted injury. Scald injury was the most common cause of both accidental and inflicted burns, mostly from tap water in children less than 2 years old. Whenever the extremities were involved, the left side was always affected. The perpetrator was the mother's boyfriend in all cases. The authors noted that inflicted burns are under-reported and often diagnosed as accidental [22].

Other Explanations for Accidental Burns

Buckles of seat belts and black vinyl car seats

These may be heated by the sun and become very hot with the risk of burn injuries. Schmitt et al. (1978) reported children who were accidentally placed in contact with hot car upholstery sustaining significant contact burns [23].

Central Heating appliances
These are mainly safe depending on the temperature set for the central heating. Small hands are more likely to be burned if trapped behind a radiator. Electric water heaters have been documented to cause burns when the child places his or her hand on the outside surface [24, 25].

Hot water bottles
The accidental leaking of a freshly prepared hot water bottle containing boiling water may cause a significant scald injury.

Local anaesthetics
These cause insensitivity to pain for several hours. Drinking very hot liquids after a local anaesthetic for dental treatment can lead to intra-oral burns.

Disability
Children with syringomyelia, spina bifida, severe developmental delay, cerebral palsy or an epileptic child in the course of a convulsion may have pain insensitivity or be unable to move away from hot surfaces or liquids that come into contact with their skin.

Congenital insensitivity to pain
Congenital insensitivity to pain is a rare condition in which a person does not perceive physical pain. Children sustain bruises, burns, fractures and other injuries. Infections are painless with often delayed diagnosis.

Folk-Healing Practices
Cupping, coining scraping/spooning and moxibustion may all cause skin burns (page 45).

Medical Conditions that May Be Confused for Burns

Dermatitis Herpetiformis
This is a chronic, papular skin condition that can be mistaken for cigarette burns. Lesions are small, clustered, intensely itchy and symmetrically distributed on the extensor surfaces of the extremities, buttocks, back, and abdomen.

Eczema
In this allergic skin condition, skin damage causes reddening with dry areas. Intense itchiness causes the child to scratch and cause injury. Reddened skin may appear as burns.

Epidermolysis bullosa
This rare group of blistering skin conditions may mimic burns. Blisters may occur spontaneously or from minimal trauma.

Impetigo
This skin infection caused by *Staphylococcus aureus* or *group A beta-haemolytic streptococcus* produces lesions that begin as pustules then form honey coloured crusts of differing sizes. The infection responds to antibiotics and heals without scarring. It is sometimes confused with cigarette burns.

Nappy rash
Severe nappy rash may mimic the denuded skin observed in scalds.

Laxatives
Loose motions which contain the laxative Senna may cause burns to the buttock and perianal area following the edges of the nappy which may be mistaken for an immersion burn.

Spiller et al. (2003) reviewed 111 children who had received the laxative Senna. Twenty-nine (33%) developed severe nappy rash. Ten (11%) had blisters and skin sloughing. Skin burns and loss were observed primarily on the buttocks and perineum, loosely following the nappy area [26]. Leventhal et al. (2001) also reported on senna induced dermatitis of the buttocks incorrectly diagnosed as inflicted burns [27].

Urticaria
Urticaria is pale red, raised, itchy rash that may lead to a burning or stinging sensation and may be confused with burns.

Phytophoto-dermatitis
When a child's skin is exposed to sunlight after contact with psoralens (chemical compounds found in limes, lemons, parsley, celery, carrots or figs) red marks appear as bruises and, if severe, burns. Lesions resemble drip marks or handprints when a child has been handled by an adult with the juice on his or her hands.

Scalded skin syndrome
Staphylococcal scalded skin syndrome is characterised by red blistering skin that looks like a burn or scald. It is caused by the release of exotoxins from strains of the bacteria *Staphylococcus aureus*.

Streptococcal toxic shock syndrome
Toxic shock syndrome is a potentially life-threatening condition caused by a bacterial toxin released from the bacteria *Staphylococcus aureus or Streptococcus pyogenes*. The characteristic rash resembles sunburn and peels after 10–14 days.

References

1. Peck MD, Priolo-Kapel D. Child abuse by burning: a review of the literature and an algorithm for medical investigations. J Trauma. 2002;53(5):1013–22.
2. McLoughlin E, McGuire A. The causes, cost, and prevention of childhood burn injuries. Am J Dis Child. 1990;144(6):677–83.
3. Purdue GF, Hunt JL, Prescott PR. Child abuse by burning – an index of suspicion. J Trauma. 1988;28(2):221–4.
4. Pawlik MC, Kemp A, Maguire S, Nuttall D, Feldman KW, Lindberg DM. Children with burns referred for child abuse evaluation: burn characteristics and co-existent injuries. Child Abuse Negl. 2016;55:52–61.
5. Al-Qattan MM, Al-Tamimi AS. Localized hand burns with or without concurrent blast injuries from fireworks. Burns. 2009;35(3):425–9.
6. Faller-Marquardt M, Pollak S, Schmidt U. Cigarette burns in forensic medicine. Forensic Sci Int. 2008;176(2–3):200–8.
7. Hathaway WE, Hay WW, Groothuis JR, Paisley JW. Current pediatric diagnosis and treatment. Norwalk: Ct. Appleton & Lange; 1993.
8. Showers J, Garrison KM. Burn abuse: a four-year study. J Trauma. 1988;28:1581–3.
9. Dressler DP, Hozid JL. Thermal injury and child abuse: the medical evidence dilemma. J Burn Care Rehabil. 2001;22(2):180–5.
10. Maguire S, Moynihan S, Mann M, Potokar T, Kemp AM. A systematic review of the features that indicate intentional scalds in children. Burns. 2008;34(8):1072–81.
11. Wilson Jones N, Wong P, Potokar T. Electric hair straightener burns an epidemiological and thermodynamic study. Burns. 2008;34(4):521–4.
12. Shavit I, Knaani-Levinz H. Images in emergency medicine: child abuse caused by cigarette burns. Ann Emerg Med. 2008;51:579, 582.
13. Alexander RC, Surrell JA, Cohle SD. Microwave oven burns to children: an unusual manifestation of child abuse. Pediatrics. 1987;79(2):255–60.
14. Ozen S, Helhel S, Bilgin S. Temperature and burn injury prediction of human skin exposed to microwaves: a model analysis. Radiat Environ Biophys. 2011;50(3):483–9.
15. Showers J, Bandman RL. Scarring for life: abuse with electric cords. Child Abuse Negl. 1986;10:25–31.
16. Zubair M, Besner GE. Pediatric electrical burns: management strategies. Burns. 1997;23(5):413–20.
17. Kini N, Lazoritz S, Ott C, Conley SF. Caustic instillation into the ear as a form of child abuse. Am J Emerg Med. 1997;15(4):442–3.
18. Fagen KE, et al. Frequency of skeletal injuries in children with inflicted burns. Pediatr Radiol. 2015;45(3):396–401.
19. Kemp AM, Jones S, Lawson Z, Maguire SA. Patterns of burns and scalds in children. Arch Dis Child. 2014;99:316–21.
20. Kemp AM, Maguire SA, Lumb RC, Harris SM, Mann MK. Contact, cigarette and flame burns in physical abuse: a systematic review version of record online: 28 June 2013. Child Abuse Rev. 2014;23(1):35–47.
21. Hobbs CJ. When are burns not accidental? Arch Dis Child. 1986;61(4):357–61.
22. Ojo P, Palmer J, Garvey R, Atweh N, Fidler P. Pattern of burns in child abuse. Am Surg. 2007;73(3):253–5.
23. Schmitt BD, Gray JD, Britton HL. Car seat burns in infants: avoiding confusion with inflicted burns. Pediatrics. 1978;62(4):607–9.

24. Chuang SS, Yang JY, Tsai FC. Electric water heaters: a new hazard for pediatric burns. Burns. 2003;29(6):589–91.
25. Drago DA. Kitchen scalds and thermal burns in children five years and younger. Pediatrics. 2005;115(1):10–6.
26. Spiller HA, Winter ML, Weber JA, Krenzelok EP, Anderson DL, Ryan ML. Skin breakdown and blisters from senna-containing laxatives in young children. Ann Pharmacother. 2003;37(5):636–9.
27. Leventhal JM, Griffin D, Duncan KO, Starling S, Christian CW, Kutz T. Laxative-induced dermatitis of the buttocks incorrectly suspected to be abusive burns. Pediatrics. 2001;107(1):178–9.

Further Reading

CORE INFO Cardiff Child Protection Systematic Reviews/www.core-info.cardiff.ac.uk/ (accessed 15.04.17)

Abusive Head Trauma (AHT)

5

Abstract

Serious accidental head trauma is generally the result of a significant fall or road traffic accident when both impact and crushing injuries may occur. Head injury in infants and young children is commonly inflicted, a result of shaking, impact or a combination of both.

In the past, abusive head trauma has been described as non-accidental head injury (NAHI) and shaken baby syndrome (SBS). Abusive Head Trauma (AHT), recent terminology proposed by the American Academy of Pediatrics, is used in this text [1].

AHT is mainly seen in children under 2 and most commonly in those under 6 months of age. It is the leading cause of trauma deaths in infants [2]. A vast majority (95%) of severe head injuries occurring in the first year of life are due to inflicted injury with a mortality rate of 21.4% and half of survivors having residual disability [3]. The same clinical findings are sometimes found in children up to 5 years of age [4].

Starling et al. (1995) reported that male victims accounted for 60.3%. Male perpetrators predominated with fathers, step-fathers, and mothers' boyfriends being responsible for over 60% of the cases. Fathers accounted for 37%, boyfriends 20.5%, female baby-sitters 17.3%. Mothers were responsible for only 12.6% of cases where the perpetrator was known [5]. Increased infant risk is associated with male gender, prematurity, low birth weight and disability.

The Royal College of Pathologists (2009) concluded that widespread bilateral retinal haemorrhages and large macular folds, thin film subdural haemorrhage and encephalopathy provided suspicion for mechanical trauma including vigorous shaking. Further, that all individual elements of the triad had a differential diagnosis and that the triad was not absolute proof of traumatic head injury [6].

© Springer International Publishing Switzerland 2017

D.L. Robinson, *Pediatric Forensic Evidence*, DOI 10.1007/978-3-319-45337-8_5

General Principles

Infants are more vulnerable than adults to intracranial injury from shaking or impact. The head is larger than an adult's in proportion to the body, the brain being 75% the weight of an average adult brain at age 2 years. Neck muscles that protect against rapid movement of the head are weak and unable to control the head's motion during acceleration-deceleration forces. The infant brain is relatively soft with high water content and a greater surface area covered by a large thin subarachnoid space providing little protection against impact.

The base of the infant skull is relatively flat, permitting the brain to move more readily in response to acceleration–deceleration forces whilst the skull bone is thin and pliable transferring impact forces across the subarachnoid space to the brain. Sutures (fibrous connections between skull bones) also permit transmission of forces to cerebral tissue.

AHT as a Result of Shaking

Shaking creates rotational movements of the head with acceleration-deceleration forces and rupture of fine vessels that cross the subdural space resulting in subdural haemorrhage with associated diffuse axonal injury and subarachnoid bleeding in some cases. The same forces produce forward and backward movements of the brain. Some infants sustain cervical hyperflexion-hyperextention (whiplash) injury which can be disabling or fatal.

In the aftermath of injury, evidence for encephalopathy may be minimal or severe. At the point of injury an infant will scream out in distress then develop symptoms that may resolve rapidly or progress. For milder cases, there may be an abnormal cry, poor feeding, respiratory symptoms, vomiting, irritability and lethargy. The infant may settle if comforted. In some cases, a sleeping infant may have altered consciousness, with carers not recognising a change in behaviour for some hours.

At the severe end of the spectrum, symptoms may progress rapidly to convulsions, altered mental state, severe breathing difficulties, coma and death. Medical assessment may reveal a full fontanelle (soft spot over skull), increased head circumference, signs of encephalopathy and other evidence of inflicted injury. Some infants present in a collapsed state due to clinical shock (inadequate organ perfusion) as a result of blood loss and neurological damage (hypoxic-ischaemic injury). Initial investigations may show anaemia (due to bleeding, fluid resuscitation or a combination of both), acidosis on blood gas analysis, a raised white cell count and C-reactive protein (CRP) as non-specific indicators of stress.

A lucid interval (consciousness between injury and collapse) may occur but where there is hypoxic-ischaemic damage, the point of deterioration is more likely to be close to the point of injury. The evolution of symptoms depends on the age of the infant, (smaller infants present more acutely) the degree of force used, resultant brain injury, compression effects and any brain stem injury (control of circulation and breathing). The absence of a history of trauma or external signs of injury may delay diagnosis.

A diagnosis of AHT must also be considered when an infant presents with unexplained Apparent Life Threatening Event (pages 173–179). Some infants may present non-acutely with an increasing head circumference where neuro-imaging shows chronic subdural haematomas or effusions dating back weeks.

Adamsbaum et al. (2010) reviewed 112 cases of AHT comparing 29 where the perpetrator confessed to violence toward the child with 83 cases in which there was no confession. In the first group shaking was described as extremely violent in 29 (100%), a single episode in 13 (45%) and repeated episodes in 16 (55%) from 2–30 times. Impact was recorded in 5 (17%). In 4 cases the perpetrator reported symptoms immediately after the shaking. In the remainder the time delay to symptoms was variable but less than 24 hours. [7].

Gilliland and Folberg (1996) reviewed postmortem findings of 80 infants with evidence of shaking on the basis of two of the following: finger-marks and/or rib fractures, subdural haematoma and/or subarachnoid haematoma, a history of vigorous shaking. The authors concluded that three mechanisms operated: namely, shaking, shaking and impact and impact. Eleven percent of cases were considered to be shaking injuries [8].

Aoki and Masuzawa (1984) described 26 infants presenting with acute subdural haematoma aged between 3–13 months. Twenty-three had convulsions (13 within 1 minute, 18 within 5 minutes). The longest delay was 15 minutes. All patients had retinal and pre-retinal haemorrhage [9].

A 3-month-old infant was admitted to hospital with widespread bruising to the back and signs of encephalopathy. Neuro-imaging showed bilateral subdural haematomas and cerebral oedema. There were retinal haemorrhages. Carers were unable to provide an explanation. However, prior to expert evidence the mother stated, 'It was 3 o'clock in the morning and I was alone with my baby who was screaming. I picked her up and tried to soothe her but the screaming got louder. I felt desperate and started squeezing and shaking her, digging my fingers into her back. The whole episode lasted about a minute. I am so sorry.'

AHT as a Result of Impact

There may be impact against a hard or soft surface with an infant being dropped from a significant height or swung in an adult grip impacting against a wall, floor or furniture. Trauma from an adult hand or another blunt implement may be responsible.

The clinical course for infants who have suffered an impact injury is similar to that described for shaking injuries although Graham et al. (2000) suggested that a lucid interval was more common after impact due to slowly evolving raised intracranial pressure [10]. Focal injuries from impact include scalp haematomas, lacerations, epidural haematomas, SDH, sub-arachnoid haemorrhage (SAH), skull fracture, and brain injury. Duhaime et al. (1987) reviewed 48 children with SDH or

SAH, retinal haemorrhages and a history indicating abuse. All children who died and 63% of survivors had evidence of impact [11].

A 'coup' injury occurs under the site of impact whilst a 'contra-coup' occurs on the side opposite the impacted area. Both may occur in AHT. Impact against a soft surface may result in AHT without signs of external injury.

Degree of Force Required

Whilst the degree of force required for AHT is not known, it is generally accepted to be far in excess of normal or rough handling with the perpetrator immediately realising that excessive force had been applied. However, it is not known for how long a child must be shaken to cause serious injury or why retinal haemorrhages result from shaking but rarely from falls.

The American Academy of Paediatrics (1993) stated that 'the act of shaking to produce these injuries must be so violent that neutral observers would recognise it as a dangerous act.'

Kemp (2002) reported that the clinical spectrum of cases varies from children with multiple injuries as a result of a severe degree of violence to those with an isolated SDH and that knowledge of the precise forces required to elicit SDH was based on small studies where perpetrators admitted shaking an infant, those where monkeys had been shaken, and modelling experiments. Cases are referred to where infants were shaken by carers unable to cope and those who had reportedly shaken to resuscitate a baby who had stopped breathing [12].

Hobbs et al. (2005) reviewed 186 infants and children aged 0–2 years reporting on the most likely causes for SDH and effusions. The authors stated there was little evidence to support the view that minor trauma caused SDH and that in accidental cases the history was of severe trauma [13] (Table 5.1).

Sauvageau et al. (2008) reported the case of a 2-year-old child on a rocking toy whilst a 6-year-old shook it from behind and a 12-year-old held the handlebars pushing the toy backwards. After some minutes the 2-year-old hit his head on the handlebars. He cried, a bruise developed on his forehead but he continued playing. During the night he was found to be breathing irregularly. In hospital, an SDH was evacuated but he died during surgery. Postmortem revealed residual right SDH, subarachnoid haemorrhage, diffuse cerebral swelling, and multiple bilateral retinal haemorrhages. The accounts given by the two children were considered truthful [14].

Denton et al. (2003) described a 9-month-old who struck his head on a concrete floor after a fall from a bed. He appeared well for 72 hours but then sadly died. Post

Cause of SDH	Number	Percentage
Non accidental head injury (AHT)	106	57%
Perinatal	26	14%
Meningitis	23	12%
Accidental	7	3.7%
Non traumatic medical condition	7	3.7%
Undetermined	17	9%

Table 5.1 Hobbs et al. [13], Subdural haematoma and effusion in infancy

mortem showed skull fracture, cerebral oedema and subgaleal haematoma. No child protection concerns were raised after investigation. [15].

Clinical Assessment

Multidisciplinary Approach
When an infant presents with signs of encephalopathy or significant head trauma, urgent neuro-imaging, skeletal survey and ophthalmic review are essential to exclude AHT and other injuries.

A multidisciplinary approach is required to include paediatrician, neurosurgeon, ophthalmologist, nurses and social care. The police will visit the family home, interview carers and collect forensic evidence.

History and Examination
A comprehensive medical history and examination should be undertaken as described in chapter 1, pages 4–6. Systems enquiries, past medical history, family history, whether Vitamin K was given at birth and reports of abnormal bleeding are all relevant. The account of an accident and its aftermath is compared with clinical findings and the developmental stage of the child.

The carer may report non-specific symptoms with either no mention of trauma or a history of minor impact. Sleepiness, poor feeding, vomiting, apnoea, a cyanotic spell or convulsion may be reported with a scalp swelling noticed. When shaking is admitted, the carer may suggest that someone else was with the infant at the time or that he or she was found not breathing with vigorous resuscitation attempts causing injury and deterioration.

Physical examination should include observation of the parent-child interaction, signs of neglect, assessment of growth and development, systems examination and a careful search for any skin marks or other injuries.

Examination specific to AHT includes a search for signs of external skull and spinal injury including soft tissue haematomas, skull/spinal deformities and bruises around the eyes, ears, neck and spine. Oro-nasal bleeding and facial petechiae are associated with shaking injuries.

A full neurological assessment should include head circumference and signs of encephalopathy or raised intracranial pressure. Where a scalp swelling is identified, its size, shape the condition of overlying skin, warmth and tenderness should all be recorded. Accurate documentation of skin marks on body maps and good quality images with a standard ruler should be undertaken.

Factors that raise concern for inflicted injury and those associated with abuse are discussed on pages 7–12. Following accidental injury, medical attention is usually sought promptly. In abuse, a delay in seeking care is more common. Other factors that raise concerns are a clinical examination that does not match the account of injury, no credible history of a memorable event and its aftermath, discrepant accounts and a history that does not fit with the child's developmental abilities. The carer may blame a sibling, the family may be known to children's social care with repeated medical attendances for injuries. There may be other injuries on the child or signs of neglect.

Bechtel et al. (2004) reported that accidental head injuries usually present with a history of trauma whilst in AHT seizures or altered mental status predominate. Bechtel reported seizures in 53% of AHT compared to 6% in accidental trauma, altered mental status in 53% vs. 1% [16].

Starling et al. (2004) reviewed 81 cases of AHT (2 weeks to 52 months) in which perpetrators admitted abuse. Shaking was the most common mechanism of injury among perpetrator admissions, 55/81 (68%). Impact was *not* described in 44/81 (54%) of cases. Where only impact was described, 60% (12/20) had a skull or scalp injury, compared with 12% (4/32) in the shaking group. In 52/57 (91%) of cases where the time to symptoms was described, these appeared immediately after the abuse. In 5 cases (9%) they occurred within 24 hours. No infant or child was described as behaving normally after the event [17].

Neuroimaging

Neuro-imaging is essential for diagnosis, monitoring, interventions and documentation.

It should be performed where has been unexplained collapse, neurological symptoms or signs, head trauma, an increasing head circumference, where there is uniformly blood stained cerebro-spinal fluid or evidence of retinopathy [18, 19]. Head ultrasound is unreliable as a means of detecting or excluding SDH.

A CT head scan is recommended for any infant under 1 year of age where there is evidence of physical abuse, and should be considered in children up to the age of 2 years. It accurately detects acute subdural bleeds differentiating between SAH and SDH, mass effect, and skull fractures.

Magnetic resonance imaging (MRI) is more accurate for smaller bleeds especially in areas less well seen on CT. It more accurately detects oedema, subacute haemorrhage, ischaemic changes, cervical spine injuries, diffuse axonal injury (DAI) and petechial haemorrhages. Dating is more accurately assessed with an MRI. A repeat MRI or CT is recommended on day 3 with a further study at 2–3 months to assess any resulting cerebral damage, chronic SDH, hydrocephalus and other abnormalities. Increasingly, an MRI spine is undertaken on day 1 (Table 5.2).

Laboratory Investigations

Suggested investigations and assessments depending on the clinical presentation are documented on page 7 and in Table 5.3. A full blood count repeated after 1–2 hours may show a low or falling haemoglobin from intracranial bleeding, fluid administration or both. Renal and liver function, serum amylase, C-reactive protein and septic screen to include blood, urine and cerebrospinal fluid cultures are basic investigations. Uniformly blood stained CSF indicates likely intracranial bleeding.

Management

Infants may present in clinical shock and require urgent resuscitation and management of the airways, breathing and circulation. For the latter, fluid resuscitation or urgent blood transfusion may be required as well as assisted ventilation. Raised intracranial pressure may require neurosurgical assessment and treatment.

If a diagnosis of AHT is considered likely, a referral to children's social care is required with local safeguarding children's board (LSCB) procedures followed.

Table 5.2 Royal College of Radiologists, Royal College of Paediatrics and Child Health (2008) [19]. Standards for radiological investigations of suspected non-accidental injury

Day 1	Cranial CT
	Skeletal survey including skull films if the child is well enough
	MRI spine (unpublished guidance 2016)
Day 3–5	If initial CT brain abnormal or ongoing neurological signs, MRI
3–6 months	Repeat MRI

Table 5.3 Suggested investigations for AHT

Full blood count
Renal and liver function tests
Serum amylase
C-reactive protein (CRP)
Septic screen to include blood, urine and cerebrospinal fluid
Standard clotting screen
Factor Assays and von Willebrand factor (page 26)
Platelet function tests (page 26)
Alpha 2 antiplasmin
Plasma amino acids
Urine organic acids
Acetyl-L-Carnitine profile (glutaric aciduria)
Urine for Toxicology
Copper and Caeruloplasmin levels
Galactosaemia screen
Skin biopsy for glutaric aciduria (rarely undertaken)
Neuro-imaging (Table 5.2)
Skeletal survey in children under 2 years with repeat chest radiograph after 10–14 days

A telephone discussion should be followed by a referral in writing on a standard form (page 16).

The Clinical Triad in AHT

Subdural Haematoma (SDH)

SDHs do not occur as spontaneous events in infants and children in the absence of an underlying medical condition that increases susceptibility. Where there is no credible history of a significant accident, they are strongly associated with AHT.

SDHs occur in the space between the dura and the arachnoid membranes, usually as a result of rupture of the bridging veins that join the surface of the brain to the dura. Focal subdural haemorrhage is more common after impact, diffuse SDH commonly seen after shaking. In the latter, SDHs are typically multiple and commonly located over the convexity of the cerebral hemispheres, inter-hemispheric or in the posterior fossa. In contrast to accidental trauma, haemorrhages are found in several locations and of mixed density.

Wells et al. (2002) reviewed SDHs in 293 infants and children under 3 years who had suffered head trauma. In 143 (49%) SDH was interhemispheric. Of these, 73% were caused by AHT and 15% by accidental head trauma including three falls from heights of over 2 metres, 12 road traffic accidents, 4 falls from infant walkers and 2 blows to the head [20].

Hymel et al. (1997) reported SDHs in 16/39 (41%) of patients in an AHT group compared to 4/39 (10%) in the accidental group [21].

Tung et al. (2006) found that mixed-density SDHs were significantly more common in AHT (67%) than in accidental trauma (18%). Homogenous hyperdense SDHs were more common in accidental injury [22].

Retinal Haemorrhages (RH)

Retinal Haemorrhages are strongly associated with, but not exclusive to, AHT. They can occur following high-velocity or crush injuries and are seen in new-borns particularly those born by vacuum or forceps with vacuum.

Watts et al. (2013) reviewed 1777 infants from 13 studies reporting RH in the following: infants born by spontaneous vaginal delivery (25.6%), vacuum extraction (42.6%) and forceps plus vacuum (52%). Haemorrhages were usually bilateral, intraretinal and restricted to the posterior pole [23].

In AHT, RH are usually bilateral, multi-layered and extend to the periphery of the retina. Those found in accidental trauma are mainly unilateral, few in number and around the posterior pole. However, there are case reports of severe crush injuries where extensive RH were found with other retinal findings [24]. Studies indicate that 83% of retinal haemorrhages in the newborn resolve by 10 days, 97% by 42 days [25].

Bechtel et al. (2004) found RH in 60% of AHT patients and in 10% following accidental head trauma. In the AHT group 40% were bilateral, 30% pre-retinal, 20% premacular and 27% extended to the periphery of retina. In the accidental group, none were pre-retinal, pre-macular or extended to the periphery of the retina and only 1.5% bilateral [16].

Other rare causes of retinal haemorrhages include leukaemia, bleeding disorders, thrombocytopenia, severe infections, extra corporeal membrane oxygenation (ECMO), raised intracranial pressure, retinopathy of prematurity, persistent foetal retinal vasculature, cardiopulmonary resuscitation, convulsions and other rare inherited conditions including glutaric aciduria Type I.

Encephalopathy

Encephalopathic features may be mild to include an abnormal cry, poor feeding, respiratory symptoms, vomiting irritability and lethargy or progress to convulsions, altered mental state, severe breathing difficulties, coma and death (page 114).

Diffuse axonal injury (DAI) is inertial brain injury from acceleration–deceleration forces causing widespread shearing to axons and small blood vessels. Axons are the neural projections that allow one neuron to communicate with another.

Hypoxic ischaemic injury is neuronal cell damage from cerebral hypoxia that may lead to hypoxic ischaemic encephalopathy (HIE). It is associated with oxygen deprivation from birth asphyxia, AHT, serious accidents and upper airways obstruction. It can be widespread and associated with cerebral oedema (brain swelling).

Brain contusions are a result of impact forces. Multifocal haemorrhagic contusions are caused by shearing forces at the time of impact. In AHT, contusions are often observed in association with diffuse axonal injury. They may be adjacent to the point of impact (coup) or on the opposite side of the brain (contrecoup).

Adamo et al. (2009) reviewed 164 cases of accidental trauma and 54 of AHT. The accidental trauma group were more likely to present with higher Glasgow Coma Scale (GCS) scores. Skull fractures were present in 57.2% of the accidental group of whom 15% had subdural collections. Skull fractures were present in 30% of the AHT group with subdural collections in 52%. Hypodense subdural collections were associated with AHT where patients were more likely to require neurosurgical intervention [26].

Kemp et al. (2011) reviewing the medical literature, found that hypoxic-ischaemic injury was 3.7 times more common in inflicted injury compared with accidental head trauma. Cerebral oedema was 2.2 times more common in AHT [27].

Vinchon et al. (2010) reviewed 45 cases of confessed AHT and 39 cases of independently observed accidental trauma (AT). Brain ischaemia was found in 26.7% of AHT with the most significant factors for AHT being SDH, severe retinal haemorrhages, and no signs of impact [28].

Thomas et al. (2013) reviewed the CT scans of 149 children younger than 2 years of age following accidental head trauma. Three children had brain parenchymal injury all from significant trauma (fall from a top bunk on to a hard surface, from a 1st-floor window on to concrete, being struck by a car and thrown 30 feet) [29].

Other Features of AHT

Subarachnoid Haemorrhages (SAH)

SAH is bleeding into the area between arachnoid membrane and the pia mater surrounding the brain. It is associated with arteriovenous malformations, aneurysms, coagulopathies, infection, and major accidental trauma. In AHT, it commonly occurs at the site of impact in association with a depressed skull fracture or brain contusion.

Ewing-Cobbs et al. (1998) reported that that inflicted SAH may result from shaking, impact, or a combination of both [30].

Reece and Sege (2000) reviewed the medical records of 287 children with head injuries injuries aged 1 week to 6.5 years. Accidents accounted for 81% of cases and

AHT 19%. The mean age of the accident group was 2.5 years and for the definite abuse group, 0.7 years. Associated injuries were as follows: SDH (10% in the accident group 46% AHT), SAH (8% accident group 31% in AHT), retinal hemorrhages (2% accident group 33% AHT). Twenty three percent of the accident group were injured in an RTA, 58% by falls, 2% in play activities. In 56% of those in the AHT group, there was no history to account for injuries. Mortality rates were 13% in the AHT group and 2% in the accident group [31].

Scalp Swellings

A *cephalhaematoma* in the newborn is bleeding between the skull and periosteum occurring more commonly after an instrumental delivery. Clinically the swelling does not cross the cranial suture lines. It must be differentiated from *caput succeda-neum* which crosses suture lines and is due to pressure of the scalp against the cervix during delivery. A *sub-aponeurotic fluid collection* presents with a scalp swelling at 3–18 weeks of age and is more often associated with an instrumental delivery. It may be mistaken for a traumatic cephalhaematoma associated with AHT. A *coagulation defect* may initiate scalp bleeding or exacerbate it after minor trauma.

A traumatic cephalhaematoma (page 66) follows direct impact by a blunt instrument or against a hard surface. King et al. (2003) reported that 54% of infants with inflicted head injury had no bruising at initial presentation [32]. Swellings may not be obvious clinically but seen on neuro-imaging. Kleinman and Spevak 1992, examined the CT scans of 35 children aged 3 months to 8 years with recent skull fractures. At least 4mm of soft tissue swelling was found in all cases [33].

Scalp swellings that are caused by impact mostly appear within minutes but may be overlooked for up to 24 hours (usually by a non-observer/perpetrator who is not on the "look out" for injuries) particularly where an infant has thick hair. They may increase in size in the 2–3 days after head injury. Some are tender to palpation for up to 72 hours and most resolve clinically by 10 days.

Rubin et al. (2003) examined 65 abused children under 2 years of age for occult head injury. All had a normal neurological examination. Inclusion criteria were one of the following: rib fractures, multiple fractures, facial injury, or age less than 6 months. Of 65 patients, 51 had neuro-imaging in addition to skeletal survey. Of these, 19 (37.3%) had an occult head injury to include scalp swelling (74%), skull fracture (74%), or intracranial injury (53%). Ophthalmic examination was performed in 14 of the 19 cases. No retinal haemorrhages were observed [34].

Other Associated Injuries

Soft tissue injuries

Bruising and abrasions, particularly to the head and neck, are associated with AHT. Barnes and Krasnokutsky (2007) reported that tears to the frenulum of the tongue or upper lip from forcing a bottle or dummy into an infant's mouth or other blunt trauma were associated with significant head injury [35].

Petska et al. (2013) described 3 infants all younger than 5 months old presenting with facial bruising which was not investigated. All three re-presented with AHT supporting a view that facial bruising in a pre-mobile infant signals the risk for further abuse [36].

Fractures

Skull fractures are due to direct impact whilst rib fractures may occur after a squeezing/shaking injury. Long bone and metaphyseal fractures have been associated with shaking. Cervical spine fractures are associated with hyperflexion-hyperextention (whiplash) injury.

Lazoritz et al. (1997) reviewed 71 children younger than 3 years of age with AHT. Thirty-two percent had extra-cranial fractures and 87% of these were multiple [37]. Bechtel et al. (2004) compared young children with serious inflicted versus non-inflicted head injury. Abused patients were more likely to have rib, long bone, and metaphyseal fractures [16].

Hobbs (1984) reported that complex skull fractures (multiple, bilateral, diastatic or depressed) were more commonly associated with AHT. Eight children in the AHT group with skull fractures had associated SDHs whilst none were seen in the non-AHT skull fracture group [38].

Apnoea

Kemp et al. (2003) reviewed 65 children under 2 years of age with an SDH secondary to AHT. Twenty-two had a history of apnoea at presentation which was associated with hypoxic ischaemic brain damage. Eighty-five percent of cases had associated injuries consistent with inflicted injury [39].

Differential Diagnosis

Accidental head injury

Both subdural and retinal haemorrhages have been reported following severe accidental injury to include high level falls, road traffic accidents and other crush injuries.

Gerber and Coffman (2007) reported that falls of more than 4 feet were associated with depressed/basilar skull fractures, SAH and cerebral contusions. In severe accidental trauma, subdural haematomas and axonal injury were reported [2].

Cranial malformations

Aneurysms, arachnoid cysts and vascular malformations may lead to intracranial bleeding with minimal trauma. Unless associated with raised intracranial pressure, retinal haemorrhages are unusual.

Meningitis, Encephalitis and Septicaemia

Post-infective effusions, subdural empyema and sepsis may be associated with retinal haemorrhages. Severe sepsis and disseminated intravascular coagulation (DIC) are associated with intracranial bleeding.

Coagulopathies and other blood disorders

Bleeding disorders may initiate both retinal and subdural haemorrhage or exacerbate them after minor trauma. Leukaemia and sickle cell anaemia are also associated with retinal haemorrhages.

Galactosaemia

This rare metabolic disorder leads to irreversible neurological damage if untreated. There are case reports of associated retinal haemorrhages.

Glutaric aciduria type I

This rare neuro-metabolic disorder is associated with widening of the subdural space and rupture of subdural vessels causing SDH often without trauma in areas of cortical atrophy. Retinal haemorrhages have been described with frontal lobe hypoplasia observed on neuro-imaging.

Hypernatraemia

SDH has been described in association with hypernatraemic dehydration from salt poisoning.

Birth trauma

SDH is more common after instrumental delivery and birth trauma. Asymptomatic subdurals sustained at birth are reported to be small, posterior and resolve by 4 weeks of age in term infants. There is no evidence that these become larger or rebleed later in infancy.

Whitby et al. (2004) examined MRI images from healthy infants born at term by normal or instrumental delivery. Fewer than 10% were found to have SDHs (9 subdurals in 111 babies). All these were in the posterior fossa by the parieto-occipital lobes, either unilateral or bilateral and just a few millimetres in depth [40].

Rooks et al. (2008) investigated 101 neonates of which 46 had SDHs detected on neuroimaging. Most were less than 3mm and resolved by 1 month (all by 3 months). All 46 had supratentorial SDHs seen in the posterior cranium. Of these, 20 (43%) had infratentorial SDHs. The authors emphasised that the pattern of SDH should not be used in isolation to distinguish between birth injury and AHT [41].

Symptomatic SDHs sustained at birth are larger and seen at any location. Infants typically present after a difficult delivery that may include emergency extraction with forceps/ventouse or emergency caesarean section. As for AHT, there is a range of clinical presentations from irritability and poor feeding to convulsions and coma. At the severe end of the spectrum (hypoxic ischaemic encephalopathy) there is a delay in establishing regular respirations/adequate heart rate with signs of encephalopathy.

Benign Enlargement of the Subarachnoid Space (BESS)

Benign enlargement of subarachnoid space may be an incidental finding on neuroimaging or present with macrocephaly (large head). BESS can increase an infant's susceptibility to SDH following minor trauma. Radiologically there is an increase in size of the subarachnoid space without ventricular dilatation.

Osteogenesis imperfecta (OI)
Parmar et al. (2007) reported that 10–30% of OI patients have a bleeding disorder which may predispose them to intracerebral bleeding [42].

Menkes disease
Kinky hair syndrome (Menkes Disease) presents with hypotonia, convulsions, failure to thrive, hypopigmentation, developmental delay and hair that is kinky, coarse, and hypopigmented. It is a progressive neurodegenerative disorder with radiographic findings that may be indistinguishable from fractures. Arteries in the brain can be distorted and brittle leading to rupture or blockage.

Other
Medical or surgical manipulations, tumours, autoimmune disorders and long-term shunting of hydrocephalus have all been associated with intracerebral bleeding.

Other Presentations

Haematomas

Chronic Subdural Haematoma
Most inflicted SDHs are resorbed over a period of days to weeks. In some cases they may evolve into a chronic subdural haematoma. Whilst chronic collections suggest a prior traumatic episode, this cannot be presumed in the absence of supporting evidence. Re-bleeds may occur in resolving SDHs but the amount of bleeding is usually small. There is no evidence that a chronic SDH may lead to large acute SDH from minor trauma.

Dias et al. (1998) reported that the time required for an acute subdural to evolve to a chronic SDH varies from days to weeks [43].

Extradural Haematoma (EDH)
Extradural (epidural) haemorrhage may occur after low-impact trauma due to tearing of the middle meningeal artery. There is bleeding into the space between the inner skull surface and dura which may progress or be self-limiting and resorb. When due to venous bleeding, EDHs are more commonly associated with accidental trauma but are also described in inflicted injury.

Subgaleal Haematoma (SGH)
An SGH is the result of bleeding between the fibrous layers of the scalp and the skull usually caused by blunt injury to the head or abusive hair-pulling that results in the scalp being lifted off the calvarium ('scalping'). It has also been associated with hair braiding.

The condition presents clinically as a boggy swelling over the scalp. There may be a skull fracture if caused by blunt injury. In the newborn, an SGH may result from vacuum extraction (ventouse delivery).

Seifert and Puschel (2006) reported a 3-year-old presenting with forehead swelling. Some hours later large bilateral periorbital haematomas developed. Ultrasound revealed extensive subgaleal haematoma. The carer confessed to pulling the child's hair [44].

Schultes et al. (2007) reported an 18-month-old boy with swelling and extensive haematoma of the forehead and eyelids. CT scan showed an extensive subgaleal haematoma. Police investigations revealed that the mother had locked the child's head firmly between her arm and chest jerking it backwards and forwards several times [45].

Onyeama et al. (2009) described a 31-month-old African American girl who presented with subgaleal haematoma a day after having her hair braided. Resolution was complete by 2 weeks [46].

Intraventricular Haemorrhage (IVH)
An IVH is bleeding into the brain's ventricular system commonly from rupture of subependymal veins as a result of a vascular malformation, coagulopathy or trauma to include surgical complications. It is common in premature infants, rare in AHT.

Intracerebral Haemorrhage (ICH)
An ICH results from ruptured intracerebral blood vessels following trauma.

Zidan and Ghanem (2011) reviewed 30 patients with ICH ranging from 1 month to 17.5 years. Trauma was the most common cause and found in 13 patients (43%), bleeding diathesis in 9 (30%), arteriovenous malformation in 5 (17%), intracranial tumour in 2 and an aneurysm in one [47].

Hygromas
Hygromas are enlarged subdural/subarachnoid spaces filled with cerebro-spinal fluid (CSF). They are observed following AHT and may develop from a chronic subdural haematoma. They may also be seen following neurosurgical procedures. Most hygromas are small and clinically insignificant. Larger ones may cause pressure effects with neurological symptoms requiring decompression.

Spinal Trauma

Infants and young children with AHT may have evidence of injury at the cranio-cervical junction causing respiratory depression. There may be damage to the lower brainstem and contusions of the spinal cord. The mechanism of injury is hyperextension–flexion as seen in shaking (page 78). Spinal cord injury is reported in fewer than 3% of child abuse cases.

Priatt (1995) described a 15-month-old who presented with quadriplegia after reportedly having fallen off a couch. There had been past history of facial burns. On examination there were multiple skin injuries, flaccid quadriplegia with anaesthesia below the neck. An MRI of the cervical spine demonstrated swelling of the spinal cord with atrophy 2 months later. There were associated fractures [48].

Hadley et al. (1989) described 13 infants following a shaking injury of whom 8 died. Of 6 postmortems there were 5 extradural and 4 sub-dural haematomas in the cervical spine with 4 contusions of the cervical cord [49].

Choudhary et al. (2012) reviewed 252 children aged 0–2 years with AHT. A second group of 70 children aged 0–2 years were treated for accidental trauma. In the AHT group 67/252 (26.5%) had spinal imaging results. Of these, 38/67 (56%) had undergone thoracolumbar imaging, with 24 (63%) having thoraco-lumbar subdural haemorrhage. This finding was rare in those with accidental trauma [50].

Outcomes Following AHT

Of all cases of AHT, 30% die, 30–50% survive with significant neurological deficits and up to 30% recover without deficit. Studies report worse outcomes for younger patients and those with cerebral injury.

Reece and Sege (2000) reported a six-fold increase in mortality (13% vs. 2%) in children with AHT versus accidental injury [51]. Ewing-Cobbs et al. (1998) reported that even in children with comparable Glasgow Coma Scale (GCS) scores, AHT resulted in more severe cognitive deficits at short-term follow-up in comparison with children with non-AHT [31].

Bonnier et al. (1995) reviewed 13 patients with AHT of whom 6 appeared to recover. However at follow-up 11/12 were diagnosed with difficulties including psychomotor delay, learning disabilities, blindness, seizures, tetraplegia, and hemi-paresis [51].

Barlow et al. (2005) reviewed cases of AHT who were followed for a mean of 59 months. Of 25 cases, 68% had abnormalities at follow-up including motor (60%), visual (48%), speech and language (64%) epilepsy (20%) and behavioural distur-bances (52%). The latter included self-injurious and self-stimulatory behaviours, hyperactivity, temper tantrums, and rage reactions. Many of these did not manifest until the second or third years of life [52].

References

1. Christian CW, Block R, Committee on Child Abuse and Neglect, American Academy of Pediatrics. Abusive head trauma in infants and children. Pediatrics. 2009;123(5):1409–11.
2. Gerber P, Coffman K. Nonaccidental head trauma in infants. Childs Nerv Syst. 2007;23(5):499–507.
3. Keenan HT, Runyan DK, Nocera M. Child outcomes and family characteristics 1 year after severe inflicted or non-inflicted traumatic brain injury. Pediatrics. 2006;117(2):317–24.
4. Duhaime AC, Christian CW, Rorke LB, Zimmerman RA. Non-accidental head injury in infants—the "shaken baby syndrome". N Engl J Med. 1998;338(25):1822–9.
5. Starling S, Holden J, Jenny C, Abusive Head Trauma: The Relationship of Perpetrators to Their Victims. Pediatrics. 1995; Vol 95/Issue 2.
6. Royal College of Pathologists. Report of a meeting on the pathology of traumatic head injury in children. 2009.

7. Adamsbaum C, Grabar S, Mejean N, Rey-Salmon C. Abusive head trauma: judicial admissions highlight violent and repetitive shaking. Pediatrics. 2010;126(3):546–55.
8. Gilliland MGF, Folberg R. Shaken babies – some have no impact injuries. J Forensic Sci. 1996;41:114–6.
9. Aoki N, Masuzawa H. Infantile acute subdural hematoma. Clinical analysis of 26 cases. Journal of neurosurgery.1984;61(2):273–80.
10. Graham DI, McIntosh TK, Maxwell WL, Nicole AD. Recent advances in neuro-trauma. J Neuropathol Exp Neurol. 2000;59:641–51.
11. Duhaime AC, Gennarelli TA, Thibault LE, Bruce DA, Margulies SS, Wiser R. The shaken baby syndrome: a clinical, pathological, and biomechanical study. J Neurosurg. 1987;66(3):409–15.
12. Kemp AM. Investigating subdural haemorrhage in infants. Arch Dis Child. 2002;86:98–102.
13. Hobbs C, Childs AM, Wynne J, Livingston J, Seal A. Subdural haematoma and effusion in infancy: an epidemiological study. Arch Dis Child. 2005;90(9):952–5.
14. Sauvageau A, Bourgault A, Raclette S. Cerebral traumatism with a playground rocking toy mimicking shaken baby syndrome. J Forensic Sci. 2008;53:479–82.
15. Denton S, Miluesnic D. Delayed sudden death in an infant following an accidental fall: a case report with review of the literature. J Forensic Med Pathol. 2003;24:371–6.
16. Bechtel K, Stoessel K, Leventhal JM, Ogle E, Teague B, Lavietes S, et al. Characteristics that distinguish accidental from abusive injury in hospitalized young children with head trauma. Pediatrics. 2004;114(1):165–8.
17. Starling SP, Patel S, Burke BL, Sirotnak AP, Stronks S, Rosquist P. Analysis of perpetrator admissions to inflicted traumatic brain injury in children. Archives of pediatrics & adolescent medicine." Arch Pediatr Adolesc Med. 2004;158(5):454–8.
18. Kemp AM, Rajaram S, Mann M, Tempest V, Farewell D, Gawne-Cain ML. What neuroimaging should be performed in children in whom inflicted brain injury is suspected? A systematic review. Clin Radiol. 2009;64(5):473–83.
19. Royal College of Radiologists, Royal College of Paediatrics and Child Health Standards for radiological investigations of suspected non-accidental injury. 2008.
20. Wells RB, Vetter C, Laud PM. Intracranial hemorrhage in children younger than 3 years: prediction of intent. Arch Pediatr Adolesc Med. 2002;156(3):252–7.
21. Hymel KP, Rumack CM, Hay TC, Strain JD, Jenny C. Comparison of intracranial computed tomographic (CT) findings in pediatric abusive and accidental head trauma. Pediatr Radiol. 1997;27(9):743–7.
22. Tung GA, Kumar M, Richardson RC, Jenny C, Brown WD. Comparison of accidental and non-accidental traumatic head injury in children on non-contrast computed tomography. Pediatrics. 2006;118(2):626–33.
23. Watts P, Maguire S, Kwok T, Talabani B, Mann M, Wiener J, Lawson Z, Kemp A. Newborn retinal hemorrhages: a systematic review. J AAPOS. 2013;17(1):70–8.
24. Watts P, Obi E. Retinal folds and retinoschisis in accidental and non-accidental head injury. Eye. 2008;22(12):1514–6.
25. Hughes LA, May K, Talbot JF, Parsons MA. Incidence, distribution, and duration of birth-related retinal hemorrhages: a prospective study. J AAPOS. 2006;10(2):102–6.
26. Adamo MA, Drazin D, Smith C, Waldman JB. Comparison of accidental and non-accidental traumatic brain injuries in infants and toddlers: demographics, neurosurgical interventions, and outcomes. J Neurosurg Pediatr. 2009;4(5):414–9.
27. Kemp AM, Jaspan T, Griffiths J, Stoodley N, Mann MK, Tempest V. Neuroimaging: what neuroradiological features distinguish abusive from non-abusive head trauma? A systematic review. Arch Dis Child. 2011;96(12):1103–12.
28. Vinchon M, de Foort-Dhellemmes S, Desurmont M, Delestret I. Confessed abuse versus witnessed accidents in infants: comparison of clinical, radiological, and ophthalmological data in corroborated cases. Childs Nerv Syst. 2010;26(5):637–45.
29. Thomas AG, et al. Patterns of accidental cranio-cerebral injury occurring in early childhood. Arch Dis Child. 2013;98:787–92.

30. Ewing-Cobbs L, Kramer L, Prasad M, Canales DN, Lovis PT, Fletcher JM, et al. Neuroimaging, physical and developmental findings after inflicted and non-inflicted traumatic brain injury in young children. Pediatrics. 1998;102(2 Pt 1):300–7.
31. Reece RM, Sege R. Childhood head injuries: accidental or inflicted? Arch Pediatr Adolesc Med. 2000;154(1):11–5.
32. King WJ, MacKay M, Sirnick A, Canada Shaken Baby Study Group. Shaken baby syndrome in Canada: clinical characteristics and outcomes of hospital cases. Can Med Assoc J. 2003;21168(2):155–9.
33. Kleinman PK, Spevak MR. Soft tissue swelling and acute skull fractures. J Pediatr. 1992;121(5 Pt 1):737–9.
34. Rubin DM, Christian CW, Bilaniuk LT, Zazyczny KA, Durbin DR. Occult head injury in high-risk abused children. Pediatrics. 2003;111(6 Pt 1):1382–6.
35. Barnes PD, Krasnokutsky M. Imaging of the central nervous system in suspected or alleged non-accidental injury including the mimics. Top Magn Reson Imaging. 2007;18(1):53–4.
36. Petska HW, Sheets LK, Knox BL. Facial bruising as a precursor to abusive head trauma. Clin Pediatr (Phila). 2013;52(1):86–8.
37. Lazoritz S, Baldwin S, Kini N. The whiplash shaken infant syndrome: has Caffey's syndrome changed or have we changed his syndrome? Child Abuse Negl. 1997;21(10): 1009–14.
38. Hobbs CJ. Skull fracture and the diagnosis of abuse. Arch Dis Child. 1984;59:246–52.
39. Kemp AM, Stoodley N, Cobley C, Coles L, Kemp KW. Apnoea and brain swelling in non-accidental head injury. Arch Dis Child. 2003;88(6):472–6; discussion 472–6.
40. Whitby EH, Griffiths PD, Rutter S, Smith MF, Sprigg A, Ohadike P, et al. Frequency and natural history of subdural haemorrhages in babies and relation to obstetric factors. Lancet. 2004;363(9412):846–51.
41. Rooks VJ, Eaton JP, Ruess L, Petermann GW, Keck-Wherley J, Pedersen RC. Prevalence and evolution of intracranial hemorrhage in asymptomatic term infants. AJNR Am J Neuroradiol. 2008;29(6):1082–9.
42. Parmar CD, Sinha AK, Hayhurst C, May PL, O'Brien DF. Epidural hematoma formation following trivial head trauma in a child with osteogenesis imperfecta. J Neurosurg. 2007;106(Suppl Pediatrics):57–60.
43. Dias MS, Backstrom J, Falk M, Li V. Serial radiography in the infant shaken impact syndrome. Pediatr Neurosurg. 1998;29(2):77–85.
44. Seifert D, Püschel K. Subgaleal hematoma in child abuse. Forensic Sci Int. 2006;157(2–3): 131–3. Epub 2005 Sep 46.
45. Schultes A, Lackner K, Rothschild MA. "Scalping": A possible indicator for child abuse [German]. Rechtsmedizin 2007;17(5):318–20.
46. Onyeama CO, Lotke M, Edelstein B. Subgaleal hematoma secondary to hair braiding in a 31-month-old child. Pediatr Emerg Care. 2009;25(1):40–1.
47. Zidan I, Ghanem A. 2011 Intracerebral hemorrhage in children. Alex J Med. 2012;48(2): 139–45.
48. Priatt JH. Isolated spinal cord injury as a presentation of child abuse. Pediatrics. 1995;96:780–2.
49. Hadley MN, Sonntag VK, Rekate HL, Murphy A. The infant whiplash-shaken injury syndrome a clinical and pathological study. Neurosurgery. 1989;24:536–40.
50. Choudhary AK, Bradford RK, Dias MS, Moore GJ, Boal DK. Spinal subdural hemorrhage in abusive head trauma: a retrospective study. Radiology. 2012;262(1):216–23.
51. Bonnier C, Nassogne M, Errard P. Outcome and prognosis of whiplash shaken infant syndrome; late consequences after a symptom-free interval. Dev Med Child Neurol. 1995;37(11): 943–56.
52. Barlow KM, Thomson E, Johnson D, Minns RA. Late neurologic and cognitive sequelae of inflicted traumatic brain injury in infancy. Pediatrics. 2005;116:e174–85.

Further Reading

Maguire S, Pickerd N, Farewell D, Mann M, Tempest V, Kemp AM. Which clinical features distinguish inflicted from non-inflicted brain injury? A systematic review. Arch Dis Child. 2009;94(11):860–7.
CORE INFO Cardiff Child Protection Systematic Reviews/www.core-info.cardiff.ac.uk/ (accessed 15.04.17).

Abdominal and Thoracic Trauma

6

Abstract

Abdominal and thoracic trauma accounts for just 5% of all cases of abuse but carries a mortality rate of up to 50%. Injury may be occult (no clinical signs) leading to delayed diagnosis. Death from bleeding, organ injury and infection including peritonitis following gut perforation have all been recorded.

Most abdominal and thoracic injuries are accidental, resulting from blunt trauma following severe falls or road traffic accidents. Sports injuries or impact against bicycle handle bars or other hard objects may cause similar injury.

In inflicted injury, impact from a blunt instrument or against a hard surface are common mechanisms. Inflicted abdominal injury is more common under 4 years of age whilst accidental injury predominates in older children. Children with inflicted thoracic injuries are usually younger than 5 years of age.

Ledbetter et al. (1998) compared 156 cases of abdominal injuries of which 11% were inflicted mainly in the younger age group (mean age 2½ years). There was a higher incidence of hollow viscus injuries [1].

High mortality rates are due to the child's susceptibility to injury, delays in seeking medical attention and often no signs of external trauma. There may be severe bleeding and co-existing injuries.

Barnes et al. (2005) reviewed 20 children with abdominal injuries due to abuse (16 less than 5 years of age) and 164 with injuries to the abdomen due to accident (112 road traffic accidents, 52 falls). Eleven abused children had an intestinal injury (6 died), compared with five (all over 5 years of age) who were injured by a fall. The authors noted that small-bowel injuries were significantly more common in abused children [2].

Trokel et al. (2004) reviewed 664 cases of blunt abdominal trauma (RTA excluded) in patients aged 0–4 years. Abuse was the commonest mechanism of injury (40.5%). Mortality rates were as follows: only abdominal trauma (8.8%),

D.L. Robinson, *Pediatric Forensic Evidence*, DOI 10.1007/978-3-319-45337-8_6

abdominal and skeletal injuries (11.1%), abdominal injuries with AHT and skeletal injury (29.6%) and abdominal with AHT but without skeletal injury (57.7%). Presumably, the presence of skeletal injuries allowed for more prompt diagnosis and improved outcomes [3].

Blunt Abdominal Trauma

Susceptibility

A child's abdominal wall is thinner than an adult's, with less fat and muscle for protection. Children may be unable to brace themselves in anticipation of injury. Ribs cover less of the abdomen and are compressible, potentially crushing organs which are proportionally larger. Solid organs in children have a weak internal structure and are damaged easily.

Gastric or bowel distention following a feed or from excessive crying may increase the risk of bowel perforation after trauma. The most susceptible organs for injury are the small bowel (particularly duodenum), liver and pancreas.

Bush et al. (1996) reviewed postmortem data of 211 children under the age of 12 years where resuscitation attempts had been made from between 5–80 minutes. The cause of death was cot death (56%), drowning (8%), congenital cardiac defects (7%) and pneumonia (4%). Fifteen children (7%) sustained injuries including retroperitoneal haemorrhage, pneumothorax, pulmonary haemorrhage, epicardial haematoma and perforation of the stomach. Rib fractures at the costochondral junction were found in one child [4].

Mode and Types of Injury

Shearing of the posterior attachments or vascular supply of abdominal organs results from rapid acceleration-deceleration forces as seen in road traffic accidents, significant falls or inflicted injury. Blows at the sites of bowel fixation may also lead to vessel disruption and severe bleeding. Intestinal perforations may occur [5].

In abuse, injuries to the bowel result from single or repeated blows to the mid-abdomen from a blunt instrument or impact against a hard surface. Hollow or solid organs may be crushed against vertebrae causing rupture with peritonitis.

Children who are restrained in seat belts that cover the lap with or without shoulder restraints, are at risk of abdominal injury. The belt may slip to rest over the abdomen not the hips as intended. Sudden acceleration-deceleration usually during an RTA may cause blunt injuries to the abdomen and spine. Children riding a bicycle at speed with sudden deceleration may fall on to the handlebars causing significant injuries to the bowel, pancreas, or liver. There will usually be a credible history of an accidental event and its aftermath.

Maguire et al. (2013) reviewed 88 studies of children aged 0–18 with inflicted visceral injuries. Of these, 64 included abdominal injuries where patients were younger (2.5–3.7 years) than accidentally injured children (7.6–10.3 years). Duodenal injuries were common in abused children but not reported following accidental injury in those less than 4 years old. Liver and pancreatic injuries were frequent. Abdominal bruising was found in only 20%. Other injuries included fractures, burns and head injuries. The mortality from inflicted abdominal injuries was 53% compared to 21% for accidental injuries [6].

Medical Assessment

Multidisciplinary Approach
Collaboration between paediatricians, surgeons and pathologists is needed to establish timing especially for hollow viscus injury with delayed presentation. Social care should be consulted early where inflicted injury is suspected. The police will visit the family home, interview carers and collect forensic evidence. Child protection protocols should be followed (pages 16–17).

History
A comprehensive medical history and examination should be undertaken, as described in chapter 1, pages 4–6. Systems enquiries, past medical and family history are all relevant. In abdominal trauma vomiting and abdominal pain are the commonest presenting symptoms. The account of an accident and its aftermath is compared with clinical findings and the developmental stage of the child.

Factors that raise concern for abuse and those associated with abuse are discussed on pages 7–12. Following accidental injury, medical attention is usually sought promptly. In abuse, a delay in seeking care is more common. The child may appear to recover, settle and sleep. Further symptoms may be delayed with carers feeling reassured that no harm had been caused.

Other factors that raise concerns are a clinical examination that does not match the account of injury, no credible history of a memorable event and its aftermath, discrepant accounts and a history that does not fit with the child's developmental abilities. There may be vague accounts of a minor injury. Falls from beds, couches or stairway falls are unlikely to result in significant abdominal injury [7]. The carer may blame a sibling, the family may be known to children's social care with repeated medical attendances for injuries. There may be other injuries or signs of neglect.

Examination and Management
Physical examination should include observation of the parent-child interaction, signs of neglect, assessment of growth and development, systems examination and a careful search for any skin marks or other injuries with documentation on body maps and medical images.

On presentation the spectrum ranges from an asymptomatic child brought by a concerned carer following injury to one with abdominal signs or clinical shock from fluid loss and sepsis.

Initial observations including temperature, pulse, blood pressure, capillary refill time, respiratory rate, oxygen saturation and mental status will identify patients in clinical shock requiring management of the airways, breathing and circulation. For the latter, fluids or urgent blood transfusion may be required with antibiotics, pain relief, assisted ventilation or surgery to identify bleeding points or perforations.

A secondary survey includes a complete examination to identify any injuries whether abdominal, head, skin or bone (page 6). Children with inflicted abdominal injuries particularly those under 1 year of age, may have associated injuries such as abusive head trauma (AHT), burns and fractures.

There may be signs of obstruction, bleeding and infection. Abdominal distention may be due to gastric air, organ injury or peritonitis. The latter is evidenced by abdominal tenderness, distention, rigidity and diminished bowel sounds. Bile (green) stained vomitus indicates likely obstruction or perforation.

Symptoms and signs depend on the location and severity of injury as well as virulence of leaked bacteria. Haematomas developing from bruising to the bowel wall may lead to obstruction or necrosis. Following some injuries the child may appear to improve then slowly deteriorate as bowel necrosis and perforation develop. Signs may be minimal at presentation with careful observation required. Strictures developing days or weeks after injury present with vomiting and abdominal distention. Acute appendicitis with bowel perforation and other abdominal pathologies must be excluded.

Many children with serious abdominal trauma have no external injury to the abdomen [8]. The absence of such injury, a vague history and non-specific abdominal symptoms may all lead to delayed diagnosis of inflicted injury with clinicians giving priority to resuscitation.

A 3-year-old child was brought by his mother to ED with breathing difficulties, fever, vomiting and abdominal pain of 24 hours duration. On examination he was in clinical shock requiring fluid resuscitation and assisted ventilation. The abdomen was tense but with no obvious bruising. Abdominal CT showed multiple linear echogenic foci within liver parenchyma with evidence of bowel ischaemia and perforation. His mother was observed to have a black eye (concealed with make-up) which she had said occurred after a fall. At operation multiple intestinal perforations were found and a diagnosis of inflicted abdominal trauma made. Child protection investigations revealed a pattern of domestic violence perpetrated by the father.

Laboratory investigations

Suggested investigations and assessments depending on the clinical presentation are documented on page 7. Anaemia indicates blood loss, haemodilution following fluid resuscitation, or both. Serial measurements of haemoglobin (haematocrit) if falling indicate continuing blood loss.

The C-reactive protein (CRP), and white cell count may be elevated with peritonitis or as non-specific indicators of stress. Platelets may be low in disseminated intravascular coagulation (DIC) or raised as a consequence of blood loss. Coagulation investigations are abnormal in DIC. A blood gas may show metabolic acidosis with raised lactate. Renal, liver and pancreatic function tests if abnormal may provide a guide to specific organ injury.

Radiological Investigations

Plain abdominal radiographs

Radiographs may show obstruction, fluid, foreign bodies, free air or bony injury. Upright or decubitis (side) views more reliably demonstrate free air as a result of perforation.

Ultrasound

Ultrasound is not as sensitive as CT but valuable in diagnosing free fluid, intestinal haematomas, retroperitoneal and other injuries.

CT scan

Abdominal contrast CT is the investigation of choice in abdominal trauma for the diagnosis of organ injury. It is less reliable in diagnosing intestinal perforations, haematomas, and mesenteric injury. Solid organ injuries may be overlooked if an abdominal CT scan is omitted.

Radionuclide scans

These are occasionally used to assess specific organ injury.

Upper Gastrointestinal Radiographs and Endoscopy

If the child is stable, upper gastrointestinal radiology and endoscopy may permit the location and extent of injuries to be visualised.

Skeletal survey and Head CT

Many children have additional injuries. A skeletal survey is required for those under 2 years of age with follow up films 10–14 days later. A CT head scan is mandatory for any infant under 1 year where there is evidence of physical abuse (with ophthalmology referral) and should be considered in children up to the age of 2 years or older if clinically indicated.

Specific Organ Injury

Urinary Tract and muscle injury

Blows to the flank or impact against a hard immoveable surface may result in renal contusions or lacerations. Kidneys are relatively protected by their location and renal trauma is often associated with other abdominal organ injury. Children present with flank pain and tenderness. There may be visible blood in the urine and a positive urine dipstick for blood, or microscopy showing red blood cells.

When the urine is positive for blood by dipstick, but microscopy shows no red blood cells, myoglobinuria or haemoglobinuria should be suspected. Myoglobinuria is the presence of myoglobin in the urine and associated with muscle destruction. A raised creatinine phosphokinase (CK) also indicates muscle damage. Trauma may also lead to haemogobinuria where haemoglobin is detected in the urine.

Traumatic rupture of the bladder or ureters leads to urine and blood leaking into the peritoneal cavity with resorption resulting in potential electrolyte imbalance, acidosis, and renal failure. Peritonitis, abscess and fistula formation may result.

Liver

The size and location of the liver makes it vulnerable to injury. Lacerations and haematomas result from blunt trauma to the upper abdomen. Penetrating injuries are rare. Small lacerations and subcapsular haematomas can be treated conservatively if bleeding is controlled. Otherwise urgent surgical exploration is required.

After blunt liver trauma, levels of the liver enzymes aspartate aminotransferase and alanine aminotransferase (AST, ALT) may rise rapidly, then decline over several days [9]. Hennes et al. (1990) reviewed the medical records of 43 children with elevated serum AST and ALT who underwent abdominal CT for blunt abdominal trauma. Nineteen (44.2%) had AST levels greater than 450 iU/L (normal range 10–40) and ALT levels greater than 250 iU/L (normal 7–56) with 17/19 having hepatic injury identified on abdominal CT [10].

Other causes for abnormal liver function including viral illnesses, hepatitis and other liver diseases must be excluded but the rapid rise and subsequent fall of liver enzymes observed following injury is not typical of these conditions. Nevertheless, the true predictive value of the above tests remains uncertain.

Spleen

Splenic injuries are uncommon in abuse and are usually associated with sports injuries, road traffic accidents and severe falls. The spleen is protected by being 'tucked' under the ribs. Injury is suspected where there is left-sided chest or upper abdominal pain. Haematomas may develop after injury with delayed rupture and potentially severe bleeding days after injury.

Pancreas

Blunt trauma to the upper abdomen may cause pancreatic injury with the body of the pancreas being crushed against the spine. Pancreatitis may result with raised amylase and lipase levels which do not correlate with the extent of injury. Other causes of pancreatitis including biliary tract disease, congenital anomalies, cystic fibrosis, infection and some medications must be excluded.

Children present with abdominal pain and distention, vomiting and fever. Evolving haematomas may lead to blood loss presenting with anaemia in an otherwise stable child. There may be delayed development of pancreatitis, pseudocyst, bowel obstruction, necrosis and perforation.

Stomach

Direct blows to the abdomen or shearing forces as a result of rapid acceleration-deceleration in road traffic accidents or severe falls may cause stomach or bowel perforations. Symptoms and signs develop rapidly with a distended, tense abdomen, and pneumoperitoneum on plain radiograph. Urgent surgery is required.

Duodenum

The commonest hollow organ injury is to the 3rd and 4th fourth parts of the duodenum which is fixed and lies close to the vertebral column. Haematomas and perforations result from blunt trauma and crush injuries against vertebrae. Bleeding and haematomas may narrow the duodenal lumen leading to partial or complete obstruction.

Abdominal pain, tenderness and vomiting may develop slowly. Signs of peritonitis following perforation may be absent because of the retroperitoneal location of the duodenum. There may be injury to the closely located pancreas. Plain radiographs may show gastric distention and decreased bowel gas with abdominal CT providing more accurate information.

Jejunum and Ileum

Perforations and haematomas of the small intestine occur after blows to the abdomen or shearing forces in both inflicted and accidental trauma. Most injuries are jejunal with signs of peritonitis and sepsis developing over hours.

A 3-month-old infant was presented for care with pallor, multiple bruises, decreased consciousness and in clinical shock. Her abdomen was distended and tense with only minor bruising. The initial blood pH was 6.9 (profoundly acidotic), haemoglobin 80 which dropped to 59 (normal 105–122). She was found to have a significant liver laceration, lung contusions, pericardial effusion, rib and femoral fractures. The first Tropinin level (cardiac enzyme) was 1300 which fell to 170 suggesting cardiac trauma. Hepatic enzymes, (ALT, AST and gamma GT) all rose rapidly then fell to normal levels in keeping with acute liver trauma. There was no history of an accident or its aftermath with the mother reporting only an unusual cry and vomiting. The infant received intensive care (no surgery) and made a full recovery.

Colon

Injuries to the colon following blunt abdominal trauma are rare. If there is rectal bleeding or other signs of trauma, a full CSA assessment is required. Peritonitis is common and surgical repair usually required.

Cardiothoracic Injuries

Susceptibility

A child's ribs are flexible and less susceptible to fractures than an adults. Bones are incompletely ossified, ligamentous attachments supple and musculature not fully developed. Within the upper airways the trachea in infancy is narrow and short. Small changes in diameter from inflammation or haematoma may lead to rapid respiratory deterioration. Inflicted cardio-thoracic injuries are more common in infants younger than 12 months with accidental injury predominating between 1–3 years.

DiScala et al. (2000) compared hospitalised children under five who had either suffered inflicted or accidental injuries. Thoracic injuries were more common following child abuse (12.5%) than after accidental trauma (4.5%) [11]. Roaten et al. 2006 reported that pulmonary contusions, rib and clavicular fractures were three times more common in inflicted (17%) than in accidental trauma (6%) [12].

Darling et al. (2014) reviewed 65 infants and toddlers with rib fractures caused by abuse or accident. Of the 65 cases, 47 (72%) were inflicted injuries. Abused children had more rib fractures whilst intrathoracic injuries were more common with accidents (55.6% vs. 12.8%). Intracranial, intra-abdominal injuries and skull fractures were equally frequent, but other extrathoracic fractures were more common with abuse (70.2% vs. 16.7%) [13].

Mode of Injury

Thoracic injuries result from accidental blunt trauma following severe falls, road traffic accidents (RTA), sports injuries, impact against bicycle handle bars or other hard objects. In abuse, injuries to the chest result from single or repeated blows from a blunt instrument or impact against a hard surface. Dysrythmias (disorganised cardiac rhythm) and collapse may follow blunt trauma to the chest.

Denton and Kalelkar (2000) reported two children aged 14 months and 3 years who collapsed and died immediately after being struck on the chest by a closed fist (commotio cordis). No external chest trauma was visible in one child [14].

Cumberland et al. (1991) reported intimal tears of the right atrium found at autopsy in six children. Three teenagers died following road traffic accidents and three were victims of abuse. All had associated liver lacerations and other signs of abdominal trauma [15].

Clinical Assessment

Multidisciplinary Approach
Collaboration between paediatricians, cardiologists, chest physicians, surgeons and pathologists is essential as children with chest injury can deteriorate rapidly requiring specialist care. Social care and the police should be consulted early if abuse is suspected. Child protection protocols should be followed (pages 16–17).

History
A comprehensive medical history and examination should be undertaken as described in chapter 1, pages 4–6. Factors that raise concern for abuse and those associated with abuse are discussed on pages 7–12.

After the initial painful aftermath of chest trauma, a child may appear to recover, settle and sleep. There may be a delay in presentation to hospital with no history of accident or vague accounts of a minor injury. Chest pain, haemoptysis (blood arising from lung tissue) and breathing difficulties are the commonest presenting symptoms.

Examination and Management
Physical Examination should include observation of the parent-child interaction, signs of neglect, assessment of growth and development, the systems examination and a careful search for any skin marks or other injuries with documentation on body maps and medical images.

On presentation, the spectrum ranges from an asymptomatic child brought by a concerned carer following chest injury to one with chest pain, breathing difficulties, haemoptysis or collapse from a cardiac cause.

Clinical findings may include oro-nasal bleeding, hypoxia, difficulty breathing, clinical shock, respiratory or heart failure. Oral bleeding from the latter may have a frothy appearance. Clinical shock is evidenced by cold peripheries, hypoxaemia, rapid thready pulse, hypotension, lethargy and coma. Myocardial dysfunction from dysrhythmias may result in sudden death. Injury to major blood vessels may rarely cause significant blood loss.

The clinical priority will be to resuscitate and stabilise the infant or child. Initial observations to include temperature, pulse, blood pressure, capillary refill time, respiratory rate, oxygen saturation and mental status, will identify patients requiring emergency treatment.

A secondary survey will include a full physical examination to identify any injuries whether chest, abdominal, head, skin or bone (page 6). This to-gether with a chest radiograph, are often sufficient to raise concerns for inflicted trauma. There may be few or no signs of external injury.

Children, particularly those under 1 year of age may have other injuries such as abusive head trauma (AHT), burns and fractures.

Patients with suspected cardiac injuries require continuous ECG monitoring. An urgent 12-lead ECG may reveal a cardiac rhythm disturbance that requires emergency management with drugs or DC shock.

Laboratory investigations

Suggested investigations and assessments depending on the clinical presentation are documented on page 7. Anaemia indicates blood loss, haemodilution following fluid resuscitation or both. Serial measurements of haemoglobin (haematocrit) if falling indicate continuing blood loss.

The white cell count, platelet count and C-reactive protein (CRP) may be elevated as non-specific indicators of stress. Platelets may be low in disseminated intravascular coagulation (DIC) or raised as a consequence of blood loss. Coagulation investigations are abnormal in DIC. A blood gas may show metabolic or respiratory acidosis with a raised lactate.

Elevated Creatinine Kinase-MB fraction (CK-MB) and cardiac troponin T (cTNT) suggests ischaemic myocardial injury.

Radiological Investigations

Chest radiograph

This may show lung contusion, infection, alveolar collapse or fractures.

Micro-laryngobronchoscopy

Visualisation of the pharynx, larynx and trachea with a flexible endoscope identifies specific injuries.

CT scan

Chest CT detects lung injury and rib fractures.

Skeletal survey and Head CT

A skeletal survey is required for those under 2 years of age with follow-up films 10–14 days later. A CT head scan is mandatory for any infant under 1 year where there is evidence of physical abuse (with ophthalmology referral) and should be considered in children up to the age of 2 years or older where clinically indicated.

Cardiac Echo

If cardiac injury is suspected, a cardiac echo should be undertaken by a paediatric cardiologist.

Specific Injuries

The most frequently observed injuries are pulmonary contusions. Penetrating injuries are rare but occasionally seen.

Ismail (2012) reviewed 472 paediatric patients with chest trauma of whom 2.1% had penetrating, 97.9% blunt trauma. The following injuries were documented: pulmonary contusions (27.1%), lacerations (6.9%), rib fractures (23.9%), flail chest (2.5%), haemothorax (18%), haemopneumothorax (11.8%), pneumothorax (23.7%). A smaller number sustained surgical emphysema, tracheo-bronchial and diaphragmatic injuries. Additional injuries included head (38.9%), fractures (33.5%), and abdominal (16.7%). The overall mortality rate was 7.2% with multiple injuries being the main cause of death [16].

Rib fractures

Rib fractures (page 67) are suspicious for inflicted injury. They are commonly the result of shaking injuries although may also result from direct impact.

Intrathoracic injury

Accidental impact from falls and road traffic accidents or inflicted chest trauma may cause focal pulmonary injury. Chest radiograph may show abnormal infiltrates.

Pneumothorax (air in the pleural cavity) may result from rib fractures but also blunt chest trauma without fractures. Tension pneumothorax may lead to hypoxia and respiratory failure requiring urgent drainage with needle thoracocentesis followed by a pleural drain.

Haemothorax (blood in the pleural cavity) may result from laceration of lung tissue following blunt chest trauma. As for pneumothorax, tension may lead to hypoxia and respiratory failure. Chylothorax results from lymph (formed in the digestive tract), leaking into the pleural cavity from damage to the thoracic duct and has been associated with shaking injuries [17, 18].

Pharyngeal, oesophageal and tracheal injuries

Damage to the upper airways, oesophagus or trachea may result from forced insertion of a foreign body (often an adult finger) into the mouth and upper airways or instillation of caustic substances (page 179). Lacerations, burns and perforations have been described. An assessment for CSA may be required.

Injury may lead to respiratory symptoms from compression by a foreign body, bleeding, infection or pneumomediastinum (air within the mediastinum). Clinical findings include respiratory difficulties, subcutaneous emphysema with neck swelling, oro-nasal bleeding and visible injury. Perforation burns from ingestion of caustic substances present with drooling, difficulty swallowing, stridor, respiratory distress and visible burns.

References

1. Ledbetter DJ, Hatch Jr EI, Feldman KW, Fligner CL, Tapper D. Diagnostic and surgical implications of child abuse. Arch Surg. 1988;123(9):1101–5.
2. Barnes PM, Norton CM, Dunstan FD, Kemp AM, Yates DW, Sibert JR. Abdominal injury due to child abuse. Lancet. 2005;366(9481):234–5.
3. Trokel M, DiScala C, Terrin NC, Sege RD. Blunt abdominal injury in the young pediatric patient: child abuse and patient outcomes. Child Maltreat. 2004;9:111–7.
4. Bush CM, Jones JS, Cohle SD, Johnson H. Pediatric injuries from cardiopulmonary resuscitation. Ann Emerg Med. 1996;28(1):40–4.
5. Kleinman PK. Visceral trauma. In: Kleinman PK, editor. Diagnostic imaging of child abuse. Baltimore: Williams and Wilkins; 1987. p. 115–58.
6. Maguire SA, Upadhyaya M, Evans A, Mann MK, Haroon MM, Tempest V, Lumb RC, Kemp AM. A systematic review of abusive visceral injuries in childhood--their range and recognition. Child Abuse Negl. 2013;37(7):430–45.
7. Joffe M, Ludwig S. Stairway injuries in children. Pediatrics. 1988;82(3):457–61.
8. Cooper A, Floyd T, Barlow B, Niemirska M, Ludwig S, Seidl T, et al. Major blunt trauma due to child abuse. J Trauma. 1988;28:1483–7.
9. Baxter AL, Lindberg DM, Burke BL, Shults J, Holmes JF. Hepatic enzyme decline after pediatric blunt trauma: a tool for timing child abuse? Child Abuse Negl. 2008;32:838–45.
10. Hennes HM, Smith DS, Schneider K, Hegenbarth MA, Duma MA, Jona JZ. Elevated liver transaminase levels in children with blunt abdominal trauma: a predictor of liver injury. Pediatrics. 1990;86:87–90.
11. DiScala C, Sege R, Li G, Reece RM. Child abuse and unintentional injuries a 10 year retrospective. Arch Pediatr Adolesc Med. 2000;154:16–22.
12. Roaten JB, Partrick DA, Nydam TL, Bensard DD, Hendrickson RJ, Sirotnak AP, Karrer FM. Nonaccidental trauma is a major cause of morbidity and mortality among patients at a regional level 1 pediatric trauma center. J Pediatr Surg. 2006;41(12):2103–5.
13. Darling SE, Done SL, Friedman SD, Feldman KW. Frequency of intra-thoracic injuries in children younger than 3 years with rib fractures. Pediatr Radiol. 2014;44(10):1230–6.
14. Denton JS, Kalelkar MB. Homicidal commotio cordis in two children. J Forensic Sci. 2000;45:734–5.
15. Cumberland GD, Riddick L, McConnell CF. Intimal tears of the right atrium of the heart due to blunt force injuries to the abdomen: its mechanism and implications. Am J Forensic Med Pathol. 1991;12(2):102–4.
16. Ismail M, Ibrahim al-Refaie R. Chest trauma in children. Arch Bronchoneumol. 2012;48(10):362–6.
17. Anderst JD. Chylothorax and child abuse. Pediatr Crit Care Med. 2007;8:394–6.
18. Geismar SL, Tilelli JA, Campbell JB, Chiaro JJ. Chylothorax as a manifestation of child abuse. Pediatr Emerg Care. 1997;13:386–9.

Further Reading

Gaines BA, Ford HR. Abdominal and pelvic trauma in children. Crit Care Med. 2002; 30(11 Suppl):S416–23.

CORE INFO Cardiff Child Protection Systematic Reviews, www.core-info.cardiff.ac.uk/ (accessed 15.04.17).

Neglect and Emotional Abuse

7

Abstract

Neglect is failure to provide nutrition, shelter, emotional support, safe living conditions, health needs and education to a child, within available resources. It is exposing a child to harm and may adversely affect physical or mental health impeding social and developmental progress [1]. The effects of neglect may be cumulative with early intervention designed to avoid long-term consequences. Substitution with sensitive care is usually followed by significant improvements in development, behaviour and social adjustment. Carers have responsibilities, as does society. Some cultural practices are unacceptable and may require intervention.

Neglect is the most common form of maltreatment. Brandon et al. (2013) reported that 60% of Serious Case Reviews over a 2-year period included the diagnosis [2].

Dubowitz et al. (2000) focussed on the shared failure of carers, family, community, and society to meet a child's basic needs encouraging professionals to concentrate on the strengths and weaknesses of a child's home environment [3].

When faced with a neglected child, support including practical, educational, medical and emotional inputs are priorities. Many infants who fail to thrive due to poor nutrition come from single-parent families with poor resources or lack of knowledge of basic child care. Non-judgemental support with a focus on the un-met needs of both family and child are starting points.

Types of Neglect

Physical

This is a failure to meet a child's basic physical needs. Inadequate nutrition leads to failure to thrive whilst unhealthy diets predispose to obesity. Lack of adequate clothing, heating and furniture pose risks. Lack of hygiene increases the chance of infection, pain and discomfort particularly when there is dental caries. Poor safety

© Springer International Publishing Switzerland 2017
D.L. Robinson, *Pediatric Forensic Evidence*, DOI 10.1007/978-3-319-45337-8_7

measures within the home pose significant risks to the child. Poverty may severely limit a carer's ability to provide essentials.

Emotional

Emotional abuse includes withholding or limiting basic emotional nurturance and affection as well as a failure to seek care for emotional or behavioural problems. There may be overprotection limiting normal social functioning or inappropriate expectations. Children may witness domestic violence and drug or alcohol misuse. There may be inadequate structure and chaotic home circumstances. Infants may be left alone and under-stimulated for many hours inhibiting their natural development.

Medical

Medical neglect is a failure to present a child for medical care when needed or delaying such care. The carer may minimise the illness or fail to administer medication or treatments prescribed. There may be illness fabrication or induction (FII).

Supervisional

Supervisional neglect is a failure to provide adequate supervision to prevent injury and to protect the child from harm. It includes leaving a child 'home alone' or repeatedly moving a child between carers or leaving him or her with others for days. Consequences can be life-threatening. Chaotic home circumstances where a carer is pressurised by domestic or psychological issues and may be in personal crisis can lead to poor supervision.

Educational

Educational neglect is failure to facilitate a child's education within legal requirements, permitting chronic absence from school or failing to attend to special educational needs. There may be neglect within the home to include poor stimulation, guidance or acknowledgment of a child's achievements.

Effects of Neglect

The effect of neglect depends on which needs are not being met, the severity and duration, the age of the child and effectiveness of interventions.

Hobbs et al. (1993) reported that neglectful parenting was evidenced by dirty, ill-fitting clothing, excessive nappy rash, a bald patch on the back of the head, poor grooming and hygiene [4].

Peterson and Urquiza (1993) reported that the effects of neglect included withdrawn affect, decreased social interactions, disorganised and aggressive interactions with peers and fewer positive play behaviours [5]. De-Panfilis (2006) reported that some children are resilient and despite being neglected mature and develop normally [6].

Adolescent neglect is associated with suicide or serious injury from risk-taking behaviours.

Physical Neglect

Clinical Assessment

Multidisciplinary Approach
Collaboration between paediatricians, nurses, social care, CAMHS, playgroup and school staff is required to gain a clear understanding of the degree of neglect and measures needed to assist the child and family. Where neglect has been severe, the police may visit the family home, interview carers and collect forensic evidence.

A referral to children's social care may be required and local safeguarding children's board (LSCB) procedures followed. A telephone discussion should be followed by a referral in writing on a standard form (pages 16–17).

History
A comprehensive medical history and examination should be undertaken (chapter 1, pages 4–6). A full medical history including a chronology with birth details, attendances, non-attendances, diagnoses, surgical procedures, accident history, use of other health services (e.g. dentist, optician) and interventions will provide an initial understanding of the child's health needs (Table 7.1).

The family and social history, including financial resources, physical and mental health, alcohol or drug use and help being offered through social care and other agencies, should all be assessed. Enquiries about development and behaviour in different settings, particularly school or play-group should be made.

The carer's understanding of child's health, development and needs should be assessed. A mother may have learning or other disabilities. She may have a serious eating disorder such as anorexia nervosa and have difficulties feeding her child

Table 7.1 Medical history where neglect is suspected

Chronology with birth details
Attendances, non-attendances
Diagnoses, surgical procedures, accident history
Use of other health services e.g. dentist, optician
Developmental history
Behaviour in different settings (home, school or play-group)
Carers:
Financial resources
Physical and mental health
Alcohol or drug use
Understanding of child's health, development and needs
Learning or other disabilities
Social pressures
Whether pregnancy was unplanned
Help being offered through social care and other agencies

adequately. She may have limited resources or other social pressures. The pregnancy may have been unplanned, perhaps unwanted. The child may have complex needs. A carer may be in personal crisis, desperate for help but fearful of criticism.

Examination and Investigations

Physical examination should include looking for signs of neglect, assessment of growth and development, systems examination and a careful search for any skin marks or other injuries. Clothes may fit poorly or be inadequate for the weather. Extremities may be red and swollen from cold damage. There may be hair loss. The level of cleanliness, severity of nappy rash, infestations or untreated dental or other conditions should be assessed. There may be signs of anaemia (iron deficiency) or other deficiencies. The affect of the child, their behaviour and interaction with the carer and vice-versa should be recorded (Table 7.2).

The child's nutritional status should be recorded by plotting weight, height and head circumference on standard charts and comparing values with previous measurements from health visitor records. Percentage median body mass index (BMI) should be assessed. Basic blood investigations (page 7) may provide additional information.

Management

Nutritional, speech and language, dental, audiology, visual and developmental assessments may all be required. Outstanding immunisations should be completed with parental consent. A telephone discussion with the health visitor and social worker will provide important information regarding evolving or past concerns, progress made and assistance being offered. A referral to child and adolescent mental health services (CAMHS) or adult psychiatry should be considered.

Table 7.2 Possible signs of neglect	
	Dirty, ill-fitting clothing inadequate for the weather
	Poor grooming and hygiene
	Excessive nappy rash
	Extremities red and swollen from cold damage
	Hair loss
	Persistent infestations
	Untreated dental or other conditions
	Anaemia or other deficiencies
	Failure to thrive
	Delayed language development
	Social, maturational, and behavioural difficulties
	Withdrawn affect
	Decreased social interactions
	Disorganised and aggressive interactions with peers
	Fewer positive play behaviours
	Suicidal thoughts in adolescents
	Serious injury from risk-taking behaviours in adolescents

Failure to Thrive (FTT)

Failure to thrive is a diagnosis given to infants or children who are underweight or who do not gain weight adequately. It usually presents in infancy and early childhood during periods of rapid growth. Weight is affected first, followed by height then head circumference.

Non-organic failure to thrive indicates inadequate dietary intake. Neglect, parental mental health disorders and adverse social circumstances may all affect the provision of adequate nutrition. The amount of money a family has to spend on food and the nutritional content of that food may affect growth. A mother may simply not know how much milk is needed or, due to limited resources, dilute feeds to make them last longer.

> A 9-week-old infant was admitted to hospital following an apparent life threatening event (ALTE) and oral bleeding. There was severe FTT and signs of neglect. The mother had recently travelled from Nigeria and was living alone with the infant in a small bed-sit with little money to buy essentials, isolated and in crisis. She admitted to diluting feeds with water as she could not afford to buy milk and did not know how to seek help. Adequate nutrition in hospital led to rapid weight gain. Oral bleeding was found to be 'on the balance of probabilities' a result of imposed upper airways obstruction.

Organic failure to thrive indicates an underlying medical disorder leading to poor growth. There may be difficulties in feeding from cleft lip and palate or problems with chewing and swallowing. Severe gastro-oesophageal reflux (GORD), malabsorption (commonly coeliac disease and cystic fibrosis) infections and other hypermetabolic states may all affect growth. Medical causes may coexist with non-organic FTT (Table 7.3).

Table 7.3 Common causes for failure to thrive

Maternal malnutrition, alcohol or drug mis-use
Prematurity
Intra uterine growth retardation (IUGR)
Poor suck or swallow
Gastroesophageal reflux
Poor appetite
Chronic infections
Chronic conditions eg: cystic Fibrosis or coeliac disease
Renal failure or renal tubular acidosis
Hypo or hyperthyroidism, diabetes mellitus
Growth hormone deficiency
Inborn errors of metabolism
Malignancy
Chromosomal abnormalities and inherited syndromes

Medical History

A comprehensive medical history and examination should be undertaken (chapter 1, pages 4–6). The type and volume of feeds, frequency and technique of both preparation and feeding should be recorded. Infant formula is available as a ready-to-feed liquid or as powder where the carer makes up the feed with the required amount of water. If the infant is breast-fed fullness and tightening of the breasts before feeding with breast softness after feeds suggests adequate breast milk. Test weighing before and after a feed is inaccurate for assessing milk intake in babies.

Examination

Physical Examination includes looking for signs of neglect, assessment of growth and development, systems examination and a careful search for any skin marks or other injuries. There may be muscle wasting with loss of subcutaneous tissue, abdominal distention, dry or cracked skin, sparse hair or dystrophic nails.

In severe cases, a decreased pulse rate and core body temperature may be found. The child may be anaemic and dehydrated with electrolyte disturbances. Poor muscle tone often improves with adequate nutrition. Developmental delay is common in motor function, language and personal-social development [7]. Substitution with sensitive care is usually followed by significant improvements in development.

> A 14-month-old boy was found at home by the police cyanosed with rapid, laboured breathing. On admission to hospital there was severe failure to thrive and other signs of neglect. He required fluid resuscitation and assisted ventilation. Haemoglobin was 20g/L (normal range 115–155) and serum Ferritin (iron) 2 (10–150). Severe physical neglect led to a life-threatening illness. In addition, there was medical neglect with carers failing to present him earlier for care.

Growth measurements should include head circumference and recumbent length up to 2 years of age, standing height thereafter. Measurements should be plotted on a standard centile chart and compared with previous values to assess growth velocity [8]. Weights for other siblings and growth patterns of the biological parents should be taken into account. A correction for height expectations based on parental size can be made [9]. A weight age is done by plotting the child's weight and assessing at what age this would be on 50th percentile. Percentage median body mass index (BMI) should be calculated using standard charts.

Two percent of healthy children grow normally below the 2nd percentile. Some babies cross centiles in the first 2 years of life remaining on the lower centile throughout childhood with good growth velocity. This is not failure to thrive. Carers may be slim with short stature and reassurance is required if the weight for height ratio is normal and the child appears well nourished.

However, depending on other clinical assessments, a low centile weight may also indicate FTT, as does a drop across at least two centiles or fluctuating patterns of normal interspersed with poor growth. Careful assessment is required to exclude underlying disease.

To correct for prematurity, the number of weeks a baby is premature (based on 40 weeks at full term) should be subtracted from the chronological age, with the weight then plotted against the corrected age. Weight is corrected to a chronological age of 12 months for infants born at 32–36 weeks and 24 months for infants born before 32 weeks. For those born after 36 weeks and 6 days, correction is not required. Many paediatricians prefer simply to correct for weight, height and head circumference up to 24 months for infants born at 36 weeks gestation or less.

In asymmetric intrauterine growth retardation (IUGR) weight is lower whilst head circumference and length are spared. In symmetric IUGR head circumference, length, and weight are all equally reduced. These infants have a poorer potential for normal growth and some remain small throughout life.

Triceps skinfold thickness provides an objective assessment of fat and muscle mass [10]. Mid upper-arm circumference can be charted and followed. Both these values are reduced in non-organic FTT and normalise with improved nutrition.

Investigations

Investigations should be guided by the clinical history and examination as they are seldom helpful in diagnosis. Basic investigations are set out in Table 7.4. Results of the newborn metabolic screen should be checked in infants. Testing for lead, vitamin D, B12 and folate levels are occasionally warranted, as are investigations for malabsorption and other medical causes for FTT. A radiograph of the hand to assess bone age (the average age at which a child reach a stage of bone maturation) in older children comparing bone development to 'standards' and chronological age can also be useful.

Berwick et al. (1982) reviewed the records of 122 infants and children (aged 1–25 months) admitted for FTT. On average, 40 laboratory and radiological investigations were performed for each child. Only 0.8% of these were considered helpful in

Table 7.4 Investigations for failure to thrive

Routine:
Full Blood Count and Ferritin
C-reactive protein (CRP)
Renal and Liver Function
Alkaline phosphatase, calcium, phosphorous
Thyroid function tests
Coeliac Screen
Stool samples for parasites and ova
Urine for culture and sensitivity
Sweat test to exclude cystic fibrosis
Other investigations occasionally warranted: Lead levels Vitamin D, B12 and Folate Complement and immunoglobulin levels Urine for amino acids/organic acids, serum ammonia Blood gas analysis
Bone age

making a diagnosis [11]. Sills (1978) reviewed 185 children hospitalised for FTT, finding that only 1.4% of all tests were of diagnostic value. No test proved useful without a specific clinical indication [12].

Assessment of Caloric intake and expected weight gain

Breast milk contains approximately 65kcal per 100mls, commercial formulas 70 and premature infant milks 80–90kcals per 100ml. Expected weight gains are tabulated in Table 7.5.

Management

A multidisciplinary approach is required, to include paediatrician, nursing staff, dietician, speech therapist, health visitor, social worker and psychologist.

A hospital admission allows observation and supervision over the amount, frequency and technique of feeding. Weight gain can be monitored daily. The infant-carer interaction can be observed and a psychosocial assessment undertaken. Depressed or anxious carers may appear disinterested and need psychological support or psychiatric referral.

Carers are usually willing to allow a short hospital stay when their infant is failing to thrive. Admission is also required where home management has failed, a carer is highly anxious, depressed or negative towards the infant, where there is malnutrition, or other signs of neglect or physical abuse.

Infants with FTT may show good weight gain with normal feeds in hospital but additional calories are occasionally required. Krugman and Dubowitz (2003) reported that for 'catch-up' growth, an additional 50% is recommended [13]. High energy milks or supplements can be used.

If an infant gains weight rapidly in hospital and investigations are normal, a diagnosis of non-organic failure to thrive can be made, reasons for this defined and the necessary help put in place.

Outpatient Management

Outpatient management may be suitable for less severe cases where the interaction between carer and child is good, help is willingly accepted, there is no evidence for neglect or abuse and weight gain is adequate over time. Home care nurses and health visitors will support carers with parenting skills to include feeding routines and making up feeds.

Non-organic FTT should be managed with non-judgemental support, careful evaluation, education and follow-up. In some cases, the carer will have a psychiatric

Table 7.5 Calorie requirements and expected weight gains at different ages

Age	Requirement	Range	Expected weight gain
0–3 months	115kcal/kg	95–145kcal/kg	27gms per day
Up to 6 months	115kcal/kg	95–145kcal/kg	20gms per day
Up to 12 months	105kcal/kg	80–135kcal/kg	12gms per day
1–3 years	95kcal/kg/day	90–102kcal/kg	5–6g per day (2kg/year)

illness, be a substance abuser or homeless, have a low IQ, and be either unable or unwilling to accept advice. They themselves may be facing a personal crisis. Child protection procedures are required where a parent is unable to provide adequate care for whatever reason or there is evidence of physical abuse or neglect.

Obesity

Failure to provide a healthy life-style for a child is increasingly recognised as being neglectful. The number of children who are clinically obese has increased three-fold in England over the past 25 years.

Obesity results from both an unhealthy lifestyle (diet, physical activity, inactivity) and genetic influences. It is associated with poorer mental health outcomes, reduced quality of life and serious diseases to include hypertension, high cholesterol, type 2 diabetes, coronary heart disease, stroke, osteoarthritis, sleep apnoea, breathing problems and some cancers.

There is an increased risk of depression and anxiety with an overall lower quality of life. Some medical conditions including Cushing's disease and polycystic ovary syndrome as well as drugs such as steroids and some antidepressants may increase susceptibility to weight gain [14].

Emotional Neglect

Overview
In emotional abuse and neglect (psychological maltreatment) the carer fails to provide a nurturing environment for psychological and emotional well-being and is emotionally unavailable to the child. Interactions including both omission and commission become harmful [15]. The child is left feeling worthless, unloved and inadequate. Anxiety, depression, fear, social withdrawal, developmental and educational delay have all been observed.

The carer may repeatedly criticise, blame, denigrate, silence, humiliate, exploit or bully the child. Cyberbullying (texts, emails or social media) is increasingly common. There may be failure to seek care for the child's emotional or behavioural problems.

Unreasonable expectations may overwhelm the child. Overprotection, poor stimulation and inhibiting peer friendships may co-exist. The child may witness domestic violence, drug and alcohol abuse or be 'used' where there is conflict with another adult. There may be illness fabrication or induction (FII). Depending on the degree of emotional abuse the child may be in crisis and dysfunctional behaviours are common.

Significant risk factors for carers include mental health disorders, domestic violence, alcohol or substance abuse, low IQ and a history of abuse in the carer's childhood. There may be poverty and social isolation with a young mother feeling overwhelmed with her own difficulties and, as a consequence, becoming emotionally unavailable to her child and others.

Emotional abuse is hard to recognise and evidence. Social workers may observe abnormal patterns in the home while teachers may report unusual behaviours in the child. Diagnosis requires careful observation and documentation of the child's affect in different settings.

Management may include removal of the child from the abusive environment with long-term mental health input. Substitution with sensitive care is often followed by dramatic improvements in behaviour and social adjustment.

Fahlberg (1994) reported that a child's behaviour could be influenced by what was experienced in the home and that the most helpful intervention for a child with behavioural difficulties was the provision of an environment which encouraged growth. Moreover, children needed to be exposed to adults with appropriate behaviours and those who had been abused or neglected required extra doses of good parenting since they were more susceptible to further damage from poor parenting practices [16].

Symptoms and signs

No symptom or sign is diagnostic of emotional abuse. Infants may have feeding difficulties, excessive crying, poor sleep patterns or delayed development. They may be irritable or apathetic. Toddlers and pre-school children may exhibit head banging,

Table 7.6 Potential features of neglect and emotional abuse

Infants
Feeding difficulties
Excessive crying
Poor sleep patterns
Irritable or apathetic
Delayed development
Toddlers and pre-school children
Head banging, rocking
Hyperactive or apathetic and clingy
Developmental delay particularly language & social skills
School children
Anti-social behaviour
Disturbed sleep
Encopresis (soiling) or enuresis (bed-wetting)
Poor educational performance and school attendance
Feelings of worthlessness, being unloved and inadequate
Anxiety and depression
Social withdrawal
Developmental and educational delay
Adolescents
Anti-social behaviour
Clinical depression
Self-harming behaviours, alcohol or drug abuse
Eating disorders
Poor self-esteem

rocking, hyperactivity or be apathetic and clingy. There may be developmental delay, particularly in language and social skills (Table 7.6).

School children may exhibit anti-social behaviour with poor educational performance and school attendance. There may be disturbed sleep, encopresis (soiling) or bed-wetting. Adolescents may be clinically depressed, express suicidal thoughts, self-harm, abuse alcohol or drugs, exhibit an eating disorder and poor self-esteem. Where there are reports of hyperactivity, unlike in ADHD abnormal behaviours are not always found in all environments. If the child is hyperactive and inattentive at home but focussed and relaxed at school, he or she is less likely to have ADHD.

The child may have emotional signs, (sad, withdrawn, depressed, anxious, over-affectionate, angry, apathetic), behavioural signs (fearful, restless, frozen and still, destructive, overactive, distant or over-friendly) or signs of developmental delay.

There may be a lack of response or extreme response to separation from the carer. Self-soothing, rocking, head banging, attention seeking and antisocial behaviours are all observed.

Management

A multi-agency approach is required, including a comprehensive medical assessment with referrals to children's social care and child and adolescent mental health services (CAMHS). Through psychotherapy, children may admit to feeling worthless, unloved, inadequate, frightened and isolated.

Medical Neglect

Overview

Medical neglect is a failure to present a child for care when needed or delaying that care. The health care needs of the child, whether for immunisations, dental care or other child health promotion programmes, are not met. Some carers choose to withhold vaccinations with explanations provided. Education and counseling is required. Failure to present a child for acute care for serious illness or injury is considered profoundly neglectful.

Neglecting the on-going care needs of a clinical condition by failing to administer prescribed medications, or not presenting a child for follow-up includes children with special needs who are not brought for physio or other therapies.

A 4-year-old boy with developmental delay and cerebral palsy was referred for physiotherapy, occupational and speech and language therapy. Over a 3-year period only 4 of 32 appointments were attended, with no reasons provided for non-attendance. The child developed severe contractures and worsening feeding difficulties, both of which will have been limited by regular therapy input. This constitutes medical neglect.

Professionals in Partnership with Carers

Illness symptoms can sometimes be subtle and fluctuate with a child appearing to improve. A carer may choose to wait before presenting a child for care, not wanting to trouble professionals and expecting improvements. A child with a fever may have either a self-resolving viral or life-threatening bacterial infection. Carers are usually not medically qualified and may underestimate the severity of an illness. They cannot always be expected to respond with accuracy to a child's medical needs.

For children with special needs, there may be multiple appointments with health, education and social care. Carers may not understand the benefit of them all. If they are consulting a specialist they may not see the need to repeat their concerns to the GP, health visitor and paediatrician or fully understand that these professionals provide an overview and co-ordinate care.

There may be financial constraints for transport to and from hospital, no social support systems, cultural beliefs, fear of a serious diagnosis or of being criticised. Some carers have learning difficulties or are overwhelmed by other pressures. They may be unhappy with the care provided and not wish to attend or complain. Carers become physically and emotionally exhausted and paediatricians taking an overview should advise on which appointments, particularly those that are duplicating, may not be necessary.

Medical interventions involve benefits but also potential risks. Carers need accurate and consistent advice about medications and whether they need to be increased, decreased or stopped. A care plan should be agreed in partnership with the carer. Asthma medications are sometimes required in the winter but not the summer. Equally, some teenagers with chronic illnesses such as diabetes can be rebellious, adjust their own medication or refuse to attend.

Dental Neglect

Failure to meet a child's basic dental needs leads to poor oral and general health. It may also affect development [17]. Dental decay affects 31% of 5-year-old children in England with each child having an average of three teeth affected. There are regional variations with 42% in Scotland and 48% in Wales affected [18].

Untreated decay results in pain, infection, difficulties with chewing, speaking and sleeping. It may affect social activities and school attendance. Impaired growth has been demonstrated in pre-school children, with improvements following treatment [19]. Children with early caries are more likely to develop further disease in both their primary and permanent teeth. For good dental health, help with brushing and oral hygiene, advice about a diet limiting sugar and dental checks for prevention and treatment are required.

Montecchi et al. (2009) reported that abused children had a significantly higher dental plaque index, gingival inflammation and a greater number of untreated decayed teeth. These children showed evidence of neglect and were less cooperative during dental visits [20].

Mansour et al. (2010) reviewed the dental records of 5045 children aged 3–8 years old finding 309 extractions in 206 children. Reasons given were dental caries (60.5%), orthodontics (11.3%), trauma (10.4%), other (17.8%) [21].

The Unborn Child

Maternal drug or alcohol use in pregnancy can affect foetal growth and lead to defects such as Foetal Alcohol Spectrum Disorder (FASD) where growth failure, visual and hearing defects, poor muscle tone, learning, social and behavioural difficulties may be observed [22]. A maternal diet deficient in folate leads to an excess of neural tube defects in the foetus. Physical assault of the mother may lead to premature delivery or damage to the unborn foetus.

Mothers who subsequently neglect their infants may book late for maternity care, have sporadic antenatal care or present only at the onset of labour. A pre-birth conference and psychiatric assessment of the mother may be needed.

Supervision Neglect

Carers have a duty to protect their child from harm. However, they themselves may have disabilities, be abusing drugs or alcohol, be depressed, have a low IQ or overwhelmed and in personal crisis. Many are desperate for help and a change of circumstances. Either way, the child suffers.

Accidents in the home are common and often unavoidable. Burns and scalds, falls, accidental ingestion of medication all occur even when carers are vigilant. However, a single emergency department (ED) attendance with a significant injury or frequent attendances for minor injury or accidental ingestions may indicate poor supervision.

Educational Neglect

This is failure to provide adequately for a child's education, whether at school or by home education. There is often associated emotional abuse and lack of stimulation within the home. A carer, overwhelmed with domestic matters may be encouraging a child to remain at home to assist with age-inappropriate tasks.

Other Conditions

Head Lice
Head lice is a common diagnosis in all social groups and not necessarily indicative of neglect. The infestations are most frequent in children aged 3–10. Itching may be

severe and scratching can cause sores which become infected. About 6–12 million children between the ages of 3 and 11 are treated annually for head lice in the USA with high levels of infestations reported in Israel, Denmark, Sweden, UK, France and Australia. The number of children per family, sharing of beds, hair-washing habits and socioeconomic status are all factors in head lice infestation.

Severe recurrent head lice, left untreated that resolves in care with the correct treatments is indicative of neglect.

Nappy Rash

Nappy rash is caused by skin disorders and irritants occurring when skin is exposed to prolonged wetness from urine and faeces. The rash is common babies but also in infants 8–12 months possibly in response to an increase in solid foods which affects faecal composition. Treatments include barrier creams and exposure.

Severe persistent nappy rash with or without secondary infection may indicate neglectful parenting particularly if with the correct treatments there is resolution in hospital or care.

Brachycephaly

Infants sometimes develop a flattened appearance to the back of the skull with hair loss as a result of spending time lying on their back. In plagiocephaly the head is flattened on one side, in brachycephaly the back of the head is flattened and the forehead may protrude. These abnormalities affect about 20% of normal babies and on their own are not an indication of poor stimulation or neglect.

References

1. Keir C, Gray J, When to suspect child maltreatment, National Institute for Health and Clinical Excellence (NICE), 2009.
2. University of East Anglia, National Society for the Prevention of Cruelty to Children. Neglect and serious case reviews. 2013.
3. Dubowitz H, Giardino AP, Gustavson E. Child neglect: guidance for paediatricians (review). Pediatr Rev. 2000;21(4):111–6.
4. Hobbs CJ, Hanks HGI, Wynne TM. Failure to thrive. In: Child abuse and neglect: a clinician's handbook. New York: Churchill Livingstone; 1993. p. 17–45.
5. Peterson MS, Urquiza AJ. The role of mental health professionals in the prevention and treatment of child abuse and neglect. Washington, DC: U.S. Department of Health and Human Services; 1993.
6. De-Panfilis D. Child neglect: a guide for prevention, assessment, and intervention. U.S. Department of Health and Human Services. Office on Child Abuse and Neglect; 2006.
7. Allen RE, Oliver JM. The effects of child maltreatment on language development. Child Abuse Negl. 1982;6(3):299–305.
8. RCPCH. UK-WHO growth charts. 2016. http://www.rcpch.ac.uk/Research/UK-WHO-Growth-Charts.
9. Tanner JM, Goldstein H, Whitehouse PH. Standards for children's height at age 2–9 years allowing for height of parents. Arch Dis Child. 1970;45:755–62.
10. Ayatollahi S-M-T, Mostajabi F. Triceps skinfold thickness centile charts in primary school children in Shiraz. Arch Iran Med. 2008;11(2):210–3.

11. Berwick DM, Levy JC, Kleinerman R. Failure to thrive: diagnostic yield of hospitalization. Arch Dis Child. 1982;57:347–51.
12. Sills RH. Failure to thrive: the role of clinical and laboratory evaluation. Am J Dis Child. 1978;132:967–9.
13. Krugman SD, Dubowitz H. Failure to thrive. Am Fam Physician. 2003;68:879–84.
14. Luppino FS, et al. Overweight, obesity, and depression: a systematic review and meta-analysis of longitudinal studies. Arch Gen Psychiatry. 2010;67(3):220–9.
15. Glaser D. How to deal with emotional abuse and neglect: further development of a conceptual framework (FRAMEA). Child Abuse Negl. 2011;35:866–75.
16. Fahlberg V. A child's journey through placement. London: British Agencies for Adoption and Fostering; 1994. p. 13–61. Attachment and bonding.
17. Harris JC, Balmer RC, Sidebotham PD. British Society of Paediatric Dentistry: a policy document on dental neglect in children. Int J Paediatr Dent. 2009.
18. British Association for the Study of Community Dentistry. 1997.
19. Sheiham A. Dental caries affect body weight, growth and quality of life in preschool children. Br Dent J. 2006;201(910):625–6.
20. Montecchi PP, Di Trani M, Sarzi Amadè D, Bufacchi C, Montecchi F, Polimeni A. The dentist's role in recognizing childhood abuses: study on the dental health of children victims of abuse and witnesses to violence. Eur J Paediatr Dent. 2009;10(4):185–7.
21. Mansour Ockell N, Bågesund M. Reasons for extractions, and treatment preceding caries-related extractions in 3-8 year-old children. Eur Arch Paediatr Dent. 2010;11(3):122–30.
22. Advisory Council on the Misuse of Drugs. Hidden harm: responding to the needs of children of problem drug users. London: Home Office; 2003.

Further Reading

CORE INFO Cardiff Child Protection Systematic Reviews/www.core-info.cardiff.ac.uk/

Fabricated and Induced Illness by Carers (FII)

8

Abstract

Medical neglect is when a carer fails to present a child for care when required. Fabricated or induced illness (FII) is when a carer seeks medical care unnecessarily or induces symptoms.

When a child is presented with symptoms, the clinician must make a diagnosis. In some cases a child may have a genuine medical problem diagnosed only at a later stage after initial concerns about FII have been raised. The term FII is child-centred, seeking to define the cause of a child's reported or actual illness.

McClure et al. (1996) collected data nationally between 1992–94. Only cases discussed at a formal child protection case conference involving illness induction were included. There were 97 FII cases with incidences quoted as 0.5/100,000 under 16 years, 1.2/100,000 under 5 years and 2.9/100,000 under 1 year [1]. Watson et al. (2000) using broader inclusion criteria, estimated a prevalence rate for FII of 89/100,000 within a Health District in Manchester [2].

Flaherty et al. (2013) reviewing FII, reported that bleeding, seizures, central nervous system depression, apnoea, diarrhoea, vomiting, fever, and rash were the most commonly reported presentations and that illnesses could involve multiple organs with numerous specialists involved [3].

The Spectrum

There are anxious carers who need time with professionals to feel fully reassured. There may be cultural aspects to illness perception and expectations. Most of these cases do not 'cross a line' that requires a safeguarding approach. However, reassurance and a non-invasive approach may not satisfy some carers who insist on further interventions, referrals or a change of doctor. There may be escalation from

© Springer International Publishing Switzerland 2017

D.L. Robinson, *Pediatric Forensic Evidence*, DOI 10.1007/978-3-319-45337-8_8

exaggeration to fabrication, falsification and illness induction. The clinician must decide at what point the child is placed at risk of harm and when a safeguarding referral is required.

Exaggeration, Half-truths and Mis-truths

A concerned carer may exaggerate symptoms to heighten the doctor's awareness and to "get his or her attention". Another family member may have had a serious diagnosis such as leukaemia leading to anxiety over trivial symptoms in the child. If the carer does not feel 'heard' or the assessment is incomplete, he or she will continue to have doubts about the child's well-being. At times, a simple blood test is reasonable if this reassures the carer and prevents escalation.

Whilst half-truths and mis-truths (eg: reporting a diagnosis of epilepsy when clinicians only suggested the possibility) may not be acted upon by medical professionals, repeated exaggeration may place the child in a "sick role" with psychological consequences and harm done.

Fabrication

Overview

Exaggeration or mis-truths may progress to fabricating non-existent symptoms with repeated presentations and demands for investigations. An internet search may heighten a carer's anxiety.

In fabrication a carer presents the child with symptoms such as pain, fits, blue spells or vomiting that are episodic and cannot be verified or explained by any known medical condition. A diagnosis is suspected but cannot be confirmed. There are repeated medical presentations often with escalating and changing symptoms.

At first, a carer may accept medical advice but then withdraw the child by not attending follow-up appointments or removing him or her from hospital against advice.

Previously reported symptoms may resolve with new ones arising that appear to require investigation. Carers may not be satisfied with negative findings. Complaints against health professionals and demands for further opinions where investigations are often repeated are common ('doctor shopping'). Both physical and emotional symptoms can be fabricated.

Roesler and Jenny (2009) concluded that FII involved a child receiving unnecessary and harmful or potentially harmful medical care at the instigation of a carer [4].

Acute Symptoms

Acute symptoms and signs are usually observed by one carer with no supporting evidence from other family members (unless there is collusion), school or medical professionals.

Disabled and unwell children

A disabled child may be presented with a more significant problem than exists or a child with a verified illness such as asthma presented with excessive symptoms and reports of increased use of inhalers. Treatments for real diagnoses may be withheld.

The 'sick role'

The carer promotes the 'sick role'. The child is exposed to concerns about his or her health at home which are shared with the school and may come to believe that he or she is unwell. Older children may fabricate, induce or somatise illness.

Examination and Treatment

Physical examination and investigations are normal with a poor response to prescribed treatments. There is an increasing mismatch between what the doctor believes are the child's needs and what the carer considers these to be.

Harmful interventions

Any potentially harmful medical intervention becomes abusive if there was no medical need for it. Fabrication may lead to unnecessary, painful, often repeated investigations and potentially harmful treatments. Blood tests, invasive procedures and unwarranted operations have all been recorded. In FII there are repeated presentations for medical care with the potential for repeated investigations and treatments by different clinicians.

Child's Daily Life

The child's daily life and activities become limited. There may be poor school attendance, social isolation or the use of unnecessary special aids – wheelchairs, buggies, specialist shoes. Carers who fabricate become knowledgeable about diagnoses and medical terms particularly if their child has complex medical needs.

Falsification

Fabrication may co-exist with, or progress to, falsifying medical information. Blood may be placed in urine specimens, vomitus on clothing. Test results and observation charts may be falsified with oxygen saturations altered to suggest hypoxia or documentation of a non-existent fever.

Illness Induction

This implies direct interference with the child. Equipment may be deliberately tampered with, medications withheld or given unnecessarily. There may be non-accidental poisoning (page 172) or intentional suffocation (page 173).

Common Presenting Features

Conditions associated with FII are those where the diagnosis rests primarily on the history provided and where reported symptoms are episodic. Key presentations identified in the Cardiff-Leeds Study are shown in Table 8.1.

Table 8.1 Key presentations identified in the Cardiff-Leeds Study [5]

Presenting feature	All FII cases
Fits	24
Apparent life threatening events (ALTE)	22
Drowsy, Coma	13
Blood loss in vomit or rectally	13
Failure to thrive, feeding difficulty	11
Bowel disturbance	9
Asthma	9
Vomiting, Gasto-Oesophageal Reflux	8
Blood loss, haemoptysis	5
Skin lesions	4
Fabricated disability	3
False allegations of abuse	3
Blood in urine	3
False disclosure of accidental overdose	3

An infant may be reported to be going blue or stopping breathing. He or she is rushed to hospital where examination and investigations are normal. During admission no blue spells are recorded unless the case has progressed to illness induction. The infant is discharged home well, only to be re-admitted at a later date with further similar symptoms reported.

A child may be reported to be having fits at home that are only observed by one carer. In the aftermath of the 'seizure' others may be present but find the child well unless there has been imposed airways obstruction. In hospital no abnormalities are found, investigations are normal and no fits observed. The carer is asked to video an episode but this never occurs.

Behavioural presentations may include reported symptoms of attention-deficit hyperactivity disorder (ADHD) or Autism Spectrum Disorder (ASD). The carer insists the child is uncontrollable at home whilst the school or nursery report that he or she quiet and attentive. However, some children may exhibit abnormal behaviour patterns as a result of FII, being anxious, confused and in crisis.

Children with a disability and complex diagnoses may be subject to FII. In some cases, the mother will have a complex obstetric history with evidence of precipitation of a premature delivery [6].

Carers

In most cases, the biological mother is the perpetrator. However, involvement of the father as perpetrator is described as is collusion between carers [7]. Anyone in a caring role for a child can potentially perpetrate FII. The absence of abuse or psychiatric illness in the carer does not preclude FII nor does being abused in childhood or having a psychiatric history necessarily mean that someone will abuse their child.

Some carers are overwhelmed by personal or social stresses and feel the need to repeatedly consult a doctor about their child. They may have depression, anxiety, or low IQ. They may have been subjected to domestic violence and seek safety in hospital by falsifying symptoms in the child. Some carers genuinely misinterpret advice offered particularly if a consultation has been hurried.

A carer may be deluded (holding a fixed unchangeable belief) that the child is ill, and fabricate symptoms believing they are doing their best for the child. Where there is a true delusional disorder an implausible history may be obvious.

A carer may logically fabricate symptoms to attention-seek, direct blame or use the situation to maintain closeness to the child. There may be financial secondary gain, including benefits such as Disability Living Allowance (DLA). Once the latter are achieved contact with health professionals and social care may be avoided although carers may also escalate matters further in order to maintain or enhance benefits.

Levin and Sheridan (1995) reported that motivations of the perpetrator are probably not uniform and may include components of help-seeking, a delusion that the illness is real, anger towards the child, healthcare providers, or significant others and other secondary gain [8].

The Child

Harm done can be both physical and emotional (Table 8.2). Repeated presentations to health professionals with often escalating parental concerns may raise anxiety in the child creating abnormal perceptions of illness with unusual behaviours.

Harm done includes hospital attendances, painful investigations and procedures with surgeons sometimes being persuaded to perform unnecessary surgery (eg. tonsillectomy). Important treatments may be withheld or unnecessary ones

Table 8.2 Potential harm done as a result of FII

Physical
Unnecessary often painful investigations
Unnecessary treatments
Unwarranted surgical procedures and anaesthetics
Withholding important treatments
Risk of under-treatment for real conditions
Significant risk of handicap or death with induced illness
Emotional:
Inappropriate often prolonged hospital admissions
Placing the child in a 'sick role' to include disability that does not exist
Disordered perceptions leading to anxiety and abnormal illness behaviour
Abnormal relationship between a child and carer
Limitations on normal activities e.g.: school attendance
Prolonged legal proceedings
The risk of further abuse
Long-term psychiatric consequences

imposed. There may be associated neglect and physical abuse. Disability from imposed upper airways obstruction has been recorded [9–11].

Children usually accept the need to visit a health professional, take medication or even use a wheelchair when this is not required, or be be excluded from school. They may collude in the deception, somatise, fabricate, induce symptoms or self-harm. Passive acceptance is more common in younger patients. Abnormal carer-child interactions and bonding are often found.

The child may assume a 'sick role', become socially isolated, confused and anxious. They may come to believe that they are unwell or disabled. Their normal daily life including friendships, school attendance and educational achievement become limited.

Health Professionals

For the vast majority of medical presentations, carers provide an accurate account of their child's symptoms to help doctors make a diagnosis. Both work in partnership for the child's benefit. Paediatricians find it difficult to acknowledge that carers are fabricating and will also be concerned that they are missing a physical diagnosis (which may be the case) and lean towards investigation and treatment. When FII occurs in children with chronic conditions who are often on multiple medications, it becomes even more difficult to distinguish between real and fabricated symptoms.

> A 7-year-old boy with special needs was reported by his mother to be having recurrent severe seizures. Symptoms improved then deteriorated with multiple fits being observed only by the mother. Concerns were raised for FII with the paediatric neurologist encouraging the carer to record an episode on her iPad. Child protection investigations then Court proceedings were commenced. During these the mother was able to record a prolonged seizure which the neurologist deemed to be sufficient evidence for epilepsy. Meticulous, often prolonged medical observation is required to exclude FII.

FII is a clinical diagnosis, based on history, examination and test results. The diagnosis emerges as a series of consultations and reported events over months, sometimes years depending on the severity and escalation of reported symptoms. Carers in this situation can be pressurising, consultations lengthy and often vexatious.

Once FII is diagnosed, doctors may feel both betrayed by what was assumed to be a trusting relationship and guilty at having allowed the situation to continue without more prompt diagnosis.

The paediatrician must first consider the possibility of FII and distinguish between an anxious carer with a tendency to exaggerate and one whose behaviour may cause harm to the child. Time is required and a busy out-patient clinic not the most suitable setting. It is often better to invite the family back for a longer consultation or recommend admission to hospital.

The suggestion of admission may raise suspicions in the abusing carer with complaints and demands for a change of consultant. A diagnosis of FII cannot be handled alone. It is useful to share the case with the named lead for safeguarding and arrange a joint assessment. Permission should be sought from carers to discuss the child's health and performance with the school.

In some cases, neither a physical diagnosis or FII can be confirmed. Older children may somatise or fabricate their own illness. Careful repeated clinical assessments are required with a timely referral to CAMHS if needed.

Clinical Management

The approach must be centred on diagnosis, safeguarding the child and providing support to the family.

Out-Patient Management

History
As for any child protection concerns, a meticulous assessment is required (chapter 1, pages 4–6). The medical history will include a chronology of care with birth details, attendances, non-attendances, diagnoses, surgical procedures, accident history, use of other health services and interventions. The paediatrician should identify any inconsistencies between the history and clinical picture. Behaviour and symptoms at school or play group should be explored with the carer's permission.

Examination and Investigations
Physical examination should include looking for signs of neglect, assessment of growth and development, systems examination and a careful search for any injuries. The affect of the child, their behaviour and interaction with the carer and vice-versa should be recorded. Limited investigations (if not already done in primary care) may be warranted (page 7).

Mian (1995) reported that decisions for investigations should be based on necessity, a consideration of risk/benefit analysis and the ability to distinguish between a true organic condition and FII [12].

If the paediatrician is unable to provide reassurances, or carers appear to accept advice but continue to seek further opinions and investigations, a medical admission is warranted to allow close observation and safeguarding where required.

Medical Admission

In FII, separation of the child from the alleged perpetrator often results in resolution of the child's reported medical problems.

If an infant is reported to be having recurrent respiratory pauses (apnoeas) at home but none are observed in hospital or a child is said to have repeated vomiting with blood but these are not observed at school or during respite, concerns are raised. If acute episodes of illness continue during hospital admission with close observation of child and carer, a genuine diagnosis must be further pursued.

Carers need reassurance that observation is necessary because of uncertainty about their child's diagnosis. If they refuse and suspect concerns about FII, a referral to social care is warranted after discussion with colleagues. The purpose of admission should be to make a clear diagnosis.

The Multidisciplinary Team

Overview
Collaboration between paediatricians, psychiatrists, nurses, health visitors, GP, social care, police (where indicated), the school and other staff is needed to gain a clear understanding of the situation and for successful diagnosis and outcome (Table 8.3).

Lead Paediatrician
One paediatrician must take responsibility for the case, with other Consultants being made aware of care plans at regular hand-overs. Tests, treatments and procedures should be requested only by the lead paediatrician. Forensic tests should be undertaken in collaboration with the police.

The lead paediatrician will decide whether there are grounds for suspecting FII and involve the multidisciplinary team. If the child is considered in need or at risk of significant harm, a referral to children's social care is required and local safeguarding children's board (LSCB) procedures followed. A telephone discussion should be followed by a referral in writing on a standard form (pages 16–17). If illness induction is suspected, an urgent referral to both social care and the police is required. An emergency protection order (page 18) may be necessary. Consent from carers is not required and informing them of concerns may put the child at further risk.

In hospital the medical history will be reviewed with a further careful examination. Concerns regarding FII should be documented as well as discussions with carers and colleagues. Carers will be told of clinical concerns and need for close observation in order to clarify a diagnosis. Permission to restrict a carer's access to medical notes may be required in order to safeguard the child.

A carer may request a change in consultant or a referral to another hospital particularly when FII is suspected. A tertiary referral may be warranted as a support to

Table 8.3 Key responsibilities in FII

Lead Paediatrician	Takes responsibility for the case and plans care
	Decides if there are grounds for suspecting FII
	Makes referral to children's social care (and police if required)
	Prepares reports
Named Paediatrician for Safeguarding	With named nurse assists the lead paediatrician
	Prepares a medical chronology
	With named nurse attends conferences
Nursing Teams	Close observation of the child and family
Teachers/therapists	Often spend long periods with the child and can make important observations
Other Consultants	'On service' for a week at a time
	Follows advice from the lead paediatrician
	Examines the child daily and responds to concerns
CAMHS	Addresses emotional or behavioural problems
	Adult psychiatry addresses relevant issues for carers
GP	Prepares chronology of medical care for the child
	Provides relevant information about carers under GMC guidance
Health Visitor	Information on vaccinations, growth, feeding, development, parent-child interaction, parenting skills
Education	Attendance records, symptoms reported at school
	Whether special educational support is being provided
	Medical concerns raised by carers
Social care	Safeguard and co-ordinate strategy discussion
Police	Involved if illness induction is suspected
	Visit the home, interview carers, collect relevant forensic samples

the lead paediatrician. For example, a paediatric neurologist may be able to exclude or confirm epilepsy where there have been reported seizures. Thereafter care must return to the lead paediatrician.

Named Lead Consultant and Nurse for Safeguarding

The named paediatrician and nurse for safeguarding will have expertise as well as contacts within social care to assist the lead paediatrician. They should be consulted as early as possible during the hospital admission and will assist in compiling a medical chronology. This may reveal patterns regarding frequent appointments, non-attendances, 'doctor shopping' and previous concerns for abuse and neglect.

Both the named paediatrician for safeguarding and the lead consultant will prepare reports/statements for social care and the police.

Paediatric Nursing and Medical Teams

Hospital admission allows for a period of close observation of the child and family. As well as providing potential evidence for FII, nursing staff may be able to exclude the diagnosis, if for example, fits are observed on the ward. Teachers and therapists will spend longer periods with the child and make important observations.

Consultants are generally 'on service' for a week at a time. During these periods they should follow advice from the lead paediatrician, examine the child daily and respond to any concerns.

Emotional or behavioural problems should prompt a referral to the local child and adolescent mental health service (CAMHS). The child should be given an opportunity to speak about his or her concerns.

Any potential forensic evidence, e.g. blood, vomitus, clothing or bedding should be collected in collaboration with the police. If symptoms are reported, a paediatrician should examine the child at the time, making careful notes and observations.

Covert Video Surveillance (CVS) involves using a hidden video camera to observe a carer who is not aware of its use. It is supervised by the police under the Regulation of Investigatory Powers Act 2000. Agreement at the multi-agency strategy discussion is required as well as close collaboration with medical staff and senior management. Whilst rarely used, it may be justified where there is doubt about the diagnosis and a need to provide sufficient evidence of FII [13, 14]. Hall et al. (2000) noted that CVS could occasionally exonerate carers previously suspected of causing harm [15].

Carers and family members should be supported and counselled regularly. However, a decision to exclude them from the ward or allow access only with supervision may be warranted. The needs of siblings should be discussed. Staff also require support and training in dealing with cases of suspected FII. The idea that a doctor or nurse has caused harm with unnecessary investigations and treatments is naturally distressing.

General Practitioners

GPs are the gatekeepers for medical care and a chronology from their records is essential. In FII, there are often frequent GP and HV presentations. In addition, there may be information regarding specialist opinions, therapy consultations, non-attendances and other concerning features. The GP should also be asked to review relevant family records as there may be a history of illness fabrication, somatisation or other relevant behaviour in a carer. GMC guidance for confidentiality must be followed [16, 17].

Health Visitor

The case should be discussed with the health visitor. The red book, containing information including vaccination status, growth, feeding, development and any concerns raised, should be reviewed.

Education

The school will be able to provide attendance records and indicate whether special educational support is being provided. They will have a record of symptoms and concerns raised by the child and those reported by carers. There may be other background information. In FII, a carer may offer medical information to the school which is at variance with the true clinical picture.

Social care

If the child is considered in need or at risk of significant harm, a referral to children's social care is required and LSCB procedures followed (pages 16–17). Social care will co-ordinate a multi-agency strategy discussion which will assess the level of risk to the child and actions required to safeguard. After the meeting the lead consultant, senior nurse and social worker will inform carers about concerns and action planned. If a criminal offence has been committed, the police will make such disclosures. If illness induction is suspected an emergency protection order will be required. Carers will need support.

Police

The police should be involved if illness induction is suspected. They will visit the family home and collect relevant forensic information such as medications. Forensic investigations should be conducted under their direction.

On-Going Care

Children

The paediatrician should continue out-patient assessments, whether the child returns home or is accommodated. Signs of disease and emotional/behavioural outcomes should be monitored. Child psychiatrists and psychologists through CAMHS help children understand what has occurred and what needs to be done to ensure their well-being. Some children are unable to recognise that fabrication has taken place. Older children may have an idea of what has occurred but feel a strong loyalty towards their carers and not wish to share feelings or be unable to do so. Others fear further abuse or removal from the family home and loss of support systems (carers, siblings, friends and school). Long-term therapeutic work is required to allow a child to express his or her feelings. Siblings should be assessed.

Carers and Families

Perpetrators often have significant medical histories with genuine diagnoses, somatisation, fabrication and mental health issues. Bools (1994) and Bass (2011) reported the following in perpetrators: factitious disorders (64%), somatisation (57–72%), self-harm (46–54%), substance misuse or addictive behaviours (11–18%), a forensic history (16–36%) and personality disorders (75–89%) [18, 19].

Carers should be encouraged to access mental health services with a referral via the GP. Psychiatrists may not identify a mental health diagnosis (axis 1 mental disorder) but often report features of a personality disorder (axis 2). With psychotherapists and psychologists they will seek to understand why a carer should fabricate or induce symptoms in the child and to ascertain their capacity to understand harm done and potential for change. Families can be helped to adjust to a new understanding of the child, past events and plans for the future.

Long-term intervention may be required to help perpetrators understand the issues and to alter motivating factors. Feelings of guilt, depression and hopelessness may be uncovered. Support groups, advice and advocacy services, police witness and victim support in proceedings may all assist the family. Practical issues such as employment or other sources of income should be explored.

Some carers are able to recognise the harm caused and alter their behaviour. It may therefore be possible to keep the child with the family or to rehabilitate in time. If there is a significant risk of recurrence the child should be separated from the perpetrator.

A previous history of FII in another child or fabrication in the mother raises concerns for the unborn child. A pre-birth conference and psychiatric assessment of the mother may be necessary.

Illness Induction

Abstract
In illness induction, a carer physically does things to a child to cause harm. This may include withholding important medications, harming a child to cause abnormal signs, injecting substances, inserting needles, inducing feeding difficulties, smothering and poisoning.

McClure et al. (1996) reported one of the 97 children diagnosed with FII had died and that 4/44 poisonings and 4/32 suffocation cases were fatal (inflicted poisoning and suffocation classified separately). An additional 15 (12%) required intensive care with 45 (35%) suffering major physical illness. There were a total of 18 deaths in siblings (10% of all siblings), five of whom had been previously classified as Sudden Infant Deaths [1].

Poisoning

Accidental poisoning is common in toddlers and young children. The child is found with a medicine bottle in his or her hand and evidence of ingestion. The carer removes what he or she can from the mouth and presents the child for medical care where few children develop symptoms. Accidental poisoning is rare under 1 year of age whilst child-safe containers provide additional safety for older children.

In deliberate poisoning, drugs prescribed for another family member (e.g.: hypnotics, tranquilisers or anti-depressants) may be given to the child. Recreational drugs may be passively inhaled or deliberately administered. In illness induction, carers have administered drugs by mouth, injection, into intravenous lines, via nasogastric/gastrostomy tubes or rectally.

Occasionally, a genuine prescribing or dispensing error will have occurred whilst remedies bought over the counter or alternative treatments may all have serious side-effects. Poisoning may also be self-administered, as with an adolescent drug overdose.

Urine, blood, gastric contents and stool should be sent for analysis. It is important to establish what prescribed drugs the child is taking and other medicines available in the family home. The police will assist by collecting relevant evidence whilst Toxbase provides accurate information regarding drug overdose and management. (https://www.toxbase.org). (accessed 16.04.17).

Symptoms of drowsiness, vomiting or disorientation are associated with hypnotics, tricyclic antidepressants, anticonvulsants, phenothiazines, methadone, cannabis, some analgesics and alcohol. An urgent blood sugar estimation is required to exclude insulin administration.

Seizures or excessive thirst due to salt intoxication are associated with high levels of sodium and chloride in the blood and urine. Hyperventilation, vomiting, seizures and pulmonary oedema suggest salicylate poisoning. Children may also present in clinical shock and require urgent resuscitation and management of the airways, breathing and circulation.

Altered consciousness requires neuroimaging, blood investigations and an urgent drug screen. Other causes for clinical shock and encephalopathy such as sepsis and abusive head trauma must be excluded.

Imposed Upper Airways Obstruction

Abstract
The term apparent life-threatening event (ALTE) refers to infants who present with apnoea, cyanosis, seizures or being unresponsive (Table 8.4).

An induced ALTE implies direct interference with the child. If an infant is presented for care with a history of being found accidentally smothered by a piece of clothing, pillow or bedding, a credible history of the circumstances and aftermath may make intentional smothering unlikely.

Table 8.4 Definitions

ALTE	Apparent life-threatening event:
	Apnoea, blue spells, fits, unresponsive
Cyanosis	Blue spell
Apnoea	Cessation of breathing, respiratory pause
Anoxic seizures	Fits from oxygen deprivation following apnoea/cyanosis
Cardiac arrest	Absent heart rate

Imposed upper airways obstruction (smothering or suffocation) carries a high risk of sudden death. A carer may place a hand firmly, possibly briefly over the infant's mouth. Cyanosis and a respiratory pause (apnoea) may follow. Smothering must persist for at least a minute to cause seizures, longer to cause neurological damage and more than 2 minutes to cause death. However, effects may be more sudden if the infant has a cardiac arrest or vomits and chokes. For survivors, subsequent behavioural disturbances are common and the risks of similar abuse to siblings high [20].

Smothering is commonest under 1 year of age and unusual over 3 years. A carer, usually the mother, but sometimes the father, may abuse a child in this manner for long periods before a diagnosis is made [21]. An adult hand, pillow or clothing is used or the carer may press the child's head against his or her chest.

Meadow (1990) reviewed 27 cases of suffocation by the mother. The diagnosis was based on observation or recording of the suffocation, maternal confession or prosecution in a Criminal Court. Of the 27 cases, 18 survived (one with severe brain damage) and 9 died. Twenty-four were reported to have had previous episodes of apnoea, cyanosis, or seizure, and 11 had 10 or more of these episodes. Repetitive suffocation mainly began between 1–3 months and continued until discovered or the child died 6–12 months later. The 27 children had 15 live elder siblings and 18 siblings who had died suddenly and unexpectedly in early life. Thirteen of the dead siblings had experienced recurrent apnoea, cyanosis, or seizures [22].

Samuels et al. (1992) reported that confrontation with the parents resulted in denial in 14 cases before CVS evidence was available. Nine of 14 cases had a history of previous factitious illness or self-harm in carers [23].

Clinical History

There is typically a history of repeated attendances for cyanosis, apnoea, seizures and unresponsiveness with or without physical evidence of suffocation. The same carer is present at the onset of each episode with others subsequently attending (Table 8.5). Recovery may be rapid with observers present in the aftermath usually seeing a well or crying child. However, depending on the length and duration of suffocation breathing difficulties, cyanosis, seizures or collapse may all be reported soon after the event. Other signs include bleeding from the upper airways or a

Table 8.5 Features that raise suspicion for imposed airway obstruction	Repeated episodes of cyanosis, apnoea, seizures and unresponsiveness
	The same carer is present at the onset of each episode
	Thereafter observers see a well, sometimes unwell infant depending on the length of airways obstruction
	Abnormal physical signs may be found at presentation
	Previous unexplained sudden deaths in infants
	Concerns for physical abuse or neglect
	Strong suspicion of fabricated illness in the child or siblings
	Parent with somatisation or abnormal illness behaviour

petechial rash over the face and neck. A careful search by paramedics for physical signs, as set out below is essential as these may have resolved by the time the infant or child arrives in the emergency department (ED).

Examination and Investigations

Signs of oxygen deprivation and stress
Oxygen saturations recorded close to the event by paramedics may be low. By the time the infant arrives in ED, saturations are usually normal, unless suffocation was prolonged.

Routine blood tests may show non-specific signs of stress including a high white cell count, raised CRP, hyperglycaemia, hypocalcaemia or transient clotting abnormalities. A blood gas may show metabolic acidosis with raised lactate. There may be changes on EEG with encephalopathic features and evidence of hypoxic-ischaemic injury on neuroimaging.

Respiratory and Neurological Complications
Immediately after asphyxiation both respiratory rate and depth increase with transient tachycardia (fast heart rate). This may be followed by bradycardia (slow heart rate). If asphyxia is prolonged, gasping (brain stem response) is seen, then deep sighing respirations.

Under the age of 6 months a respiratory pause (apnoea) is more common. Those over 6 months of age are more likely to struggle, become cyanosed, unresponsive and suffer seizures when a slower recovery is expected.

Rosen et al. (1983) described the case of a 4-month-old girl reported to have daily episodes of cardiopulmonary arrest requiring resuscitation by her mother. At 7 months of age, covert video surveillance (CVS) revealed that following respiratory obstruction by the mother the infant was moving for 90 seconds. Bradycardia commenced 30 seconds into the event and EEG slowed and flattened after 90 seconds at which time the infant was limp and apnoeic, requiring resuscitation [24].

Southall et al. (1987) described two children where intentional suffocation was captured on CVS. The first was a 20-month-old who had suffered weekly cyanotic episodes since the age of 4 months. The mother smothered the child with a T-shirt who awoke and struggled violently. Gross movements stopped at 70 seconds into the event, the EEG flattened just after 70 seconds and gasping respirations began. In the second case a similar pattern was observed [25].

Other respiratory complications include aspiration pneumonia, pulmonary haemorrhage, pneumothorax and rib fractures. A chest radiograph may show pulmonary oedema.

Bleeding
Following airways obstruction, blood vessels may rupture in the mouth, pharynx, lower airways or lung tissue. Bleeding from the nose/mouth or upper airways is bright red whilst regurgitated swallowed blood appears darker. Pulmonary secretions

are pink and frothy. For the latter, lung infiltrates may be found on chest radiograph. (non-cardiogenic pulmonary oedema). Onset and resolution (both clinical and radiological) are more rapid than found in aspiration or infection.

Becroft et al. (2001) reviewed 385 cases of SIDS (sudden infant death syndrome) finding nasal haemorrhage in 60/385 (15%). Pulmonary haemorrhage was found in 47% of 115 cases studied, being severe in only 7%. Both nasal and intrapulmonary haemorrhages were associated with younger infant age, bed sharing, and the infant being placed non-prone to sleep. Becroft suggested that smothering was a possible common factor for such haemorrhages although was unlikely to be the cause in most cases presenting as SIDS [26].

McIntosh et al. (2007) reviewed 16 nose bleeds and 3 cases of haemoptysis (blood originating from lung tissue) from 77,173 emergency department attendances over 10 years in children under 2 years of age. All cases of haemoptysis were associated with significant coughing bouts and respiratory infections. Nose bleeds in 8 cases were associated with visible trauma and in 4 cases with blood disorders. In 2 cases, an associated ALTE was described and in 2, there was an associated upper respiratory tract infection. Review of case notes suggested that 7 cases diagnosed as accidental injury might have been caused by abuse [27].

In a further study, McIntosh et al. (2010) reported cases of suffocation and oro-nasal haemorrhage (ONH) over a 10-year period. ONH was recorded as follows: haemorrhage arising from the nose or mouth (N/M) (65), haematemesis (11), haemoptysis (3) and pulmonary haemorrhage (9). Five cases were thought to be have been caused by airways obstruction. Of haemorrhage arising from the nose or mouth, (N/M), 40/65 were associated with trauma, of which 15 were thought to be probable abuse. Four cases had coagulation abnormalities. In the N/M group, 8 of 65 had a respiratory tract infection and 4 of these presented with an ALTE [28].

Rees et al. (2016) reviewed 6 studies representing 30 children with asphyxiation related epistaxis (nose bleeds) and 74 children with non-asphyxiation related epistaxis. The proportion of children presenting with epistaxis post asphyxiation was 7–24%. Features associated with asphyxiation included malaise, altered skin colour, respiratory difficulty, and chest radiograph abnormalities. The authors concluded that whilst that there was an association between epistaxis and asphyxiation in young children, epistaxis did not in itself constitute a diagnosis of asphyxia [29].

Krous et al. (2001) described oro-nasal blood in 28 (7%) of 406 cases of sudden infant deaths that may have been attributed to cardiopulmonary resuscitation (CPR) in 14 cases. The authors noted that oro-nasal blood not attributable to CPR occurred rarely in SIDS when the infant is sleeping supine in a safe environment. They added that oro-nasal blood observed before CPR may be a sign of accidental or inflicted suffocation [30].

In a further study, Krous et al. (2007) reported that differentiating SIDS from accidental or inflicted suffocation might be impossible in some cases. The authors reviewed all post-neonatal cases of SIDS or suffocation. There were 444 cases including SIDS (405), accidental suffocation (36) and inflicted suffocation (3). Pulmonary intra-alveolar haemorrhage was graded as absent (0) to severe (4). Grades 3 or 4 occurred in

33% of deaths attributed to suffocation, but in only 11% of the SIDS cases. However, all grades of pulmonary hemorrhage occurred in both groups. Among SIDS cases, those with a pulmonary haemorrhage of Grade 3 or 4 were more likely to bedshare, and with more than one co-sleeper [31].

Petechiae

Petechiae are small pinpoint bruises on the skin and mucosal surfaces (blood spots). They develop within a few minutes of injury, may disappear rapidly and usually by 72 hours (page 37). Following upper airways obstruction, they may be found on the face, neck, upper chest and conjunctivae resulting from raised intravascular pressure, lack of oxygen and retention of carbon dioxide.

Meadow (1990) reviewed the cases of 27 children who had been suffocated. Five had facial petechiae and two had bruises on the neck, while 14 had no external findings related to suffocation [22].

Neglect and other signs of trauma

There may be evidence of neglect or other signs of injury including abusive head trauma (AHT). Hand pressure may leave thumb marks or fingerprints around the nose and mouth as well as abrasions inside the mouth and bruising to the gums. The labial frenulum may be torn.

Cardiac Arrest

Oxygen deprivation leads to cyanosis, apnoea, convulsions, cardiac arrest and death. Other causes for cardiac arrest must be considered (Table 8.6).

Sudden Unexpected Death in Childhood (SUDC) is a child death that was not anticipated but may subsequently be explained by medical diagnosis or at postmortem. Sudden Unexpected Death in Infancy (SUDI) carries the same definition for an infant. Where no cause is identified, the term Sudden Infant Death Syndrome (SIDS) is used. Sudden Infant Death Syndrome is defined as 'the sudden death of an infant under 1 year of age which remains unexplained after a thorough case investigation including a complete autopsy, examination of the death scene and review of the

Table 8.6 Causes for cardiac arrest in infants and children

Oxygen deprivation	Airways obstruction, accidental or imposed
Loss of fluids	Hypovolaemia from e.g.: gastroenteritis or blood loss
Electrolyte disturbances	e.g.: high potassium, low sodium
Hypothermia	Temperatures below 20°C
Tension pneumothorax	Spontaneous or traumatic
Therapy	Drug associated arrest
Cardiac tamponade	Compression of the heart by fluid in the pericardial sac
Cardiac disease	eg. cardiomyopathies, rhythm disturbances
Trauma	Chest trauma

clinical history'. SIDS is uncommon under a month of age rising to a peak during the second month with 90% occurring by 6 months. Some are reported between 6 and 12 months with very few after a year. The rate of SIDS has declined in the UK by 75% since 1991 with the introduction of advice to include placing the infant on his or her back to sleep, preventing overheating and avoidance of parental smoking.

Other Causes for Apparent Life-Threatening Events (ALTE)

An ALTE refers to apnoea, cyanosis, seizures or being unresponsive. Often, no cause is found. A careful history, examination and thorough investigations are required particularly if there have been multiple episodes.

Infection
Infants with respiratory tract infections such as bronchiolitis and whooping cough, bowel infections such as rotavirus enteritis, those with viraemia or septicaemia to include meningitis may all present with ALTE.

Cardiac
Infants with cardiomyopathy, rhythm disturbances, prolonged QTc interval on ECG or congenital heart disease may present with an ALTE as the first clinical indication of disease.

Neurological
Epilepsy may present with convulsions, apnoea or unconsciousness. Head injury (including AHT), meningitis, encephalitis and neuromuscular disorders can lead to central hypoventilation and ALTE.

Gastro-oesophageal reflux (GORD)
In GORD, stomach contents reflux into the oesophagus causing repeated vomiting, crying, occasional failure to thrive, coughing, irritability, poor feeding, pain and breathing problems in the early months of life. Most infants are substantially improved by 12–24 months.

Semmekrot et al. (2010) reported 115 cases of ALTE mean age 11.4 weeks of which 110 were analysed. The most frequent diagnoses were gastro-oesophageal reflux (37.3%) and respiratory tract infection (8.2%). Change of colour, choking, gagging and breathing difficulties were the main symptoms observed by carers. Choking/gagging was observed in 17.3%, apnoea in 14.6%. Thirty-four percent of carers shook their infants whilst 12% reported either mouth-to-mouth breathing, tapping, squeezing, blowing, or holding the infant upside down. There were no deaths and no infant needed resuscitation on presentation. Other features reported by carers before the incident included excessive vomiting (25.5%), common cold (28.2%), feeding problems (19.1%), drowsy (7.3%), fever (7.3%), vaccination less than 24 hours prior (4.5%), apnoea (5.5%), poor growth (3.6%), excessive crying (2.7%), other (19%). Ten percent had recurrent ALTE [32].

Wenzl et al. (2001) studied 364 GORD episodes in 22 infants. Forty-nine apnoeas were associated with GORD and 11 (22.4%) of these showed acid reflux (pH < 4) [33]. Arad-Cohen et al. (2000) studied 67 infants up to 6 months with ALTE. No significant reflux was found in 32 whilst 14 had such prolonged reflux that the relationship with apnoeas could not be evaluated. In the 21 remaining infants with apnoea and reflux, for 81% of episodes there was no relationship to GORD [34].

Ear Nose and Throat

Laryngomalacia, a sensitive larynx, floppy epiglottis, pooling of pharyngeal secretions are all possible causes. Micro-laryngobronchoscopy (MLB) combined with an overnight sleep study recording any significant oxygen de-saturations will aid diagnosis.

Metabolic/Endocrine

Takahashi et al. (2015) investigated patients who presented with ALTE or Sudden Unexpected Death in Infancy (SUDI) ages 7 days – 3 years. Inborn errors of metabolism were detected in 3/196 (1.5%) of infants with SUDI, and in 7/167 (4.2%) of patients with ALTE. Nine had a history of poor feeding during the neonatal period with cough, fever or vomiting during infancy [35].

Idiopathic

In many cases no cause is found. Presentations are usually single and rarely seen after 12 months.

Abusive Head Trauma (AHT)

A shaking or impact head injury may result in an ALTE. Neuro-imaging may show subdural haematomas with retinal haemorrhages observed on ophthalmic examination (chapter 5).

Illness Fabrication

Reports of repeated ALTE may be exaggerated or fabricated. Symptoms are episodic with acute symptoms observed usually by one carer.

Other Causes of Oro-Nasal Bleeding

Possible causes of oro-nasal bleeding are listed in Table 8.7. Accidental, inflicted or medical causes are all possible. Blood may originate from the mouth, nose, upper airways, lung, oesophagus or stomach.

Infants with an *upper respiratory tract infection* occasionally present with blood streaked sputum. Minor bleeding may also occur after rough handling with a feeding bottle particularly when the infant has oral thrush. In *inflicted injury,* a perpetrator may force an infant's face on to a hard surface, insert a blunt or sharp instrument into the mouth or instil hot or caustic substances (Fig. 8.1). Injuries to the nose, mouth, teeth, palate, pharynx and frenulum have been described leading to

Table 8.7 Causes of bleeding from the nose mouth, larynx, lower airways and GI tract

Airways
Upper airway obstruction (accidental or imposed)
Resuscitation
Severe coughing
Upper respiratory tract infection (usually minimal bleeding)
Lung contusion
Spontaneous vessel rupture
Congenital haemangioma
Pneumonia and pulmonary oedema
Shaking injury
Direct trauma
Gastro-intestinal tract
Gastro-oesophageal reflux (GORD) with oesophagitis
Mallory Weiss syndrome
Nasal Bleeding Oral blood directed down the nostril
Physical abuse
Infection Spontaneous vessel rupture/congenital malformations
Other
Illness induction (FII)
Bleeding disorders
Rare medical causes

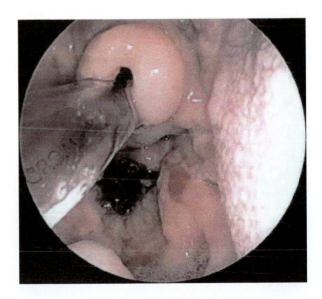

Fig. 8.1 Micro-laryngo-bronchoscopy demonstrating a blood clot following forced insertion of an adult finger into an infant's mouth and pharynx

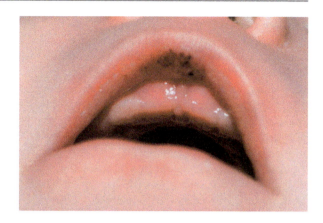

Fig. 8.2 A 4-month-old infant was brought to ED with oral bleeding and torn upper frenulum. Associated injuries were a skull fracture, SDH and retinal haemorrhages

significant bleeding. A *shaking injury* may result in oral bleeding due to rupture of small vessels in the mouth, upper airways or oesophagus.

The *labial frenulum* is a fold of tissue that secures and restricts the motion of the lips. The upper frenulum lies inside the upper lip, the lower one lying under the tongue. Force feeding, twisting the lip or a direct blow may all cause frenular injuries (Fig. 8.2).

In the aftermath, the infant will cry out in pain but settle if fed and comforted. Bleeding may initially be severe but usually ceases within a few minutes.

Tears to the frenulum of the tongue or upper lip may be found after accidental trauma in children beginning to mobilise following falls on to hard surfaces. In pre-mobile infants, they are more likely to be inflicted and part of a pattern of more extensive injury. Congenital abnormalities of the frenulum may be mistaken for a tear.

Maguire et al. (2007) reviewed nine studies documenting inflicted torn labial frenula in 27 infants and children of whom 24 were fatally abused. Only a direct blow to the face was confirmed as a mechanism of injury. Inflicted intra-oral injuries were widely distributed to the lips, gums, tongue and palate. Two studies reported torn labial frenula, both from intubation. The authors concluded that abuse could not be based on a torn labial frenulum in isolation [36].

Morrison et al. (1998) reported the case of a 3½-year-old who suffered significant head and neck injuries as a result of a protective airbag during a *collision*. Injuries included multiple abrasions, a torn labial frenulum, conjunctival petechiae, skull fractures, subgaleal and subarachnoid haemorrhages, cortical contusions, subluxation of the atlanto-occipital joint, and fracture of the C4 vertebral body [37].

Lopez et al. (2014) prospectively studied all *intubated patients* younger than 3 years of age. Of 105 patients, 12 had oral, jaw, or neck injury. One had a hard palate injury from a pen cap in his mouth during a seizure. Another broke a tooth biting the laryngoscope blade. The remaining 10 patients were considered to have suffered inflicted trauma. The incidence of injury directly from intubation was 0.9% [38].

Haematemesis (blood in vomitus) may result from swallowed blood which is then regurgitated. Gastro-oesophageal reflux (GORD) may present with bleeding when associated with oesophagitis. Acute stress gastritis is caused by a sudden illness or injury such as extensive skin burns.

Mallory Weiss syndrome is characterised by mucosal lacerations usually in the last part of the oesophagus and is associated with forceful retching. Bak-Romaniszyn et al. (1999) examined with endoscopy 2,720 children aged 5 months - 18 years who presented with haematemesis. Mallory-Weiss syndrome was diagnosed in eight (0.3%) [39].

Nasal bleeding may result from accidental or intentional smothering, a bleeding disorder, congenital malformations and rhinitis (common cold). Oral bleeding may be re-directed down the nostrils. In abuse, a carer may force an infant's face on to a hard immovable surface, pinch, or twist the nose or impact the child's face with a blunt instrument (Table 8.7).

Paranjothy et al. (2009) reported 36 cases of nosebleeds, (median age 12 weeks). Twenty-three were found to have a cause (trauma 5, coagulation disorder 4, congenital 2, rhinitis or coryza (common cold) 11, abusive smothering 1). No cause was identified in 13 cases. Coagulation disorders were excluded in seven of the 13 infants with the remainder not tested. Child abuse was suspected but excluded in 4 of the 13 cases [40].

> A 6-week-old infant was admitted to hospital with oral bleeding. Microlarygobronchocopy (MLB) revealed pharyngeal burns which were considered to be from a caustic substance. A repeat MLB a week later was inconclusive and child protection procedures were halted. Two years later, a sibling presented with recurrent oral bleeding found to have been caused by a caustic substance.

Prognosis and the Risk of Further Harm in FII

The prognosis in FII depends on the extent and length of time the child has endured abuse. Long-term psychological problems, disability, physical illness, death or neuro-disability from poisoning or smothering have all been recorded. There are risks of further abuse.

Sheridan (2003) reviewed 154 case reports concluding that 6% of cases resulted in death with 7.3% experiencing long-term or permanent injury. Of siblings, 25% died and 61.3% had illnesses similar to those of the victims [10].

Bools et al. (1993) followed up 54 children known to have suffered FII. A range of emotional and behavioural problems were found whether or not the child was accommodated. Of 30 children living with the original abuser, 10 suffered further fabrication. Outcomes for children who had a period in foster care following diagnosis were better than for those who remained continuously with their carer [41].

Berg and Jones (1999) reported the outcomes of 13 children admitted to an inpatient family unit after diagnosis. Families were engaged in therapeutic work where there was a likelihood of a successful outcome. It was recommended that 10 children should be reunited with their biological parents and 3 should be placed in alternative care. At an average of 27 months after discharge from the unit, the children had done well for development, growth and adjustment [42].

Gray and Bentovim (1996) reported good outcomes for children where cases were managed within a child protection framework and long-term therapeutic interventions were focused on the protection of the child [43].

References

1. McClure RJ, Davis PM, Meadow R, Sibert JR. Epidemiology of Munchausen syndrome by proxy, non-accidental poisoning and non-accidental suffocation. Arch Dis Child. 1996;75:57–61.
2. Watson S, Eminson DM, Coupe W. Quoted as personal communication. In: Eminson M, Postlethwaite RJ, editors. Munchausen syndrome by proxy abuse: a practical approach. Oxford: Butterworth Heinemann; 2000.
3. Flaherty EG, MacMillan HL, Committee On Child Abuse and Neglect. Caregiver-fabricated illness in a child: a manifestation of child maltreatment. Pediatrics. 2013;132:590.
4. Roesler T, Jenny C. Medical child abuse: beyond Munchausen syndrome by proxy. American Academy of Pediatrics; 2008.
5. Davis P. The Cardiff Leeds study of alleged Munchausen syndrome by proxy, non-accidental poisoning and non-accidental suffocation. Welsh Paediatr J. 2000;13:32–41.
6. Jureidini J. Obstetric factitious disorder and Munchausen syndrome by proxy. J Nerv Ment Dis. 1993;181(2):135–7.
7. Meadow R. Munchausen syndrome by proxy abuse perpetrated by men. Arch Dis Child. 1998;78:210–6.
8. Levin AV, Sheridan MS, editors. Munchausen syndrome by proxy: issues in diagnosis and treatment. New York: Lexington Books; 1995.
9. Rosenberg DA. Web of deceit: a literature review of Munchausen syndrome by proxy. Child Abuse Negl. 1987;11:547–63.
10. Sheridan MS. The deceit continues: an updated literature review of Munchausen syndrome by proxy. Child Abuse Negl. 2003;27(4):431–51.
11. Davis PM, McClure RJ, Rolfe K, Chessman N, Pearson S, Sibert JR, Meadow R. Procedures, placement and risks of further abuse after Munchausen syndrome by proxy, non-accidental poisoning and non-accidental suffocation. Arch Dis Child. 1998;78:217–21.
12. Mian M. A multidisciplinary approach. In: Levin AV, Sheridan MS, editors. Munchausen syndrome by proxy: issues in diagnosis and treatment. New York: Lexington Books; 1995. p. 271–86.
13. HM Government. Regulation of Investigatory Powers Act. 2000.
14. Shabde N, Craft AW. Covert video surveillance: an important investigative tool or a breach of trust? Archives of Disease in Childhood 1999;81(4):291–4.
15. Hall DE, Eubanks L, Meyyazhagan LS, Kenney RD, Johnson SC. Evaluation of covert video surveillance in the diagnosis of Munchausen syndrome by proxy: lessons from 41 cases. Pediatrics. 2000;105(6):1305–12.
16. General Medical Council. Protecting children and young people: the responsibilities of all doctors. 2012.
17. General Medical Council. 0–18 years: guidance for all doctors. 2007.
18. Bools C, Neale B, Meadow R. Munchausen syndrome by proxy: a study of psychopathology. Child Abuse Negl. 1994;18:773–88.

19. Bass C, David J. Psychopathology of perpetrators of fabricated or induced illness in children: case series. Br J Psychiatry. 2011;199(2):113–8.
20. McGuire TL, Feldman KW. Psychological morbidity of children subjected to Munchausen syndrome by proxy. Pediatrics. 1989;83:289–92.
21. Makar AF, Squier PJ. Munchausen syndrome by proxy: father as a perpetrator. Pediatrics. 1990;85:370–3.
22. Meadow R. Suffocation, recurrent apnea, and sudden infant death. J Pediatr. 1990;117:351–7.
23. Samuels MP, McClaughlin W, Jacobson RR, Poets CF, Southall DP. Fourteen cases of imposed upper airway obstruction. Arch Dis Child. 1992;67(2):162–70.
24. Rosen CL, Frost JD, Bricker T, Tarnow JD, Gillette PC, Dunlavy S. Two siblings with recurrent cardiorespiratory arrest: Munchausen syndrome by proxy or child abuse? Pediatrics. 1983;71:715–20.
25. Southall DP, Stebbens VA, Rees SV, Lang MH, Warner JO, Shinebourne EA. Apnoeic episodes induced by smothering: two cases identified by covert video surveillance. Br Med J. 1987;294:1637–41.
26. Becroft DM, Thompson JM, Mitchell EA. Nasal and intrapulmonary haemorrhage in sudden infant death syndrome. Arch Dis Child. 2001;85(2):116–20.
27. McIntosh N, Mok JY, Margerison A. Epidemiology of oro-nasal hemorrhage in the first 2 years of life: implications for child protection. Pediatrics. 2007;120(5):1074–8.
28. McIntosh N, Mok JY, Margerison A, Armstrong L, Mathews A, Robertson AK, Street J, Sweeney S, Chalmers J. The epidemiology of oro-nasal haemorrhage and suffocation in infants admitted to hospital in Scotland over 10 years. J Arch Dis Child. 2010;95(10):810–6.
29. Rees P, Kemp A, Carter B, Maguire S. A systematic review of the probability of asphyxia in children aged <2 years with unexplained epistaxis. J Pediatr. 2016;168:178–84.
30. Krous HF, Nadeau JM, Byard RW, Blackbourne BD. Oro-nasal blood in sudden infant death. Am J Forensic Med Pathol. 2001;22(4):346–51.
31. Krous HF, Chadwick AE, Haas EA, Stanley C. Pulmonary intra-alveolar hemorrhage in SIDS and suffocation. J Forensic Leg Med. 2007;14(8):461–70.
32. Semmekrot BA, van Sleuwen BE, Engelberts AC, Joosten KF, Mulder JC, Liem KD, Rodrigues Pereira R, Bijlmer RP, L'Hoir MP. Surveillance study of apparent life-threatening events (ALTE) in the Netherlands. Eur J Pediatr. 2010;169(2):229–36.
33. Wenzl TG, Schenke S, Peschgens T, Silny J, Heimann G, Skopnik H. Association of apnea and non-acid gastroesophageal reflux in infants: investigations with the intraluminal impedance technique. Pediatr Pulmonol. 2001;31(2):144–9.
34. Arad-Cohen N, Cohen A, Tirosh E. The relationship between gastroesophageal reflux and apnea in infants. J Pediatr. 2000;137(3):321–6.
35. Takahashi T, Yamada K, Kobayashi H, Hasegawa Y, Taketani T, Fukuda S, Yamaguchi S. Metabolic disease in10 patients with sudden unexpected death in infancy or acute life-threatening events. Pediatr Int. 2015;57(3):348–53.
36. Maguire SA, Hunter B, Hunter LM, Sibert JR, Mann MK, Kemp AM. Diagnosing abuse: a systematic review of torn frenum and other intra-oral injuries. Arch Dis Child. 2007;92(12):1113–7.
37. Morrison AL, Chute D, Radentz S, Golle M, Troncoso JC, Smialek JE. Air bag-associated injury to a child in the front passenger seat. Am J Forensic Med Pathol. 1998;19(3):218–22.
38. Lopez MR, Abd-Allah S, Deming DD, Piantini R, Young-Snodgrass A, Perkin R, Barcega B, Sheridan-Matney C. Oral, jaw, and neck injury in infants and children: from abusive trauma or intubation? Pediatr Emerg Care. 2014;30(5):305–10.
39. Bak-Romaniszyn L, Małecka-Panas E, Czkwianianc E, Płaneta-Małecka I. Mallory-Weiss syndrome in children. Dis Esophagus. 1999;12(1):65–7.
40. Paranjothy S, Fone D, Mann M, Dunstan F, Evans E, Tomkinson A, Sibert J, Kemp A. The incidence and aetiology of epistaxis in infants: a population-based study. Arch Dis Child. 2009;94(6):421–4.
41. Bools CN, Neale BA, Meadow R. Follow up of victims of fabricated illness (Munchausen syndrome by proxy). Arch Dis Child. 1993;69(6):625–30.

42. Berg B, Jones DP. Outcome of psychiatric intervention in factitious illness by proxy (Munchausen's syndrome by proxy). Arch Dis Child. 1999;81(6):465–72.
43. Gray J, Bentovim A. Illness induction syndrome: paper I – a series of 41 children from 37 families identified at The Great Ormond Street Hospital for Children NHS Trust. Child Abuse Negl. 1996;20(8):655–73.

Further Reading

Royal College of Paediatrics and Child Health. Fabricated or induced illness by carers (FII): a practical guide for Paediatricians. 2009 (Review date: October 2012).

Child Sexual Abuse

9

Abstract

This chapter provides an overview of an increasingly specialised and complex area where the understanding of physical signs is advancing and opinions changing. Detailed guidance on the assessment of children and young people for CSA is described in the RCPCH document 'The Physical Signs of Child Sexual Abuse – an evidence based review and guidance for best practice' [1].

A child is sexually abused when he or she is forced or persuaded to observe or take part in sexual acts including online activities. The Sexual Offences Act makes it an offence, where a child is under the age of 13 years, for a person to rape (the penetration by the penis of a child's vagina, anus or mouth), sexually assault by penetration (penetrate sexually the vagina or anus of a child with a part of the body or object), sexually assault by touch or cause or incite a child to engage in sexual activity whether or not the child consented to the act [2].

Sexual abuse presents in many ways and children who suffer in this manner are often coerced into secrecy for many years. Presenting symptoms may be general (e.g. abdominal pain, enuresis, behavioural problems) or more specific (e.g. vaginal bleeding or a sexually transmitted infection).

A child may make a disclosure or be unwilling or unable to do so. Grooming and threats from a perpetrator may maintain secrecy. Disclosures are rarely fabricated and must always be taken as significant. When a child resides with an adult known to pose a risk to children, vigilance is required.

A meticulous assessment by a paediatrician with specialist and appropriate training is essential.

© Springer International Publishing Switzerland 2017
D.L. Robinson, *Pediatric Forensic Evidence*, DOI 10.1007/978-3-319-45337-8_9

Clinical Assessment

Multidisciplinary Approach

When an infant or child presents with suspicions for CSA, urgent assessment, investigations and photo-documentation are essential in order to obtain the required forensic evidence and safeguard the child.

A multidisciplinary approach is required to include paediatricians, forensic specialists, nurses, microbiologists, psychologists, social care and the police.

Medical History

Police interviews should ideally take place before medical assessments, so long as they do not delay examination. A comprehensive medical history and examination should be undertaken (chapter 1, pages 4–6). Systems enquiries, past medical and family history are all relevant.

Questions specific for suspected CSA include any sexual and or menstrual history as well as use of sanitary towels or contraception. The child's account of any abusive event must be carefully taken including whether and where ejaculation occurred, if a condom or lubricant was used, whether pain, bleeding or other sensations were felt, and in the aftermath whether passing urine or opening bowels was painful and associated with bleeding. It is important to document whether the child has washed, cleaned his or her teeth or changed any clothing since the alleged event (Table 9.1).

Examination

Physical Examination should include observation of parent-child interaction, signs of neglect, assessment of growth and pubertal stage, systems examination and a careful search for any skin or other injury. The child's development, behaviour and

Table 9.1 Medical history

Sexual and menstrual history, use of sanitary towels and contraception
Present, past and family history
Account of any event and the nature of the alleged abuse
Whether and where ejaculation occurred
Whether a condom or lubricant was used
Pain experienced
Bleeding or other sensations
Whether passing urine or opening bowels after the alleged event was associated with bleeding or pain
Has the child washed, cleaned teeth or changed clothes since the alleged event

emotional status should be documented. The child should not wash until assessments are complete.

The paediatrician must decide whether a specialist forensic medical examination is urgent or can be planned for a suitable time by the local designated paediatrician for safeguarding in an appropriate setting. The forensic examination must be performed only once. When the alleged sexual abuse has occurred within 72 hours or there is bleeding/acute injury a forensic examination is considered urgent in order to optimise the chance of obtaining forensic evidence. Non-urgent examinations are appropriate where there has been a historical disclosure of abuse, sexualised behaviours or other relevant concerns.

Urgent assessments can be conducted jointly by the consultant paediatrican and forensic medical examiner or by the local designated paediatrician for safeguarding. Sexual Assault Referral Centres (SARCs) provide specialist and urgent assessments to include a forensic examination with photo-documentation and relevant investigations. Competences required for doctors are set out in the FFLM RCPCH (Faculty of Forensic and Legal Medicine, Royal College of Paediatrics and Child Health) guidelines [3].

The forensic medical examination is most likely to detect abnormal signs within 72 hours of the alleged event. DNA is more likely to be recovered in pre-pubertal children less than 24 hours from the time of the alleged assault.

The 'chain of evidence' protects forensic specimens from contamination. The person collecting the specimens completes, dates and signs a form with details of the patient. Anyone handling the sample should sign and date the same form.

A child may need management of acute trauma, post-exposure prophylaxis for HIV, Hepatitis B and bacterial infections or emergency contraception (consent required). Some children may need follow-up examinations for acute injury or sexually transmitted infections.

Social care

Child protection procedures must be commenced. An urgent telephone referral to social care should be followed by a written referral. Local safeguarding children's board (LSCB) procedures should be followed (pages 16–17).

Police

The police should be involved whenever a criminal act is suspected. They will visit the home and collect relevant forensic information including medications, bedding, and clothing or retain these if provided by the hospital. Forensic investigations such as DNA analysis should be conducted under their direction.

Therapeutic support

The child and family will need psychological support. An urgent referral to CAMHS will allow specialist psychotherapeutic support to be provided.

Genital Signs of Sexual Abuse in Girls

The interpretation of abnormal genital signs is a highly specialised and complex area where the understanding of physical signs is advancing and a high degree of medical expertise required. A knowledge of anatomical terms (Table 9.2), normal findings (Tables 9.3 and 9.4 and Fig. 9.1) and conditions that may be mistaken for abuse (Table 9.5) is essential.

Table 9.2 Anatomical terms

Labia majora	Outer lips, outer boundaries of the vulva
Labia minora	Inner lips, enclosed within the labia majora
Vestibule	Cavity containing vaginal opening & urethra
Vulva	External genitalia
Vaginal canal	Canal that extends from the hymen to the cervix
Fourchette	Junction of the two labia minora inferiorly
Urethral orifice	External opening of the urethral canal from the bladder
Hymen	Membrane surrounding the hymenal orifice
	Partially covers the vaginal orifice
Perineum	Lies between the posterior fourchette and the anus in a girl
Perineal body	The central tendon of the perineum
	Lies between the vestibule and the anus in the female
Fossa navicularis	Depression between the posterior margin of the vaginal opening & the fourchette

Table 9.3 Hymenal anatomy and findings that may be normal

Notch/cleft	'V' shaped indentation found superiorly or laterally on the hymenal membrane
Bump or mound	Rounded thickened area on the edge of the hymen
Annular	Hymen extends around circumference of the entire vaginal orifice
Crescentric	Hymen is attached at 11 o'clock and 1 o'clock positions
	No hymenal tissue between these two attachments
Imperforate	Hymen has no opening
Micro-perforate	Hymen has one or more small openings
Septate	One or more septae across the hymenal opening
Redundant	Multiple flaps, folding over each other
Hymenal tag	Elongated projection of tissue arising from the hymenal rim (may be abnormal)
Smooth rim	Rim appears relatively narrow
Bands	Periurethral or vestibular bands

Table 9.4 Other normal findings

Linea vestibularis	Pale line through the fourchette and fossa navicularis.
	May be mistaken for a scar
Urethra	Dilation of the urethral opening
Ridges	Intravaginal ridges or columns

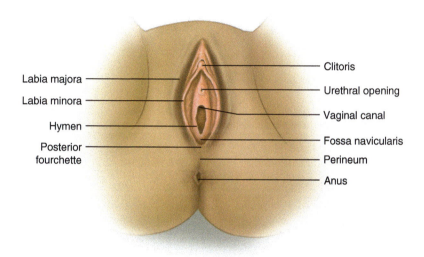

Clitoris

Labia majora

Urethral opening

Labia minora

Vaginal canal

Hymen

Posterior fourchette

Fossa navicularis

Perineum

Anus

Fig. 9.1 External Structure of the Female Genital Area

Table 9.5 Conditions that may be mistaken for abuse

Urethral prolapse
Lichen sclerosus et atrophicus
Vulval ulcer
Erythema, inflammation, and fissuring due to infection
Failure of midline fusion (perineal groove)
Rectal prolapse

Normal Findings on Examination

Detection of abnormal physical signs is dependent on the timing of the examination. Abnormal signs are more likely to be found within 72 hours of an event. Many children who have suffered CSA will have normal findings particularly when the assessment has been delayed. There is no basis for a conclusion that sexual abuse can be diagnosed only in the presence of abnormal physical findings.

Bowen and Aldous (1999) examined 393 children of whom 190 (48.3%) had a definite or probable history of sexual abuse. A further 130 (33.1%) had a suspicious history whilst 73 (18.6%) had no such history. Regardless of accounts provided, examination findings were normal or non-specific in 83.5–94.4% of cases [4].

Hobbs et al. (1995) examined 109 prepubertal girls suspected of being sexually abused. Fifty-nine had abnormal physical signs consistent with blunt trauma including a hymenal transection most commonly at the 6 o'clock position, a major notch, scar, or hymenal attenuation [5].

Watkeys et al. (2008) assessed 257 children with alleged penetrative abuse with 114 being seen within 7 days including 23 children who disclosed penetrative anal abuse. Of these, 13 (56.5%) had abnormal findings compared with 9/50 (18%) seen more than 7 days after the alleged anal abuse. Ninety-two girls reported penetrative vaginal abuse within the previous 7 days of whom 46 (50%) had abnormal findings compared with 31 (30.7%) of 101 seen more than 7 days after the alleged abuse. Thirty three girls seen within 7 days had other signs of likely assault [6].

Muram (1989) observed abnormal genital signs in 11 of 18 (61%) girls mean age 9.1 years), where the perpetrator confessed to vaginal penetration compared with 3 of 13 (23%) girls when penetration was denied. In 7 of 18 girls (39%) with perpetrator admission genital appearances were normal or non-specific [7].

Erythema and Oedema

Erythema presents as redness of the skin or mucus membranes. Common causes are trauma, infection or infestations. Some skin conditions, allergies and poor hygiene may lead to inflamed areas. As a physical sign, erythema is a subjective finding and varies with skin pigmentation. It may resolve quickly with more abnormalities found within 24 hours of an alleged abuse.

Oedema is swelling of tissues or mucous membranes from serum due to infection or trauma. Following acute sports injury, swelling is at its worst a few hours to 48 hours after injury with pain and tenderness subsiding after 72 hours.

Muram (1989) reviewed 31 girls where there was a perpetrator confession. Of these 21 were examined within 7 days of the assault. Inflammation/irritation was observed in nine. By contrast, no inflammation was observed in the ten children examined after 7 days [7].

Adams et al. (2001) assessed 214 adolescent girls, 90% of whom gave a history of penile/vaginal penetration. The examination took place within 72 hours of the assault in 87%. Erythema of the labia minora, hymen, cervix and posterior fourchette was noted by the nurse examiner in 18% – 32% [8]. In a previous study Adams and Knudson (1996) reviewed 204 girls aged 9–17 who reported a history of penile-vaginal penetration. Abnormal genital findings were found in 32% but were more common when there was reported bleeding at the time of the assault or when the examination occurred within 72 hours of the abuse. Erythema was observed in 27/204 (13%) [9].

Emans et al. (1987) compared genital findings in 3 groups of girls both pubertal and pre-pubertal. Erythema was reported in 41/119 (34%) of girls who disclosed sexual abuse, 40/59 (68%) of those seen with genital complaints and 16/127(13%) of those seen for routine health examination. Emans noted that skin pigmentation might have influenced findings [10].

Finkel (1989) reported oedema of the hymen, perihymen, fossa navicularis, clitoral hood and labia minora in 2 girls with reported accidental straddle injury which resolved 5–8 days after presentation [11].

McCann et al. (2007) studied the healing process of non-hymenal trauma, sustained by 239 girls aged 4 months–18 years. Injuries in the 113 pre-pubertal girls were accidental (21), abusive (73) and unknown (19). All 126 pubertal girls were victims of sexual assault. Oedema was observed on the labia, perineum and posterior fourchette in 4/126 of these but by the fifth day was present in only 1 of 4 girls [12].

Bruising

A bruise is the escape of blood from ruptured blood vessels, usually capillaries, caused by trauma damaging the skin and blood vessels (page 23). Bruises cannot be aged by colour. Oedema (swelling), tenderness and petechiae indicate that an injury is likely to have occurred within 72 hours of presentation (page 33). Lichen Sclerosus et Atrophicus (LSA), haemangiomas and some pigmented lesions may be mistaken for bruises. When genital bruising is found, in the absence of an underlying haematological disorder it is usually the result of trauma and more likely to be detected within 72 hours of the alleged event.

Heppenstall-Heger et al. (2003) examined 13 boys and 81 girls referred with a history of sexual assault or ano-genital trauma. There were 14 genital/anal abrasions and 6 haematomas in those reporting penile-vaginal penetration (34) and 13 genital abrasions/7 haematomas in those reporting digital-vaginal penetration or fondling (19). In the straddle injury group (25) there were 10 abrasions but no haematomas [13].

McCann et al. (2007) examined both accidental and inflicted trauma (both hymenal and non-hymenal) sustained by 239 girls of whom 164 (64%) were seen within 24 hours, 208 (87%) within 48 hours and 31 (13%) between 48–72 hours. There were 126 pubertal girls who were victims of sexual assault. Hymenal injuries included haematoma in 13 (10%), blood blisters in 7 (5%), sub-mucosal haemorrhage in 67 (53%) and petechiae in 65 (50%).

McCann reported that hymenal injuries healed with little evidence of previous trauma. Petechiae resolved within 48 hours in pre-pubertal girls and 72 hours in adolescents. Abrasions and "mild" submucosal haemorrhages resolved within 3–4 days, whilst "marked" haemorrhages persisted for 11–14 days. A blood blister was observed at 34 days in an adolescent. Of non-hymenal injuries, petechiae disappeared by 24 hours, abrasions by day 3, oedema day 5, bruising between 2–18 days depending on severity [12, 14].

Palusci et al. (2006) evaluated 190 children under 13 years of age urgently referred for CSA assessment and compared them to non-urgently referred children. Semen or sperm was identified from body swabs only from non-bathed, females older than 10 years of age or on clothing or objects. Of the 190 children seen urgently, 13.2% had abnormal signs (including 4 with bruising) and 4.8% were confirmed to have a sexually transmitted infection [15].

Myhre et al. (2010) examined 31 girls at age 5–6 with re-examination at 11–12 years. There were no concerns for abuse and all denied sexual activity. One reported a painful insertion of a tampon and was found to have a probable transection in her hymen. Otherwise there were no abnormal findings [16].

Abrasions

An abrasion is a superficial injury involving the outer layers of the skin/mucous membrane.

Heppenstall-Heger et al. (2003) reported 10 abrasions in 24 girls with a history of penile-vaginal penetration seen within 72 hours. There were 13 abrasions in 19 girls with a history of digital-vaginal penetration/fondling and 9 abrasions in 25 girls with straddle injury [13].

McCann et al. (2007) found hymenal abrasions in 2/126 of pubertal victims of sexual assault. There were a total of 63 non-hymenal genital abrasions in various locations. Abrasions resolved by the third day after injury [12, 14].

Lacerations

The terms transection, tear and laceration have been variably used in the literature. A laceration is caused by blunt force splitting the skin or mucous membrane. A first-degree tear is limited to the fourchette and superficial perineal/vaginal mucosa. A second-degree tear extends beyond the skin and mucosa to the perineal muscles but not the anal sphincter. In a third-degree tear the fourchette, perineal skin, vaginal mucosa, muscles and anal sphincter are affected.

Hymenal and non-Hymenal Lacerations

Heppenstall-Heger et al. (2003) observed two lacerations to the hymen in 24 pre-pubertal girls reporting vaginal penetration and in 4/19 girls reporting digital vaginal penetration/fondling (in addition 12 transections were reported). Four transections were reported in the straddle injury group (25) [13].

Muram (1989) observed hymenal/vaginal tears in 11/18 girls who described vaginal penetration compared with 3/13 of those who denied penetration [7].

McCann et al. (2007) reported 87 non-hymenal lacerations in 126 pubertal victims of sexual assault. Superficial lacerations were observed in the labia minora/majora in 9 (4%), vestibule in 6 (9%). Lacerations to the fossa navicularis were seen in 38 (30%). In a further study, 80 hymenal lacerations were observed amongst 126 pubertal victims of sexual assault, in all hymenal locations but more commonly on the posterior half of the hymenal rim [12, 14].

Maguire et al. (2009) examined 164 females aged 13 or older who were victims of sexual assault. A total of 35 hymenal lacerations were observed, 1 to the labia majora, 4 to the fossa navicularis/posterior fourchette and 25 anal/perianal tears [17].

Myhre et al. (2003) reviewed genital findings in pre-pubertal girls where there was no evidence for abuse. No genital lacerations were found in 195 girls aged 5–6 years of age [18].

Fourchette/Fossa Navicularis

Lacerations to the posterior fourchette or fossa navicularis have been reported in pre-pubertal girls with a history of vaginal penetration but not in non-abused females.

Heppenstall-Heger et al. (2003) reported on injuries in 43 girls with a history of vaginal penetration/fondling, 25 with straddle injury and two with surgical trauma. Fourteen lacerations to the posterior fourchette were observed with penile-vaginal penetration. In those with digital-vaginal penetration/fondling 4 lacerations were observed. In 24 girls with straddle injury, there were 14 lacerations to the posterior fourchette [13].

Adams et al. (2001) found tears to the posterior fourchette in 36% of 214 adolescent girls, examined following a sexual assault mostly within 72 hours [8].

Bleeding

Vaginal bleeding is normal in the first few weeks of life as the infant withdraws from maternal hormones. Following this, until puberty, it is abnormal and requires careful medical assessment.

Trauma and infections are the commonest causes of vaginal bleeding. The latter includes streptococci, haemophilus, staphylococcus aureus, shigella, candida, campylobacter and sexually transmitted diseases. Anorectal bleeding from constipation or haematuria (blood in the urine) may be misinterpreted as genital bleeding. Other causes are listed in Table 9.6.

Lichen Sclerosus et Atrophicus (LSA) is a chronic condition affecting the genital skin of females. Small ivory shiny spots develop on the vulva. The fragile skin becomes damaged, inflamed and raw. A referral to an experienced gynaecologist should be made if there is clinical doubt and skin biopsy may be required

Table 9.6 Causes of genital bleeding

Trauma	Accidental or inflicted
Infections	Bacterial, fungal and sexually transmitted diseases
Foreign objects	Within the vagina
Menstruation	Normal or premature menarche
Bleeding disorders	See pages 25–26
Urethral prolapse	Evagination of the lining of the urethra
Lichen sclerosis et atrophicus	Chronic condition affecting the genital skin
Skin tags	May occasionally bleed
Rare tumours	Polyps or solid benign growths
Anatomical	Congenital abnormalities
Other	Rectal bleeding or haematuria confused with genital bleeding

to confirm the diagnosis. Genital bleeding has been reported in 20–33% of girls with LSA. Loening Baucke (1991) described 10 girls with LSA including 2 with vulval bleeding [19].

The onset of premature menarche is defined as vaginal or menstrual bleeding before the age of 9.5 years. Diagnoses include premature activation of gonadotropins, McCune Albright Syndrome, congenital adrenal hyperplasia, tumours and hypothyroidism.

Transections and Scars

A transection is a break in the hymenal membrane extending through the width of the hymen to its base. A scar is fibrous tissue that develops in the course of healing.

A majority of acute injuries as a result of CSA heal without residue. Therefore the finding of a transection or scar is highly suggestive of previous trauma.

Berenson et al. (2000) reviewed 192 prepubertal girls reporting vaginal penetration and 200 who denied abuse. Either a hymenal transection, perforation, or deep notch was observed in 4 children, all of whom were abused. Berenson notes that genital examination of the abused child rarely differs from that of the non-abused child and that legal experts should focus on the child's history [20].

Adams et al. (2004) described deep notches (extending more than 50% of the hymen) and complete clefts (extending through the width of the hymen) in adolescent girls, 27 of whom gave a history of consensual intercourse with 58 denying previous intercourse. Posterior hymenal notches and clefts were found in 13/27 (48%) of those admitting past consensual intercourse and in 2/58 (3%) of those denying this but describing a painful first experience with tampon insertion [21].

Myhre et al. (2003) found no transections in 195 non-abused girls aged 5 and 6 years [8].

Other Hymenal Findings

Appearance and Size

The hymen is a membrane partially covering the vaginal orifice. The rim of the hymen in a child should be smooth and intact. In newborns, maternal oestrogen gives it a fleshy appearance whilst in infancy and early childhood, low oestrogen levels cause it to thin. As puberty approaches, it again thickens, elasticity increases and an irregular appearance with ruffled edges may be seen.

Attenuation (thinning of the hymen) is an inconsistent finding. The hymenal orifice can vary in size and shape depending on the anatomy, position of examination and relaxation of the child. Measurements of the hymenal orifice are considered unreliable.

Berenson (1995) followed 134 girls from birth to 3 years finding an annular hymen in 74% of newborns, crescentic hymen in 1%. At 3 years 55% had a crescentic hymen, 38% annular [22].

Berenson et al. (2002) reported that 189 pre-pubertal children with a history of digital or penile-vaginal penetration had a significantly larger transverse opening compared to 197 non-abused girls when examined in the knee chest position but not in the supine position. There was an overlap in measurements between the 2 groups and no significant differences were noted in the size of the vertical diameter [23].

Notches and Mounds

Clefts, notches or concavities are various descriptions for indentations of the hymen. A hymenal notch is an indentation on the edge of hymenal membrane. A superficial notch is defined as one that extends <50% of the hymenal membrane and must be distinguished from a transection.

A bump or mound is a rounded thickened area of tissue on the edge of the hymen most commonly found in annular or crescentic hymens and often observed in non-abused pre-pubertal girls.

Berenson et al. (2000) reported superficial notches (<50% of the width of the hymenal membrane) in 13/192 (7%) of children (aged 3–8 years) with a history of digital or penile penetration and 10/200 (5%) of non-abused girls [20].

In a previous study, Berenson et al. (1992) reviewed 202 non-abused children aged 1 month – 7 years. Notches were observed in 16/202 (8%) with an annular or crescentic hymen, mainly between the 11 - 1 o'clock positions on the hymenal rim, but not between the 4–8 o'clock positions [24].

Friability

When genital traction is applied, the skin or mucous membranes may break causing bleeding. Vulvitis, poor hygiene, LSA and topical steroids are possible causes.

Berenson et al. (2000) found friability in both non-abused children aged 3-8 years, and those reporting digital or penile-vaginal penetration infrequently (7/200 vs 1/192) [20].

Labial Fusion

Labial fusion is the partial or complete adherence of mucosal surfaces of the labia minora. It is seen in infants and young children wearing nappies but is unusual after 6–7 years of age when it may be related to chronic irritation. Causes include incontinence, vulvo-vaginitis, poor hygiene or friction. It is seen in both pre-pubertal girls reporting vaginal penetration and in non-abused girls.

Berenson et al. (2000) reviewed girls aged 3–8 years finding complete labial fusion in 4/196 (2%) of those with a history of penile/digital-vaginal penetration and in 8/208 (4%) of non-abused girls. Partial labial agglutination was found in 24/192 (13%) of those with a history of penile/digital-vaginal penetration and in 14/200 (7%) of those denying abuse [20].

Vaginal Discharge and Foreign Bodies

Infants up to 3 months of age often have a mucus discharge due to the effects of maternal oestrogen. With the onset of puberty when oestrogen levels increase, a light discharge is also common. Other causes include infections and infestations, foreign bodies, lack of hygiene and trauma.

Vulvovaginitis (discomfort, redness, discharge and itching) is common in girls and usually culture negative. However, both discharge and vulvovaginitis are commonly reported in CSA. When a child repeatedly presents with symptoms, a full assessment is required.

Berenson et al. (2000) reported vaginal discharge more often in girls aged 3–8 years with a history of penile-vaginal penetration compared to those reporting digital-vaginal penetration or non-abused girls (14% vs 7% vs 4%) [20]. In a previous study of non-abused infants and children aged 1 month – 7 years, Berenson et al (1992) found a vaginal discharge in 1/202 with a further 7/202 reporting discharge which had resolved with treatment [24].

Anal Signs of Child Sexual Abuse

Erythema

Common causes for redness of the perianal skin and mucosa are trauma, infection, poor hygiene, soiling, diarrhoea, milk and lactose intolerance, excessive washing and eczema. Rarer causes include Lichen Sclerosus et Atrophicus and inflammatory bowel disease. Erythema is an unreliable sign in CSA and is also found in non-abused children.

Watkeys et al. (2008) reported on 257 children with alleged penetrative abuse of whom 114 were seen within 7 days. Thirteen of 23 (56%) children with alleged penetrative anal abuse within the previous 7 days had abnormal findings, including 1 with erythema compared with 9 (18%) of the 50 children seen more than 7 days after anal abuse [6].

McCann and Voris (1993) reviewed 4 girls aged 4–8 who had been anally abused. Perineal erythema was found in all cases in the first 24 hours but disappeared within 8 days in 3 girls. The fourth had a herpes simplex infection [25].

Adams et al. (2001) reviewed the records of 214 abused girls of whom 13% reported anal penetration. Anogenital redness was observed more frequently in girls seen at 72 hours following abuse than those seen within 24 hours (20% vs 12%). The authors noted that redness is a subjective observation [8].

Bruising

A bruise is the escape of blood from ruptured blood vessels, usually capillaries following trauma. Haematological disorders may increase a child's susceptibility to bruising (page 24). Lichen Sclerosus Atrophicus (LSA), and some other skin lesions, may be mistaken for bruises.

Anal bruising is usually the result of trauma and as for other signs of CSA is more likely to be detected within 72 hours of an alleged abuse.

Watkeys et al. (2008) reported perianal bruising in 7/23 (30%) of cases of penetrative anal abuse presenting within 7 days [6]. Pierce (2004) reported anal/perianal bruising in 5/50 (10%) of children with a history suggestive of anal penetration [26].

Palusci et al. (2006) reported on 190 sexually abused children (21% anal penetration) younger than 13 years who were examined within 72 hours. Perianal bruising was found in 2/190 (1%) [15].

Fissures and Scars

An anal fissure is a split in the perianal skin radiating from the anal orifice. The terms 'fissure' and 'laceration' are interchangeable. Causes include hard or large stools dilating the anal sphincter, trauma, chronic bowel disorders, some skin conditions and infection.

A fissure may result in rectal bleeding which is also caused by inflammatory bowel disease, infective diarrhoea, polyps or other benign tumours. Failure of midline fusion (perineal groove) is seen as a sulcus of mucosal tissue anywhere between the vagina and the anus and may be mistaken for a fissure.

Pierce (2004) reported six fissures in 13 children (46%) where the perpetrator confessed to anal abuse. There were 19/37 (51%) lacerations where abuse was strongly suspected but not proven [26].

Watkeys et al. (2008) reviewed 257 referrals for alleged sexual abuse. Of these, 62 alleged penetrative anal abuse with 11 reporting both anal and genital penetration. Fissures were found in 6/23 (28%) who were examined within 7 days. Fifty children were examined following alleged penetrative anal abuse more than 7 days prior. Nine (18%) had healed fissures or scars [6].

Myhre et al. (2013) reported anal fissures in 21/197 (10.7%) of children where anal penetration was thought probable and in 25/908 (2.8%) where it was thought unlikely. Anal lacerations were observed in 9/197 (4.6%), penetration thought probable and in 3/908 (0.3%), penetration thought unlikely. Forty-seven percent were examined within 72 hours of the alleged abuse [27].

Hobbs and Wynne (1986) reviewed 35 children with a history and physical signs of anal penetration describing fissures in 23. In 4 these were multiple [28].

Bruni (2003) reviewed 50 children where anal abuse had been either admitted or a successful prosecution made. Anal scars were observed in 84%, anal tags 32%, reflex anal dilatation/venous congestion in 33%. In 6% there were no abnormal signs [29].

Constipation

Constipation is the passage of hard, painful motions. Overflow (retentive encopresis or soiling) occurs when loose motions pass around a constipated stool. Clinical findings may include palpable stool on abdominal examination, stool visible around the anus and a lax anal sphincter. A small number of constipated children have underlying conditions such as Hirschprung's disease whilst those who soil may have developmental or behavioural problems.

When a child passes a hard motion, a fissure may result which may bleed. There is pain, particularly when the child attempts to open his or her bowels again. The child becomes reluctant to defaecate leading to further symptoms and worsening constipation.

Mellon et al. (2006) reviewed 466 children aged 4–12 years diagnosed with sexual abuse, 429 referred to psychiatry for other reasons and 641 normal children. CSA was ruled out in the last two groups. Soiling rates were 10.3% for the abused group, 10.5% for those referred to psychiatry, 2% for normal children. Rates of sexualised behaviour were reported more often in the abused group, compared to both the psychiatric and normal groups and were a better predictor of abuse [30].

Agnarsson et al. (1990) investigated the perianal appearances of 136 constipated children. Warts, perianal oedema, redness, blueness and visible veins were all recorded. Fissures were found in 35 (26%) and tags in 7 (5%). Anal dilatation was found in 24 (18%) [31].

Scars and Tags

Lacerations may heal without trace or result in scar tissue. Scars appearing in the midline can be confused with a median raphe. Anal tags outside the midline raise concerns for anal abuse as do perianal scars particularly if these are away from the midline.

Watkeys et al. (2007) identified scars in 10/73 (14%) of children who had reported anal abuse, 9 of whom were examined more than 7 days after the alleged abuse [6]. Bruni (2003) reported on 50 children where there was perpetrator confession of anal penetration. Six confessed to penile and 44 to digital penetration. Scars were found in all positions around the anus (38% midline, 36% away from the midline, 26% in both locations). There were 24 skin tags of which 22 (92%) were away from the midline. [29].

Pierce et al. (2004) found 16 anal scars in 50 children with a convincing history of anal penetration. No scars were found in 81 children with abusive or accidental injury but no allegation of CSA [26].

Perianal Venous Congestion

This refers to blood in the venous plexus of the perianal tissues which appears purple and blanches on pressure. The degree of venous distension varies over time and is observed in both children who report CSA and in non-abused children.

Pierce (2004) reviewed the records of 214 children (two young adults) examined up to 6 years after alleged abuse. Large perianal veins were recorded in

4/50 (8%) where there was a strong history of anal penetration. Four preverbal children had similar signs which resolved on separation from the alleged perpetrator. Large perianal veins were not recorded in 83 children who disclosed sexual abuse but denied anal interference nor in 81 abused (not CSA) or accidentally injured children [26].

Myhre et al. (2001) described venous pooling in 70/198 (35.4%), penetration probable and in 312/910 (34.3%), penetration not probable [27].

Hobbs and Wynne (1986) studied 35 children aged 14 months to 8 years, where anal abuse was disclosed by the child or perpetrator in 27. Venous congestion/engorgement was described in four cases [28].

Anal Dilatation

Static dilatation refers to the physical finding of dilatation or laxity where the anal canal or rectum can be seen. Dynamic dilatation refers to reflex anal dilatation. Other terms have been used in various studies making analysis and comparison difficult.

Reflex anal dilatation (RAD) refers to the opening of the anal sphincter following buttock traction. With the child lying on his or her side, the buttocks are parted and inspection performed for at least 30 seconds. RAD may be observed in non-abused children with severe constipation and in some neurological disorders. It may vary depending on the position of examination. It has been observed more often in children who have alleged anal abuse than in non-abused children.

Pierce (2004) found RAD in 5/50 (10%) of children who gave a history of anal abuse but not in 81 children without evidence of sexual abuse. In a third group of 83 children who alleged CSA but denied anal abuse, one had slight anal dilatation and a history of constipation [26].

Bruni (2003) reviewed 50 children where there was a history of digital-anal penetration in (44), or penile-anal penetration in (6). RAD was observed in 17 (34%) of those examined 4 weeks – 14 months after the alleged abuse [29].

Hobbs and Wynne (1986) studied 35 children aged 1–12 years where anal abuse was disclosed by the child or perpetrator in 27. Anal dilatation was found in 18, a further 2 had wide dilatation and in 3 there was absence of sphincter [28].

Inguinal and Peno-Scrotal Injuries (Fig. 9.2)

Overview

When inguinal and genital injuries in boys are accidental, they will be reliably associated with a credible history of an event and its aftermath. Straddle injuries whilst riding a bike, sports injuries, falls and accidents with zips have all been recorded.

In abuse, a child may be punched, kicked, impacted with a blunt instrument or against a hard surface. Penile bruising may be caused by an adult grip as an inflicted

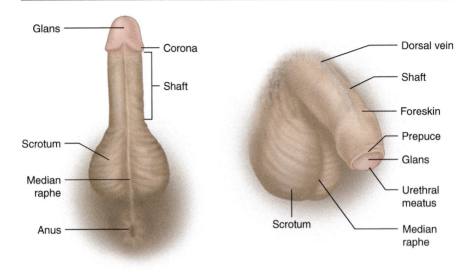

Fig. 9.2 External structure of the male

injury or CSA. Grabbing, squeezing, pulling or twisting actions have all been recorded.

A 1-year-old boy was presented for care with genital injuries to include a 1cm laceration to the scrotum, penile and scrotal bruising with petechiae. The mother stated she noticed bruising at nappy change. There was no history of an accident or its aftermath. Father denied any knowledge of injury. Other diagnoses to include balanoposthitis (page 203) were excluded with physical signs suggestive of inflicted trauma. CSA could not be ruled out. The father was deemed to be the perpetrator.

Hobbs and Osman (2007) reviewed 86 boys (average age 62.7 months) with penile or scrotal injuries. In 41 of them, the injury was unexplained or described by family members as 'accidental'. A sibling was alleged to have caused the injury in 13. The injury was judged to be inflicted in 63, suspicious in 17 and accidental in 6. Injuries were mainly to the penis and included burns/scars (7), bruises/petechiae (27), wounds, lacerations or scars (39), and other injuries to include fissures, reddening and thickening of perianal tissues (27). Abnormal anal signs were observed in 28 children. In 17 children there were >10 bruises, burns in 12, mouth injuries in 4, brain and retinal haemorrhages in 1 and poor nourishment in 14. There were three fractures thought to be inflicted. There was a single genital injury in 57, two in 15, three in 12 and more than three in 2. Hobbs stated that sexual abuse of boys includes anal penetration, oro-genital contact, and manual-genital contact by the perpetrator [32].

Other Conditions

Balanoposthitis is inflammation of the glans penis and the foreskin (prepuce) presenting with irritation, pain, penile discharge, groin rash, and pain on passing urine. Poor genital hygiene, aggressive cleaning and prolonged antibiotics all predispose to the condition, usually caused by streptococcal or candida infections. Symptoms develop over hours and not acutely as in injury. A fever, raised white cell count and C-reactive protein are common findings. Treatment with antibiotics leads to improvements within 24–48 hours.

In *paraphimosis* the foreskin becomes trapped behind the glans penis and cannot be pulled back to its normal position covering the end of the penis. The foreskin may be pulled back during experimentation, masturbation, intercourse, abuse, cleaning or medical procedures. If untreated, the area becomes swollen, tender, and purple with a bruised appearance. Surgery may be required.

Testicular torsion presents with severe testicular pain and tenderness. Scrotal bruising may be observed.

Other Presentations

In addition to the physical signs of CSA, presenting symptoms may be general (eg. abdominal pain), behavioural or psychological.

Whilst soiling, constipation and bedwetting are common paediatric problems, they may all have more profound psychological causes as well as being a physical a manifestation of sexual abuse. CSA must always be considered as a possible diagnosis with a full assessment and early referral to CAMHS.

A 9-year-old girl was presented for assessment with nocturnal and diurnal enuresis. A brief visual genital inspection was performed which showed hymenal disruption, dilatation and scarring. Child protection procedures were commenced and a urologist advised reconstructive surgery for extensive vaginal scarring. The carers from another part the UK returned to their home town for discussions with the extended family. A male relative confessed to having sexually abused the child, including penile-vaginal penetration, over a number of years.

A child may self-harm, be anxious or depressed, aggressive with poor school performance or exhibit sexualised behaviours. When young children of similar age superficially touch each other's genitalia in exploration, this is normal. It is also normal for children to explore their bodies and masturbate. It is abnormal if this is performed excessively or in public.

Sexualised behaviours, including mimicking sexual acts, are more common in children who have been sexually abused. Friedrich et al. (1998/2001) and Cosentino et al. (1995), reported that children who have been the victims of CSA may display sexualised behaviours: masturbating openly and excessively, exposing their genitals, hugging and kissing strangers, and attempting to insert objects into their genitals. A subgroup was described who forced sexual activities on siblings and peers. Other behavioural problems described included fear, aggression, and nightmares in young school-age children, depression in older children [33, 34].

Friedrich et al. (1998) reported that fewer than 1.5% of non-abused children exhibited any of the following: putting mouth on genitals, asking to engage in specific sex acts, imitating intercourse, inserting objects into the vagina or anus and touching animal genitals [35].

References

1. Royal College of Paediatrics and Child Health. The physical signs of child sexual abuse. An evidence-based review and guidance for best practice. 2008.
2. HM Government. Sexual Offences Act. 2003.
3. Faculty of Forensic and Legal Medicine, Royal College of Paediatrics and Child Health. Guidelines on paediatric forensic examinations in relation to possible child sexual abuse. 2012.
4. Bowen K, Aldous MB. Medical evaluation of sexual abuse in children without disclosed or witnessed abuse. Pediatr Adolesc Med. 1999;153(11):1160–4.
5. Hobbs CJ, Wynne JM, Thomas AJ. Colposcopic genital findings in pre-pubertal girls assessed for sexual abuse. Arch Dis Child. 1995;73(5):465–9.
6. Watkeys JM, Price LD, Upton PM, Maddocks A. The timing of medical examination following an allegation of sexual abuse: is this an emergency? Arch Dis Child. 2008;93(10):851–6.
7. Muram D. Child sexual abuse: relationship between sexual acts and genital findings. Child Abuse Negl. 1989;13(2):211–6.
8. Adams JA, Girardin B, Faugno D. Adolescent sexual assault: documentation of acute injuries using photo-colposcopy. J Pediatr Adolesc Gynecol. 2001;14(4):175–80.
9. Adams JA, Knudson S. Genital findings in adolescent girls referred for suspected sexual abuse. Arch Pediatr Adolesc Med. 1996;150(8):850–7.
10. Emans SJ, Woods ER, Flagg NT, Freeman A. Genital findings in sexually abused, symptomatic and asymptomatic, girls. Pediatrics. 1987;79(5):778–85.
11. Finkel MA. Ano-genital trauma in sexually abused children. Pediatrics. 1989;84(2):317–22.
12. McCann J, Miyamoto S, Boyle C. Healing of non-hymenal genital injuries in pre-pubertal and adolescent girls: a descriptive study. Pediatrics. 2007;120(5):1000–11.
13. Heppenstall-Heger A, McConnell G, Ticson L, Guerra L, Lister J, Zaragoza T. Healing patterns in ano-genital injuries: a longitudinal study of injuries associated with sexual abuse, accidental injuries, or genital surgery in the pre-adolescent child. Pediatrics. 2003;112(4):829–37.
14. McCann J, Miyamoto S, Boyle C. Healing of hymenal genital injuries in pre-pubertal and adolescent girls: a descriptive study. Pediatrics. 2007;119(5):1094–116.

15. Palusci VJ, Cox EO, Shatz EM, Schultze JM. Urgent medical assessment after child sexual abuse. Child Abuse Negl. 2006;30(4):367–80.
16. Myhre AK, Myklestad K, Adams JA. Changes in genital anatomy and microbiology in girls between age 6 and age 12 years: a longitudinal study. J Pediatr Adolesc Gynecol. 2010;23(2):77–85.
17. Maguire W, Goodall E, Moore T. Injury in adult female sexual assault complainants and related factors. Eur J Obstet Gynecol Reprod Biol. 2009;142(2):149–53.
18. Myhre AK, Berntzen K, Bratlid D. Genital anatomy in non-abused preschool girls. Acta Paediatr. 2003;92(12):1453–62.
19. Loening-Baucke V. Lichen sclerosus et atrophicus in children. Am J Dis Child. 1991;145(9):1058–61.
20. Berenson AB, Chacko MR, Wiemann CM, Mishaw CO, Friedrich WN, Grady JJ. A case-control study of anatomic changes resulting from sexual abuse. Am J Obstet Gynecol. 2000;182(4):820–31.
21. Adams JA, Botash AS, Kellogg N. Differences in hymenal morphology between adolescent girls with and without a history of consensual sexual intercourse. Arch Pediatr Adolesc Med. 2004;158(3):280–5.
22. Berenson AB. A longitudinal study of hymenal morphology in the first 3 years of life. Pediatrics. 1995;95(4):490–6.
23. Berenson AB, Chacko MR, Wiemann CM, Mishaw CO, Friedrich WN, Grady JJ. Use of hymenal measurements in the diagnosis of previous penetration. Pediatrics. 2002;109(2):228–35.
24. Berenson AB, Heger AH, Hayes JM, Bailey RK, Emans SJ. Appearance of the hymen in pre-pubertal girls. Pediatrics. 1992;89(3):387–94.
25. McCann J, Voris J. Perianal injuries resulting from sexual abuse: a longitudinal study. Pediatrics. 1993;91(2):390–7.
26. Pierce AM. Anal fissures and anal scars in anal abuse–are they significant? Pediatr Surg Int. 2004;20(5):334–8.
27. Myhre AK, Adams JA, Kaufhold M, Davis JL, Suresh P, Kuelbs CL. Anal findings in children with and without probable anal penetration: a retrospective study of 1115 children referred for suspected sexual abuse. Child Abuse Negl. 2013;37(7):465–74.
28. Hobbs CJ, Wynne JM. Buggery in childhood–a common syndrome of child abuse. Lancet. 1986;2(8510):792–6.
29. Bruni M. Anal findings in sexual abuse of children (a descriptive study). J Forensic Sci. 2003;48:1343–6.
30. Mellon MW, Whiteside SP, Friedrich WN. The relevance of fecal soiling as an indicator of child sexual abuse: a preliminary analysis. J Dev Behav Pediatr. 2006;27(1):25–32.
31. Agnarsson U, Warde C, McCarthy G, Evans N. Perianal appearances associated with constipation. Arch Dis Child. 1990;65(11):1231–4.
32. Hobbs CJ, Osman J. Genital injuries in boys and abuse. Arch Dis Child. 2007;92(4):328–31.
33. Friedrich WN, Fisher JL, Dittner CA, et al. Child sexual behaviour inventory: normative, psychiatric, and sexual abuse comparisons. Child Maltreat. 2001;6:37–49.
34. Cosentino CE, Meyer-Bahlburg HF, Alpert JL, Weinberg SL, Gaines R. Sexual behaviour problems and psychopathology symptoms in sexually abused girls. J Am Acad Child Adolesc Psychiatry. 1995;34(8):1033–42.
35. Friedrich WN, Fisher J, Broughton D, Houston M, Shafran CR. Normative sexual behavior in children: a contemporary sample. Pediatrics. 1998;101(4):E9.

Further Reading

Royal College of Paediatrics and Child Health. The physical signs of child sexual abuse. An evidence-based review and guidance for best practice. May 2015.

Index

A

Abdominal bruising, 37, 133
Abdominal CT scan, 135
Abdominal trauma
  blunt abdominal trauma, 131–133,
    136, 138
  clinical assessment, 139–142
  laboratory investigations, 135, 140
  mode and types of injury, 132–133
  radiological investigations, 135
  specific organ injury
    bladder, 136
    colon, 138
    duodenum, 137
    jejunum and ileum, 137
    kidney, 136
    liver, 136
    muscle, 136
    pancreas, 136–137
    spleen, 136
    stomach, 137
Abusive head trauma (AHT)
  accidental head injury, 116, 123
  associated injuries
    fractures, 123
    soft tissue, 122–123
  chronic subdural haematoma,
    115, 125, 126
  clinical assessment, 117–119
  clinical triad, 119–121
  degree of force required, 116
  encephalopathy, 114, 115, 117, 120–121
  extradural haematoma (EDH), 125
  general principles, 114
  hygromas, 126
  impact, 113–115, 117, 119, 121–123, 125
  intracerebral haemorrhage (ICH), 126
  intraventricular haemorrhage (IVH), 126
  investigation of, 119
  medical causes

benign enlargement of the subarachnoid
  space (BESS), 124
birth trauma, 124
coagulopathies and other blood
  disorders, 124
cranial malformations, 123
galactosaemia, 119, 124
glutaric aciduria type I, 124
hypernatraemia, 124
meningitis/encephalitis and
  septicaemia, 123
outcomes following AHT, 127
retinal haemorrhages (RH), 113, 115, 116,
  119–124
Royal College of Pathologists,
  2009, 113
scalp swellings, 117, 122
shaking injuries, 115, 117, 123, 127
spinal trauma in children, 126–127
subarachnoid haemorrhages (SAH),
  121–122
subdural haemorrhage (SDH), 115,
  119, 124, 127
subgaleal haematoma (SGH),
  116, 125–126
Acceleration–deceleration forces, 114, 121
Accidental
  bruises, 23, 26–27, 31, 40
  burns, 97, 105, 108–109
  head injuries, 117
Accidental *vs.* inflicted bruising, 26–30
Accidental *vs.* inflicted burns, 26–27
Adoption order, 18
Aftermath and observers
  AHT, 97–99
  bruises, 23, 30–31
  burns, 114, 117
  fractures, 64, 68, 72, 74–75
Ageing bruises, 31–33
Alagille syndrome, 86

© Springer International Publishing Switzerland 2017
D.L. Robinson, *Pediatric Forensic Evidence*, DOI 10.1007/978-3-319-45337-8

CPI Antony Rowe
Chippenham, UK
2017-11-23 21:42